Ernst Jünger's Philoso[

"Blok's book is a major contribution to the field of phenomenology and continental philosophy. With impeccable scholarship, Blok brings Ernst Jünger's understanding and critique of technology into the forefront, showing how his insights not only interface with those of Martin Heidegger, but also in certain ways diverge in yielding new avenues to address humanity's place in a globalized world."

—Frank Schalow

This book examines the work of Ernst Jünger and its effect on the development of Martin Heidegger's influential philosophy of technology. Vincent Blok offers a unique treatment of Jünger's philosophy and his conception of the age of technology, in which both world and man appear in terms of their functionality and efficiency. The primary objective of Jünger's novels and essays is to make the transition from the totally mobilized world of the twentieth century toward a world in which a new type of man represents the gestalt of the worker and is responsive to this new age. Blok proceeds to demonstrate Jünger's influence on Heidegger's analysis of the technological age in his later work, as well as Heidegger's conceptions of will, work and gestalt at the beginning of the 1930s. At the same time, Blok evaluates Heidegger's criticism of Jünger and provides a novel interpretation of the Jünger-Heidegger connection: that Jünger's work in fact testifies to a transformation of our relationship to language and conceptualizes the future in terms of the Anthropocene. This book, which arrives alongside several new English-language translations of Jünger's work, will interest scholars of twentieth-century continental philosophy, Heidegger, and the history of philosophy of technology.

Vincent Blok is associate professor in Business Ethics and Philosophy of Management, Technology & Innovation, Wageningen University (The Netherlands). He holds a PhD in philosophy of technology from Leiden University. His work has appeared in *Journal of the British Society for Phenomenology, Philosophy & Technology, Environmental Ethics* and other journals. See **www.vincentblok.nl** for his current research.

Routledge Studies in Twentieth-Century Philosophy

Ernst Jünger's Philosophy of Technology

Heidegger and the Poetics of the Anthropocene

Vincent Blok

LONDON AND NEW YORK

First published 2017 by Routledge

2 Park Square, Milton Park, Abingdon, Oxfordshire OX14 4RN
52 Vanderbilt Avenue, New York, NY 10017

Routledge is an imprint of the Taylor & Francis Group, an informa business

First issued in paperback 2019

Library of Congress Cataloging-in-Publication Data
A catalog record for this book has been requested

ISBN: 978-1-138-73759-4 (hbk)
ISBN: 978-0-367-88874-9 (pbk)

Typeset in Sabon
by Apex CoVantage, LLC

Dedicated to my teacher
Wouter Oudemans
November 25, 2016, Voorburg

Contents

Acknowledgments

Earlier versions of proportions of Chapter 1, "The Ontological Meaning of Gestalt: Understanding *The Worker*," appeared as the following articles: "Der ontologische Sinn der Gestalt. Zum Verständnis des Arbeiters," *Les Carnets Ernst Jünger* 10 (2005), pp. 173–192. An earlier version of proportions of Chapter 2, "Intermezzo: The Will to Power in Nietzsche," appeared as Section 8 of: *Rondom de Vloedlijn. Filosofie en Kunst in het Machinale Tijdperk. Een Confrontatie tussen Heidegger en Jünger.* (Soesterberg: Aspekt 2005). An earlier version of proportions of Chapter 3, "The Transformation of the Type of the Worker as Representative of the Gestalt of the Worker," appeared as the following article: "Die Bändigung des Elementaren—Der Wille zur Macht als Kunst in Ernst Jüngers *The Workerr*," *Existentia*, Vol. XVIII (2008), pp. 83–98. An earlier version of proportions of Chapter 4, "Stereoscopy and Trigonometry: Jünger's Method in the Light of the 'Sicilian Letter to the Man in the Moon,'" appeared as the following chapter: "Stereoskopie und Trigonometrie. Jüngers Methode im Licht des *Sizilischen Briefes an den Mann im Mond*," *Ernst Jünger—eine Bilanz*, ed. N. Zarska, G. Diesener and W. Kunicki. (Leipzig: Leipziger Universitätsverlag, 2010) pp. 58–73.

An earlier version of proportions of Chapter 5, "Jünger's Fundamental Metaphysical Position," and of Chapter 7, "Jünger's Concept of the Gestalt of the Worker as the Consummation of Modernity," appeared as the following article: "An Indication of Being—Reflections on Heidegger's Engagement with Ernst Jünger," *The Journal of the British Society for Phenomenology*, Vol. 42, No. 2 (2011), pp. 194–208. An earlier version of Chapter 6, "Heidegger's Ontology of Work," appeared as the following article: "Heidegger's Ontology of Work," *Heidegger Studies*, Vol. 31 (2015), pp. 109–128. An earlier version of Chapter 8, "Establishing the Truth—Heidegger's Reflections on the Gestalt," appeared earlier as "Establishing the Truth: Heidegger's Reflections on Gestalt," *Heidegger Studies*, 27(2011), 101–118. An earlier version of proportions of Chapter 9, "Controversies over Language: The One-Sidedness of Heidegger's Examination of Ernst Jünger," appeared as the following article: "Kontroversen über die Sprache—Die Einseitigkeit von Heideggers Auseinandersetzung mit Ernst Jünger," *Existentia*, Vol. XVII (2007), 19–30.

I would like to thank Harriett Jernigan for her great help in translating and editing my work in proper English, Martijn Pietersma for proofreading, and Wageningen University for its support while I was writing this book. Finally, I would like to thank my wife and children, Petra, Gudrun, Storm and Demian for their support, love and understanding while I was working the weekends to finalize this book.

Introduction

This book studies how Ernst Jünger—one of the greatest German authors of the twentieth century—envisioned the technological age we currently live in. In the trenches of World War I, he experienced the destruction of the age of Enlightenment and the emergence of a new era in which technology, functionality and work are the dominant categories. Valuable categories like rationality, equality and freedom are no longer valid and make space for a *total mobilization* of the natural world and of human existence, in which both world and man appear in terms of their functionality and efficiency.

The first reason to study Jünger's concept of the age of technology is that his novels and essays provide an impression of the scope of the age of technology, i.e., the *totality* of the mobilization of natural and human resources in the technological age. Although this totally mobilized world is meaningless and testifies of nihilism according to Jünger, he does not romantically long for the day of old, nor does he seek exceptions or alternatives for the technological age. The second reason to study Jünger's concept of the age of technology is that he tries to describe the world as it actually *is*.

Amidst the totally mobilized world, however, Jünger surmises "a new turning of being." He calls this "being" the gestalt of the worker, i.e., a metaphysical category that is able to provide meaningfulness to the totally mobilized world we currently live in. The primary objective of Jünger's novels and essays is to make the transition from the totally mobilized world we currently live in toward a world in which a new type of man—the type of the worker—represents the gestalt of the worker and is responsive to this new turning of being. The third reason to study Jünger's concept of the age of technology is that he asks for the meaning or sense of the technological age we currently live in. This reflection on the sense of the technological age is today as relevant as it was in Jünger's days.

Jünger's work had a great impact on one of the major philosophers of the twentieth century, Martin Heidegger. Jünger influenced not only Heidegger's analysis of the technological age in his later work, but also his reflections on the concepts of will, work and gestalt at the beginning of the 1930s. At the same time, Heidegger can be considered one of Jünger's fiercest critics. He raises several questions and remarks regarding Jünger's strategy to overcome the totally mobilized world of nihilism. This controversy becomes clear in *Across the Line,* in which Jünger conceptualizes the totally mobilized world of nihilism as a zero point or zero line and raises the question of whether we can cross this line and overcome the totally mobilized world, and in Heidegger's response to Jünger in *Concerning 'the Line,'* Heidegger accuses Jünger of identifying the subject of study—work—and the strategy or method of his study—work; Jünger's descriptions move unnoticed from *what* is described ("being" as work) to *how* it is described ("thinking" as work) and so mutually define one another.

The fourth reason to study Jünger's concept of the age of technology is that it enables us to reflect on our methodological access to phenomena like the age of technology. This reflection on methodology is as relevant today as it was in Jünger's days, because the identification of the subject of study and the method of study holds not only for Jünger's work, but also for more recent efforts to envision a turning of being—whether it is about the vibrancy of matter (Jane Bennett), the emergence of hyperobjects (Timothy Morton) or the anthropocene (Bruno Latour).

In the end, Heidegger rejects Jünger's strategy to envision the technological age, because his efforts to cross the line of nihilism still testify to the language of modern metaphysics. Instead, Heidegger raises the question as to whether such a crossing would presuppose a transformation of our method of saying and with this a transformation of our relation to language. Contrary to most of the existing interpretations of the Heidegger-Jünger controversy, the main hypothesis of this study is that Jünger's work in fact testifies to such a transformation of the method of saying and of our relation to language. By providing a methodological reading of Jünger's work in this study, we can not only reflect on the technological age we currently live in, but also reflect critically on the strategies and methods that enable us to have access to totalizing phenomena like "the technological age" we currently live in, and to say something about phenomena that still have to come, i.e., the turning of being across the line. Although such a turning is often envisioned in current philosophical work, it is exactly this methodological reflection on the method of philosophy that is often missing. The fifth reason to study Jünger's concept of the age of technology is, therefore, that he provides concrete strategies and methods to envision the future. Furthermore, Jünger is one of the first authors who conceptualizes this future in terms of the anthropocene.

In Part I, we first explore Jünger's concept of the age of technology, the turning of being he envisioned, and the methods he deploys in order to have access to this hidden dimension of the gestalt in his early work. In Part II, we discuss Heidegger's critical reflections on Jünger. It will become clear how Heidegger's conceptualization of will, work and gestalt at the beginning of the 1930s is influenced by Jünger. More importantly, Heidegger's reflections deepen our understanding of these concepts. At the same time, we will point at a bias in Heidegger's reading of Jünger. Because he takes Jünger's writings a priori as *metaphysical* reflections in light of Nietzsche's metaphysics of the will to power, Heidegger does not see that Jünger is on the way to a non-metaphysical method to envision the turning of being, and to a non-metaphysical concept of language that is much closer to Heidegger's than he would admit. In Part III, we return to Jünger's concept of the age of technology and the turning of being he envisions *at the time wall* in his later work. In this context, we explore Jünger's non-metaphysical method and his non-metaphysical concept of language to envision the future.

Part I

The Age of Technicity and the Gestalt of the Worker

"I am a Stranger on Earth"

(*Psalm 119:19*)

Introduction

Like no one else, Hermann Hesse revealed in his novel *Demian* the umbilical cord of the "war fever" in Germany. The liberation of the German youth, which took place with the outbreak of the First World War, was described by Hesse as the experience that "fate and adventure called us and that soon the world needed *us* to revolutionize."[1] This revolution of the world is not so much related to the geographical redefinition of Europe, but to the paradoxical intuition that a new future, a new humanity would emerge in this war. The First World War was widely hailed as a liberating way out of the meaninglessness of bourgeois existence, in which the Enlightenment ideals of the French Revolution from 1789 were rejected and "the birth of a new Germany" was inaugurated.[2]

Such a war ideology was not limited to the Germans. It could also be seen on thousands of French and English faces who, packed on boats and trains, said goodbye to their families to sacrifice themselves in the struggle of "civilization against barbarism" (Henri Bergson) and against a "world full of devils" (Paul Natorp). It concerned "the war to end all wars" (H.G. Wells) or, more generally, the liberation of the world.

A great deal of historical research has already been done about the so-called war fever of 1914 and the related war ideology. Some historians, such as Wolfgang Kruse and Jeffrey Verhey, have convincingly shown that both concepts are in fact the product of war propaganda.[3] Verhey shows for instance, based on a statistical analysis of utterances in the press, that the enthusiasm for the war was a constructed myth created by the politics of war.[4] Kruse comments on this in the following way: "The beginning of the war, which was long before stylized into a downfall of the world, was now interpreted as a world-verdict and at the same time as the start of an all-embracing renewal of the world, that a 'chosen' people has to execute in war."[5] Others, like Reinhard Rürup, recognized the role of propaganda, but pointed to the fact that the ideology of war resonated to a widespread demand in Germany, and therefore should not be reduced to a mere construction.[6] The "Spirit of 1914" could indicate a profound societal crisis, which eventually became the prelude to National Socialism in Germany. The question is: what is the nature of this societal crisis?

The work of Ernst Jünger can give an indication of the real meaning of this societal crisis. In this chapter, we explore Jünger's concept of this crisis, which he calls the age of technology, and the turning of Being—the emergence of the gestalt of the worker—he surmises in the technological world we currently live in (Chapter 1). Because Jünger is heavily influenced by Nietzsche, we will focus on Nietzsche's metaphysics of the will to power first (Chapter 2), before we move on to Jünger's transition from the totally mobilized world we currently live in toward a world in which a new type of man—the type of the worker—represents the gestalt of the worker (Chapter 3). We end the chapter with a methodological reflection on the question of how Jünger can have access to a gestalt of the worker which is not there and still has to come.

Notes

1. Hesse, Hermann, *Demian* (Frankfurt am Main: Suhrkamp, 1981) 158.
2. Cf. Kruse, W., "Kriegsbegeisterung? Zur Massenstimmung bei Kriegsbeginn," *Eine Welt von Feinden. Der große Krieg 1914–1918*, ed. W. Kruse (Frankfurt am Main: Fischer Verlag, 1997) 159–166; Rürup, R., "Der 'Geist von 1914' in Deutschland. Kriegsbegeisterung und Ideologisierung des Krieges im Ersten Weltkrieg," *Ansichten vom Krieg. Vergleichende Studien zum Ersten Weltkrieg in Literatur und Gesellschaft*, ed. B. Hüppauf (Königstein: Verlag Anton Hain Meisenhem, 1984) 1–30.
3. Kruse, W. "Kriegsbegeisterung? Zur Massenstimmung bei Kriegsbeginn," 160.
4. Verhey, J., *The "Spirit" of 1914: The Myth of Enthousiasm and the Rhetoric of Unity in World War I Germany* (Berkeley: PhD thesis, 1991).
5. Kruse, W. "Kriegsbegeisterung? Zur Massenstimmung bei Kriegsbeginn," 170. Cf. 165–170.
6. "The year 1914 was without a doubt a turning point in European history and world history. But it was not the 'Spirit of 1914' that gave it its meaning. 1914 brought the bourgeois world together, ended a historical epoch that had begun in 1789" (Rürup, "Der 'Geist von 1914' in Deutschland," 29). Cf. Leed, E.J., *No Man's Land: Combat and Identity in World War I* (Cambridge: Cambridge University Press, 1979) 39–72.

1 The Ontological Meaning of Gestalt

Understanding *the Worker*

In 1932, Ernst Jünger, like no other before him, envisioned the technological age in *The Worker*. He describes the technological age as "total mobilization." When he speaks of total mobilization, Jünger means nihilism, which in our world has become the "normal state."[1] Jünger's achievement consists of the fact that he accepts it without hunting for alternatives or excuses, and attempts to stay in the world as it *is,* rather than what he strives for it to be.

Although he affirms it, he senses the meaninglessness of our working world. "The work-world expects, hopes for its meaning,"[2] and that is the primary concern *The Worker.* This *meaning* is found in a new "purpose" of Being, which Jünger believed to have encountered in the First World War and calls the "gestalt of the worker." It is understood as "unity that can ensure a new security and rank order of life."[3] In total mobilization, he suspects an *ontological difference* between the gestalt as a new unity and the things in the world. The primary concern in *The Worker* is consequently the concept of the *gestalt* of the Worker.

This first chapter centers on the question of how the mysterious gestalt in Jünger's work can be understood. In doing so we will concentrate on *The Worker,* from 1932. First we will examine Jünger's experience of the First World War (Section 1.1), in which he sees the demise of the ideals of the Enlightenment of man as *animal rationale* and the completely meaningless world of nihilism that remains after this demise. Section 1.2 deals with the incommensurability of the First World War: the world and the human encounter that go with it appear now *totally mobilized.* Jünger calls the totally mobilized world *meaningless* and asks about the hidden *meaning* of the millions of victims of the First World War (Section 1.3). He finds it in that which he calls the "gestalt of the worker." Its precursor is the new type of warrior that fought in the First World War and who is familiar with the world of technology. Section 1.4 deals with the occasion that moved Jünger to a concept of a gestalt: the Battle of Langemarck, in which he experienced a *gestalt-switch.* Section 1.5 asks what a gestalt actually is. It will be argued that it centers on the ontologically different unity that gives the world meaning. According to Jünger, it embodies the meaning of the First World War.

Its realization allows the *transition* from total mobilization to a world in which the new race of man—the type of the worker—represents the gestalt of the worker.

1.1 The Destruction of the Platonic *Idea* in the "Shaking of the World Order"

Like many of his contemporaries, Ernst Jünger, full of idealism, dove enthusiastically into the First World War as though in a trance:

> We had left lecture halls, school desks and work tables and in those few short weeks of basic training had been merged into one large, keen body. Having grown up in an era of security, we all longed for the unusual, the greatest danger. And the war caught us up like a drug. We departed under a shower of flowers, in an atmosphere of roses and blood. The war would give us what we craved, the great, the strong, the solemn. It seemed like a manly thing to do, a jovial fraternity duel on a flowery meadow dewy with blood. "There is no finer death in all the world. . . ." Anything not to get stuck at home, to be allowed to go![4]

An experience speaks from his novels and essays that reaches far beyond the historical experience of the war.

He speaks about it as the "shaking of the world order." Jünger sees it in its most concentrated form at the Battle of Langemarck—later called the Massacre of the Innocents. In the winter of 1914, around 3,000 boys went willingly to their deaths, students who left the lecture halls to rally around the flags and fight for "German culture":

> We see here a classical attack breaking down, regardless of the strength of the will to power that enlivens the individual and the moral and intellectual values through which they are distinguished. Free will, education, enthusiasm and the thrill of death-defying acts do not suffice to overcome the gravity of the few hundred meters on which the magic of mechanical death reigns. . . . In essence, the operation in Langemarck formed the basis for the entry of a cosmic opposite that continually repeats itself when the world order shakes, and which expresses itself here in the symbols of a technological era.[5]

This is not about the actual destruction of the German troops by the English forces, rather about the experience of nihilism. That is apparent in that "shaking" refers to world *order*. It becomes clear what kind of shaking when we first ask about the *measurement* or the unity, within which the world becomes visible as order.[6]

The metaphysical tradition finds this measurement in the ontological determination of the nature of things; of the transcendental horizon of the

Platonic *idea*. In it is the *idea* or category the fixed measurement, within which the world has order and meaning. So appear, for example, in the light of the *idea* "man" different people *as* man, and we can recognize the different people *as* such. The *idea* "man" is thus not himself a man, rather it means the metaphysically given measurement within which the multiplicity of people manifests itself *as* unity, i.e., *as* man. Thus there are significant differences in the metaphysical tradition between the *idea* or category and the things that thanks to these can show themselves *as* themselves.

Animal rationale is what we call those people who understand themselves and the world in the light of the transcendental essence of things. Jünger is speaking namely of bourgeois individuals (*Bürger*), but means with that the essential nature of man as *animal rationale*, the being gifted with reason, for which the ideals of the Enlightenment, of reason and humanity, of morality and individual freedom are essential. In the light of these categories every war seems a *mistake* that discipline (resolutions and military intervention) and enlightenment could avert and heal, and whose results will be the "United Nations" of an equally good and rational humanity. So the First World War is for the *animal rationale* a war of defense, in which one should definitely settle old scores with barbarians who know nothing of reason and morality.

Jünger in contrast has the experience that the First World War is determined by a large amount of action and a small amount of "Why and what for?" which means that one can no longer see the war as a mistake or a one-time military intervention.[7] Through the shaking of the world order, he experiences, in other words, that the First World War can no longer be understood *within* the categories of the *animal rationale*.[8] The English were not better equipped than the German soldiers, nor were they strategically superior. Free will, the thrill of death-defying acts and chivalrous courage were no longer categories that had any importance.[9] That the operation of the "individual" or a "mass" of individuals was no longer relevant is shown by the example of the "three old soldiers behind an intact machine gun who weren't unsettled by the message that an entire battalion was advancing."[10]

Basic concepts such as "individuality," "courage," "chivalry" and "reason" had no meaning in the First World War, and that points at the destruction of the categories of the *animal rationale*. "Whoever really experienced that could no longer doubt that not this or that State, this or that system, rather a world-view, the moral tenor of an entire period of a culture, is breaking down."[11] With the shaking of the world order, a final line was drawn underneath the era of the *animal rationale*. After its downfall, the only thing remaining was an emptiness, a wilderness, namely the nihil of the given measurement for things. This experience of emptiness can be understood as the experience of nihilism.[12] Jünger calls nihilism a "new, terrible principle,"[13] because it destroys and denies every tie to the transcendental essence of things. Our ontologically indifferent world is incommensurable, that is, incomparable with the world of the *animal rationale*, which is permeated by ontological difference. In this context, he speaks of "the loneliness of man in a new, unexplored world, whose steely law will be felt as meaningless."[14]

The nature of this otherness is made concrete in the example of the First World War: "And so does gun powder produce an altered image of war, which however does not let itself say that it is superior in rank to the images of chivalric warfare. Nevertheless, it is from here on absurd to go into the field without cannons."[15] The *incomparability* is expressed in Jünger's example: It cannot be said anymore that a cannon is more effective than a sword. Where one no longer fights man to man on a manageable battleground, rather cities full of citizens have to fear enemy attacks from massive distances, one can no longer say that one battle method is superior to the other.

The first meaning of the shaking of the world order is the experience of nihilism, the meaningless world, which remains after the downfall of the *animal rationale*. In this way, Jünger experiences that we find ourselves in the process of an unprecedented world transition. What exactly changed him afterward, so that this war could no longer be understood within the categories of the *animal rationale,* but instead appears as the absolutely meaningless?

1.2 Total Mobilization

The destruction of the difference between the ontic and the ontological is made clear in "Total Mobilization," published in 1930. In this essay, which one can regard as a preliminary draft for *The Worker,* Jünger focuses on the mobilization in the First World War. Its character of totality did not derive from the fact that *all* resources and forces were devoted to the war. Although one could insert the individual measures at the beginning of the war as evidence—the large-scale deployment of volunteer soldiers and reservists, censorship regulations and export bans—the total mobilization had differed only *gradually* therein from the partial mobilization of the monarchy at the time.[16]

Jünger invokes a "growing conversion of life into energy" for the benefit of the movement of fleeting, nascent connections.[17] It does not mean the destruction of *things,* rather the destruction of the Platonic horizon of the transcendental *essence* of things, to which the *animal rationale* was known to be bound. The meaning of the world is no longer derived from a fixed value or a fixed measure, rather it is potential energy whose worth manifests itself in the measurements of how profitable it is in different situations. In *Total Mobilization* and *The Worker,* Jünger shows us that nothing is excluded from this conversion of life into potential energy.

For example, according to Jünger, technology can no longer be understood in a fixed category such as "progress" or "humanity." The invention of the motor and the locomotive as "an organ of progress" have their dark sides in the fact that one could transport a tank or a company of soldiers with them as well. "By the same token, the artistic depiction of nitrogen operates in both the agricultural and explosives senses."[18] The "twofold reality of technology" reveals that the locomotive or the chemical industry appears as *potential energy*, whose worth demonstrated itself in the measurement of how it functions or how profitable it is.[19] This functionality of the potential energy can consist of the manufacture of perfume just as easily as the production of poisonous gasses.

Mobilization in the First World War lends the conversion of life into energy "an ever increasingly radical character."[20] With that, the world and the war manifest themselves *as* function or—in the language of *total mobilization*—*as* work. Because of the character of work, the commitment of all available resources becomes enabled and necessary:

> So the horrific increase of the costs makes it impossible to deny the waging of war from one concrete war chest; it is much more the tension of all credit, the strain of credit, the acquisition of even the last spare penny is necessary in order to maintain the machinery. So does the image of war as an armed negotiation flow more and more into the broader image of a giant work process. Alongside the armies that encounter each other on the battlefield arise the new armies of transport, food, armament industry—the army of work. In the last phase, at the end of this war, as previously mentioned, no more movement occurs—down to the seamstress who works at home—that is not in some way involved with the war effort. In this absolute acquisition of potential energy that turns the warring industrial States into volcanic forges, the emergence of the era of the worker perhaps most clearly shows itself—it turns the World War into a historical event whose significance is superior to that of the French Revolution. In order to elicit energy of such a scale, it no longer suffices to simply cover one's weapon arm with chainmail—one must arm oneself to the marrow, down to the smallest nerve.[21]

Total mobilization thus primarily has the effect of engendering ontological indifference, since every connection to the transcendent essence of things is destroyed—Jünger also speaks of a "decrease of types"—in favor of dynamization or potential energy.[22] Because total mobilization relates to the way reality is structured and understood *as* work, there is no longer a difference between work and leisure or cultural life as a welcome change from the workday. He calls the character of work a "total pull";[23] "there are no boundaries to the workspace, just as the workday consists of 24 hours," which means "from this viewpoint" there is no state "that is not understood as work."[24] Our *ontologically indifferent* world is incommensurable with the *animal rationale's* world that is interspersed with an *ontological difference*.

1.3 The Meaning of the World

Because the meaning of people and things are measured by their functionality in our working world, Jünger calls the ontologically indifferent world *meaningless*.[25] He seeks the hidden *meaning* of total mobilization. Giving the war meaning is "a holy duty with respect to the fallen,"[26] he formulates after the First World War. Are the millions of fallen the result of a relatively coincidental short-circuit in European relationships, and with that meaningless, or are the horrors of the war part of a meaningful order "whose unity escapes us"? If there was a hidden meaning behind the "material battles," then the deaths of millions of soldiers—and lastly the destruction of the categories of the *animal rationale*—were in no way meaningless, rather *legitimized* and in fact a *sacrifice.*[27] "The working world expects, hopes to be given meaning."[28]

What does Jünger mean by *meaning*? In the metaphysical tradition, the *idea* or category is the fixed measurement or unity in which things have their order and significance, their *meaning*. Although such a meaning cannot be achieved in total mobilization, the working world nevertheless has a hidden *meaning* for it.[29] He finds the foundation of his belief in the meaning of the world in the law of the conservation of energy, which Jünger understands metaphysically. Because it is impossible "that the sum, the potency of the life force lessens," he is convinced that "every departed space"—nihilism as our normal state, in which every *idea* is destroyed—"is filled by new forces."[30] We shall see that Jünger finds this new force in the gestalt of the worker. The millions of fallen would have then not given up their lives for nothing, rather they would have been *sacrificed* in the total mobilization for the rise of the gestalt of the worker. The gestalt is the "source of meaning" and characterizes "a meaningful order."[31] Which cause did Jünger actually have for the concept of a gestalt (Section 1.4), and what is it actually (Section 1.5)?

1.4 The Experience of the *Gestalt-Switch* at the Battle of Langemarck

Jünger sees a reference to the gestalt in the Battle of Langemarck. In total mobilization he suspects a *gestalt-switch*, a transformation of the appearance of the world and the human responsiveness to the world as a unity. The shaking of the world order reveals itself namely not only in the transformation of the way the world appears in the First World War, when the world presents itself as totally mobilized. The *perception* of total mobilization is also included in this transformation, since Jünger suddenly sees himself therein *as* a functionary in the middle of total mobilization *as* a worker.[32] It not only destroys the categories of the *animal rationale*, but at the same time a type of warrior emerges that is completely adapted to and *is responsive* to the totally mobilized world.[33]

The new warrior no longer avails himself of the categories of the *animal rationale*. The soldier on the front no longer employs all means to seek possibilities in order to adjust the action and further regulate it, rather he is ready for battle. In that, Jünger sees how *another* type or race looms on the horizon. This new type manifests itself in the altered relationships that warriors have with death. The drive for individual self-preservation is foreign to the new warrior; he is capable of using his body beyond self-preservation as an *instrument*. "His fighting strength is no individual value, rather a functional one; one no longer falls, rather one gives out."[34] One gives out like an apparatus that has lost its function. Here, another race comes to light that is connected with the totally mobilized world and corresponds to this as functionary or worker. The shaking of the world order thus points to not only the transformation of the appearance of the world, but also contains the "a priori" of an altered thinking, and that is the reason for Jünger to speak of a gestalt.[35]

When namely the characteristics of the world *and* human responsiveness to the world change at the same time, this change can no longer be understood as another world-*view*. It does not relate primarily to *thought*, rather the categories within which the world *and* human responsiveness to the world appear, a simultaneous transformation of Being and thought. It then makes sense to speak of a gestalt; the *gestalt*, not man, mobilizes the world that corresponds to the new warrior. That means that the mobilization of the world through the gestalt and the mobilization of the warriors through the same gestalt run parallel. Jünger experienced this *gestalt-switch* in the Battle of Langemarck, and this experience is the original meaning of the shaking of the world order. It evokes in him the supposition of a new purpose of Being[36] in the middle of total mobilization—the gestalt of the worker—that could guarantee "a new security and rank order of life."[37] This gestalt is the ontologically different in relation to things and people, which first become visible in the light of this gestalt-switch.[38]

1.5 The Gestalt of the Worker as the Ontologically Different

In *The Worker*, Jünger asserts that "in the epoch we now enter, the stamping of space, time, and man can be attributed to . . . the gestalt of the worker."[39] But what does "stamp" mean? He describes the gestalt as a summarizing unity or measure within which the world appears as ordered. For the gestalt of the worker, this unity must be sought in work, that is, in the stamped *appearance* of reality *as* work.

Work cannot be identified with the work-character of our totally mobilized world. As we have seen, our working world, which has been interspersed with ontological *in*difference, has neither unity nor measure for the ordered appearance of the world. In contrast, in the epoch of the worker, "work" would be the ontologically different unity or the standard in whose light the world shows itself as ordered (work) and man finds his determination (worker). The gestalt relates to space, time and man, that is, it is the appearance of the world *as* work and human responsiveness to the world *as* worker.

How do the unity of the gestalt and the world as its abstraction relate to each other? The gestalt is not the cause of the ordered appearance of the world. According to Jünger, the world is ordered by the more decisive—that is *ontological*—law of stamps and imprints.[40] It can be compared to a coining machine. This machine stamps a type of token—Euros and Euro cents—into coins. What is typical of such a series of stamped coins? We do not find the type through the abstraction of concrete coins in order to find its archetype. For a comparison of different coins with each other, we need, if we wish to compare coins with *coins* rather than, for example, coins with a wallet, a basis of comparison. We have always *seen,* with other words, the coin *as* coin. The type is a model or a measure within which the multiplicity—the different coins that come off the production line—appear *as* the same. That the coins appear as the same is not an issue of the coins, but rather of the type.

So where does the difference between the gestalt and the type lie if they both are evidence of a "unity" or "standard?" In *The Worker*, the word "type" implies a new race—the type of the worker—which finds its determination in the "representation" of the gestalt of the worker (I will come back to this representational relationship presently). The type of the worker thus relates to the unity of the essence of man in the epoch of the worker, and Jünger sees its precursors in the new warrior, who emerges in the First World War and is responsive to total mobilization.

Although Jünger speaks of the gestalt of the *worker* rather than the gestalt of *work,* the unity of the gestalt is not reserved for man. The unity of the gestalt touches upon the description of the characteristics of the world and human responsiveness to the world, such as became clear in the example of the totally mobilized world and the new race of warriors. "The simultaneity of certain resources with a certain humanity does not depend on coincidence, rather is contained in the frame of a higher-ranking necessity. The unity of man with his resources is therefore the expression of a unity of a high-ranking type."[41] The unity of the gestalt lies in the structure of Being and thinking through the stamp of our technological reality *as* technological space and of human responsiveness to the world *as* the type of the worker (see Chapter 3 for a closer determination of this coordination).

The unity of the gestalt is thus not itself again that of the type, for the type is first type thanks to the stamp of the gestalt—the gestalt is *type-formation power*[42]—that relates not only to people, but also to the characteristics of the world. Because the gestalt relates to the characteristics of the world and human responsiveness to the world *as belonging together,* as *unity,* this unity of the gestalt of Jünger's is also called a *totality.*[43]

That the gestalt is not only related to the way the world appears, but at the same time relates to human responsiveness to the world, also shows the relationship between the gestalt, the type and the individual. Let us return to the example of the minting machine. The coins, which were minted with the help of the coin punch, are its expression and with that can be called the agent or representative of the coin punch. The relationship between the type and the gestalt is understood in the same manner, although the gestalt does not itself belong to the inventory of the world. As we usually only see the coin but not the coin punch, we would at best see the stamp of the gestalt, but never the gestalt itself.[44] Jünger calls the gestalt therefore also the environment that determines the order without being able to be captured itself: "Our view lies on this side of the prism, which breaks the colored ray into colorful lights. We see the filings, but we do not see the magnetic field, whose reality determines their order."[45] The gestalt is not of this world, rather *presents itself only in the representation* through the type. Jünger thus also speaks in *The Worker* of the *type of the worker as representative of the gestalt of the worker*. The individual also has gestalt insofar as he appears in the light of the gestalt as its representative.[46]

Now it should be attempted to explicate the ontological relevance of the unity of Being and thinking, which is under consideration with the gestalt-switch. Jünger describes such a gestalt-switch in the example of time in *The Hourglass Book*.[47]

In *The Hourglass Book,* Jünger portrays how time becomes visible in elemental clocks and the mechanical clock in fundamentally different ways. The characteristic of time orients itself in elemental clocks towards the "human masses" like the cyclical movements of the sun or the flowing of sand in an hourglass. Time, as the mechanical watch indicates, is in contrast chronologically predictable, calculable, and in this sense differentiated from cosmic and earthly time. "It is not time that is given, like sunlight and elements, rather time that man gives to himself and accepts."[48]

When the mechanical watch came into use, not only did the characteristics of time change with it, but also human responsiveness to the world. "Where such a transition takes place, one may assume that not only the assessment of time has changed, but also the sense of time— the swing of the pendulum in man's heart."[49] The transition of cyclical time to chronologically calculable time is thus also the "a priori of an altered thinking."[50] The *gestalt-switch* with that means a *transformation of the appearance of the world and the human responsiveness to the world as belonging together, as a unity.*[51]

The ontological relevance of the gestalt becomes clear when one considers that the gestalt-switch is not the *consequence* of the discovery of the mechanical watch. It is "an external sign of *decisions* that must have *struck lonely spirits in their cells around the year 1000.*"[52] The *decisions* are determined by the incomparably differently stamped *way of appearance* of reality and the human responsiveness to the world *as* chronological allocatability of the gestalt. The invention of the mechanical watch is an "external sign" of this gestalt-switch; that means that the lonely monks could first discover the mechanical watch therein; first when time, space and the human responsiveness to the world appear as chronological allocatability does the invention of the mechanical watch have a meaning *as* a time counter. "The switches" are contrived with the transformation of our understanding of time, "and with that all points that can be reached are determined."[53] The *decision* itself concerns the incomparably different way time is structured by the gestalt, and the ontological relevance of the gestalt reveals itself in this appearance of a new understanding of time.

The discussion of the gestalt shows that it is not a being that can be discovered in addition to the already known things of the world, rather it reveals itself as the *ontologically different*. That becomes clear when we ask ourselves how, according to Jünger, the gestalt becomes *accessible* to us. The unity of the gestalt cannot be described in a *developmental history,* nor is it accessible through comparison with other gestalts. These manners of access are suited to thematize beings, but not the gestalt as the complete *Otherness* of beings, i.e., *Being.* We will now briefly explicate why Jünger believes the gestalt lies beyond development and value.

The gestalt lies *beyond* development, because developments unfold one at a time *within* time, while the gestalt stamps the appearance of time itself. The gestalt is understood as a "dormant Being."[54] Unlike beings, Being is not subject to increase or decrease, birth or death, in short to no development, nor can any developmental history of this gestalt be described.[55] "History brings forth no gestalts," rather the characteristic of time changes through the influence of the gestalt.[56] That the gestalt does not depend on development, however, does not mean that no developments appear in the world. The gestalt does not depend on time, but determines the development of nascent life.[57]

Just as the gestalt stands beyond development, because it relates not to beings, but to Being, so it stands equally beyond value. Although, in the epoch of the worker, the gestalt stamps the world *as* technological space *and* human responsiveness to the world *as* the type of the worker, we gain no insight into the gestalt through the comparison of different eras. The gestalt possesses namely no characteristics or features that, like things in the world, would become comprehensible through comparison.[58] The gestalt lies beyond value; that means that the eras which have been informed by the gestalt are definitively disparate and with that, cannot be compared.[59]

That the gestalt lies beyond development and value thus means that it is neither a being nor can be accessible *as* a being, rather relates fully to the incomparable, i.e., Being. Because total mobilization primarily has the effect of engendering ontological indifference, the *seeing* of the gestalt as the ontologically different in the middle of total mobilization necessitates a "new opening of the eyes."[60] This opening of the eyes is a *stamping* by the gestalt, which enables Jünger to see the incomparably changed unity of the appearance of the world (work) and the way humans cope with it (worker)—and with this the *gestalt-switch*.[61] This happened to him during the Battle of Langemarck, and in this sense, the "shaking of the world order" can be considered a date in the original sense of the word, namely a *gestalt-switch* that emerged and was *given* or *passed* to human thought, which from his side corresponds to this switch as representative of the gestalt.

Notes

1. Jünger, Ernst, "Über die Linie. Martin Heidegger zum 60. Geburtstag," *Sämtliche Werke*, vol. 7 (Stuttgart: Klett-Cotta, 1980) 264 (hereafter cited as: *ÜdL*, 264).
2. Jünger, Ernst, *Maxima—Minima. Adnoten zum "Arbeiter."* *Sämtliche Werke*, vol. 8 (Stuttgart: Klett-Cotta, 1981), 325 (hereafter cited as: *MM*, 325); Jünger, Ernst, *Der Arbeiter. Herrschaft und gestalt. Sämtliche Werke*, vol. 8 (Stuttgart: Klett-Cotta, 1981) 65 (hereafter cited as *Arb*, 65).
3. *Arb*, 99.
4. Jünger, Ernst, *In Stahlgewittern. Sämtliche Werke*, vol. 1 (Stuttgart: Klett-Cotta, 1978) 11 (hereafter cited as *Sta*, 11).
5. *Arb*, 113–114.
6. In this study Jünger's biographical information and his political positions during the years between the wars will not be further discussed. In 1932, for example, Jünger believed that the emergence of the worker was related to the rise of Germany (*Arb*, 31, cf. 42–45). Later he said politics refers to real power, on which the concept of the gestalt as a *metaphysical* power has no or only indirect influence (cf. Jünger, Ernst. *Type, Name, Gestalt. Sämtliche Werke*, vol. 13 (Stuttgart: Klett-Cotta, 1981) 85, 149 (hereafter cited as: *TNG*, 85, 149). Karlheinz Hasselbach demonstrates with convincing arguments that *The Worker* included in contrast to the opinions of many interpreters, above all "considerations of the unpolitical (Hasselbach, K., "Das weite Feld jenseits von rechts und links: Zum konservativ-revolutionären Geist von Ernst Jüngers *Der Arbeiter. Herrschaft und Gestalt*," *Literaturwissenschaftliches Jahrbuch*, Volume 36, 1995: 229–242; cf. Bein. S., "Der Arbeiter. Type—Name—Gestalt," *Wandlung und Wiederkehr. Festschrift zum 70. Geburtstag Ernst Jüngers*, ed. H.L. Arnold (Aachen: Verlag Dr. Rudolf Georgi, 1965) 109–110). Because the primary concern in *The Worker* is the concept of the gestalt, we leave the "political," "accidental" and "polemic" aspects of this work outside of consideration (cf. *Arb*, 11–13). See also the study by Schwarz, H.-P. *Der konservative Anarchist. Politik und Zeitkritik Ernst Jüngers* (Freiburg im Breisgau: Verlag Rombach, 1962). For biographical information cf. Meyer, M., *Ernst Jünger* (München/Wien: Carl Hanser Verlag, 1990) and, more recently, the thorough biographies of Kiesel, H., *Ernst Jünger. Die Biographie* (München: Siedler Verlag, 2007) and Schwilk, H., *Ernst Jünger. Ein Jahrhundertleben* (München/Zürich: Piper, 2007).
7. *Arb*, 115.
8. Cf. *Arb*, 59–61, 161–165, 209; Jünger, Ernst, "Feuer und Bewegung," *Sämtliche Werke*, vol. 7 (Stuttgart: Klett-Cotta, 1980) 110 (hereafter cited as: *FB*, 110); Jünger, Ernst, *Das Wäldchen 125. Eine Chronik aus den Grabenkämpfen 1918, Sämtliche Werke*, vol. 1 (Stuttgart: Klett-Cotta, 1978) 330 (hereafter cited as: *W*, 125, 330); Jünger, Ernst, *Feuer und Blut. Ein kleiner Ausschnitt aus einer großen Schlacht, Sämtliche Werke*, vol. 1 (Stuttgart: Klett-Cotta, 1978) 451 (hereafter cited as: *FBl*, 451).
9. Cf. *Sta*, 72, 132, 204, 206, 272–273, 285; *W*, 125, 304–306, 309, 354–356; *FBl*, 441–446, 487–489, 491.
10. *Arb*, 119.
11. Jünger, Ernst. *Politische Publizistik 1919 bis 1933* (Stuttgart: Klett-Cotta, 2001) 105 (hereafter cited as *PP*, 105).
12. The discussion of whether the basis for Jünger's worker lies in the experience of nihilism is still underway. While Heidegger in *The Question of Being* directly and plainly determines that *The Worker* "has provided a description of European nihilism in its phase following the First World War" (Heidegger, Martin, "Zur Seinsfrage," *Wegmarken*, Gesamtausgabe, vol. 9 [Frankfurt am Main: Vittorio Klostermann, 1976] 389 [tr. 294]), Günter Figal believes Jünger

found this basis in the *new orientation* regarding the gestalt of the worker: "So his thinking about nihilism in the interim, the directionless fixedness between no-longer and not-yet, is completely foreign to him." Figal, Günter. "Der metaphysische Charaktere der Moderne. Ernst Jüngers Schrift *Über die Linie* (1950) und Martin Heideggers Kritik *Über'die Linie'* (1955)," *Ernst Jünger im 20. Jahrhundert*, ed. H.-H. Müller and H. Segeberg (München: Wilhelm Fink Verlag, 1995) 188. This study explores the thought that Jünger's fundamental experience is thoroughly that of nihilism (cf. *Arb*, 88, 99, 100–101), but that he first experienced a *gestalt-switch* during the First World War. The experience of *The Worker* is thus thoroughly one of an interim in which the gestalt of the worker can only be divined.

13. *Arb*, 113–114.
14. *Arb*, 113–114.
15. *Arb*, 93–94; cf. *Arb*, 98.
16. Mobilization previously had the character of a partial measure, because only soldiers had been sent to the front, and the costs of the war, "albeit extraordinary, had in no way meant a limitless expense from the available forces and resources" (Jünger, Ernst, *Die Totale Mobilmachung. Sämtliche Werke*, vol. 7 (Stuttgart: Klett-Cotta, 1980), 124 (hereafter cited as *TM*, 124).
17. *TM*, 125; cf. *Arb*, 224.
18. *Arb*, 167.
19. *Arb*, 176–177; cf. *PP*, 86.
20. *TM*, 125.
21. *TM*, 125–126; cf. *Arb*, 153.
22. *TNG*, 87; cf. 113–114; *Arb*, 12; *ÜdL*, 256–261.
23. Cf. *PP*, 95.
24. *Arb*, 95.
25. Jünger, Ernst. *Sturm. Sämtliche Werke*, vol. 15 (Stuttgart: Klett-Cotta, 1978) 17 (hereafter cited as *Stu*, 17).
26. *PP*, 50.
27. Cf. *Arb*, 42, 71–72, 77–78; *PP*, 12, 22. For the meaning of the victim in Jünger's writings, cf. Koslowski, Peter, *Der Mythos der Moderne. Die dichterische Philosophie Ernst Jüngers* (München: Wilhelm Fink Verlag, 1991) 37–45.
28. *MM*, 325; *Arb*, 65–66.
29. *Arb*, 65–66; *MM*, 325; *PP*, 200–203, 320; *ÜdL*, 271.
30. *Arb*, 98; cf. 221; *MM*, 321, 323; *TNG*, 113; *ÜdL*, 259; *W*, 125, 321.
31. *Arb*, 158, 308.
32. Cf. *Sta*, 13; Heumakers, A. and Oudemans, Th.C.W., *De horizon van Buitenveldert* (Amsterdam: Boom, 1997) 118.
33. *Arb*, 59–63; *KE*, 37, 54–61, 73, 89–90, 102–103; *Sta*, 99, 149; *W*, 125, 354, 356; *FBl*, 446; *Stu*, 25–27.
34. *Arb*, 115–118, 157–158.
35. *Arb*, 61, 244; cf. *ÜdL*, 251–252. We will come back to this issue in Part III.
36. Jünger speaks in *The Worker*, for example, of an "existential revolution."
37. *Arb*, 99.
38. Most of the secondary literature on Jünger overlooked this ontological dimension of the gestalt and highlights the political aspects of the concept. For an overview, cf. Droste, V., *Ernst Jünger: "Der Arbeiter." Studien zu seiner Metaphysik* (Mainz: Dissertation, 1980) 46–52, 98–106.
39. *Arb*, 37.
40. *Arb*, 37, 236.
41. *Arb*, 244.
42. *TNG*, 88; *MM*, 327, 395.
43. The word "totality" is misleading, since it seems to mean the sum of all things and people. Jünger in contrast speaks of the gestalt as a whole "that comprises

more than the sum of its parts." (*Arb*, 37–39). Jünger compares it with the example of man. "A man is more than the sum of atoms, limbs, organs and fluids of
which he is composed." (*Arb*, 39). We know similar examples from sociology:
society is more than the sum of its members, a forest is more than the sum of its
trees. With these models, Jünger tries to show that the gestalt is more than the
sum of temporal and spatial things in the world. The totality of the gestalt now
refers precisely to the appearances of things and the human responsiveness to
the world as a *unity, as a whole* (*Arb*, 37, 42). As a result, it also becomes clear
in which sense Jünger's gestalt cannot be oriented towards "gestalt psychology,"
which had many adherents. Gestalt psychology opposes the thought that psychic
life is built from elements (for example, perceptions and feelings). In contrast,
it regards everything that man experiences as a unity, as an indivisible gestalt
(cf. Metzger, W., "gestalt," *Historisches Wörterbuch der Philosophie*, eds. J.
Ritters, K. Gründer, and G. Gabriel, vol. 3 (Basel: Schwabe & Co, 1974) 3, 547.
Although Jünger concedes that in the nineteenth century the view begins to open
for this majority—and we can assume that he meant gestalt psychology with
that—there is no *essential* difference to the thinkers who relegate this excess "to
the realm of dreams": "certainly the majority of the opponents of logicians and
mathematicians of life also moved to a level, to the one that they battled, with
no difference in rank. For there is no difference, whether one refers to a detached
soul or a detached idea instead of a detached person" (*Arb*, 39). In contrast to
Heidegger's thesis—"You understand the word *gestalt* initially in the sense of
the *gestalt* psychology of the time, as 'a whole that contains more than the sum
of its parts'" (Heidegger, "Zur Seinsfrage," 394 (tr. 298)—the gestalt cannot
be understood from a psychological totality. That is seen in that the gestalt is
related to the unity of the delineation of things *and* the human responsiveness
to the world, rather than to a detached psychological totality of the person who
is being. For this reason, the history of the term of the gestalt will not be further
examined here either. (cf. *TNG*, 134).

44. *Arb*, 37, 89; *TNG*, 86.
45. *Arb*, 89; cf. *TNG*, 141–142.
46. It is of great important to recognize that this relationship of representation
    between the gestalt, the type and the individual is *concrete* and not *abstract*. Just
    as we find the type of coin not through abstraction of the concrete coin, so does
    Jünger show in the example of man that the individual is included in the totality
    of the gestalt. "Man possesses gestalt insofar as he is understood as the concrete,
    the tangible individual" (*Arb*, 38). The abstraction of concrete man produces
    only the unity of the term "man." This unity of the term can never describe
    something concrete. The totality of the gestalt in which the individual is included
    describes on the other hand a *concrete* relationship: the individual owns the
    gestalt, insofar as he appears in the light of the gestalt as its representative. This
    is to be calculated "neither through multiplication nor through division—many
    people have yet to produce a gestalt, and no division of the gestalt leads back
    to the individual" (*Arb*, 38). That also explains why Jünger explicitly differen-
    tiates the gestalt from the *idea* (*MM*, 373). In doing so he also understands the
    idea, as Heidegger remarks, in the modern sense as the notion of the subject
    (Heidegger, "Zur Seinsfrage," 395). The gestalt is not interchangeable with the
    "idea," because the idea, in contrast to the *concrete* gestalt is *thought* and not
    experienced (Bein, "Der Arbeiter. Type—Name—Gestalt," 109). The gestalt as
    ontological difference, however, is to be identified with the Platonic *idea*: "On
    the other hand, for you too *gestalt* is accessible only in a seeing. The seeing in
    question is that which the Greeks call ἰδεῖν, a word that Plato uses to refer to a
    seeing that catches sight not of that which is changeable and can be perceived
    by the senses, but of the unchangeable, being, the ἰδέα. You too characterize
    gestalt as 'being that is at rest.' The *gestalt* is not an 'idea' in the modern sense,

and thus not a regulative representation of reason in Kant's sense of the word. For Greek thinking, being that is at rest remains purely distinguished (different) from changeable beings. This difference between being and beings then appears, when seen starting from beings and moving toward being, as transcendence, i.e., as the meta-physical" (Heidegger, "Zur Seinsfrage," 395 (tr. 298)).

47. Jünger, Ernst, *Das Sanduhrbuch, Sämtliche Werke,* vol. 12 (Stuttgart: Klett-Cotta, 1979) 101–250 (hereafter cited as *SB,* 101–150).
48. *SB,* 140–141.
49. *SB,* 136; cf. 138.
50. *Arb,* 61, 244; cf. *ÜdL,* 251–252.
51. Jünger also speaks in this context of "inclusion" and "belonging" (*Arb,* 154–155). "All of that points to the fact the word 'time' possesses the most different meanings. But the issue is not only of meaning, but also of layers that beleaguer and saturate us like a labyrinth" (*SB,* 109; cf. *Arb,* 93–97).
52. *SB,* 138.
53. *SB,* 138.
54. *Arb,* 40; cf. 50.
55. Although the further question of the type as product of developmental history at this point leads too far, one should here think of Wilhelm Dilthey. He is an exponent of those thinkers who began in the nineteenth century to see totality as "more than the sum of its parts." Totality develops, and we can see it thanks to the method of comparison: "Not the assumption of a rigid a priori of our ability to recognize, rather only a developmental history that departs from the totality of our essence can answer the question that we all turn towards in philosophy." Dilthey, W., *Einleitung in die Geisteswissenschaften. Gesammelte Schriften,* vol. 1 (Göttingen/Zürich: Teubner/Vandenhoeck & Ruprecht, 1962) xviii. This method is, however irrevocable the thought of a "detached soul"—the physical context—arrested, which the world *discovers* (Cf. also: Dilthey, W., *Ideen über eine beschreibende und zergliedernde Psychologie. Gesammelte Schriften,* vol. 5 [Göttingen/Zürich: B.G. Teubner/Vandenhoeck & Ruprecht 1964] 156). According to Jünger, the totality of the gestalt cannot be understood in this way. On the contrary, our considerations and speaking of the gestalt are involved in this totality, *belong* to it (*Arb,* 38).
56. *Arb,* 86; cf. 143–144.
57. *Arb,* 125; *TNG,* 147; *MM,* 332; *SB,* 109.
58. Moreover, *we* do not have the standard with which such a comparison can ultimately succeed. The gestalt stamps space, time *and* man in it: "A new era decides what counts as art, what counts as standard. That which distinguishes two eras is not the higher or lesser value, rather plainly the otherness" (*Arb,* 87–88; cf. 93).
59. Cf. *SB,* 153.
60. *Arb,* 38.
61. In later works, Jünger also called the new impact of the eyes influenced by the gestalt "Divination" (*TNG,* 152, 155, 169), the "approaching" (*TNG,* 162) or the "overwhelming" (*TNG,* 151, 164). Cf. Chapters 3 and 4.

2 Intermezzo
The Will to Power in Nietzsche

Because Jünger tries to find an answer to "European nihilism" as it was inaugurated by Friedrich Nietzsche, and this answer is heavily indebted to his doctrine of the will to power, we will briefly introduce Nietzsche's thought as an intermezzo in this chapter.[1] In the next section we can ask then what is the specific nature of the human responsiveness to the turning of being which is at stake in *The Worker;* the representation of the gestalt of the worker by the will to power as art.

Nietzsche is affected by nihilism, i.e., the experience that the Platonic horizon of the transcendental *idea* or the essence of things is being erased.[2] This experience is eminently discussed in "The Parable of the Madman" in *The Gay Science,* where Nietzsche speaks about the death of God.[3] The death of God does not indicate the death of the Christian God nor the growing atheism. "God" is first and foremost the name of the Platonic horizon of the transcendental *idea* or essence of things:

> Who gave us the sponge to wipe away the whole horizon? What did we do when we loosened this earth from its sun? Whither does it now move? Whither do we move? Away from all suns? Do we not dash on unceasingly? Backwards, sideways, forwards, in all directions? Is there still an above and below? Do we not stray, as through infinite nothingness?[4]

Nietzsche speaks of a decoupling of the earth from its sun and our wiping away the whole horizon. The question is what concepts like sun and earth actually mean here. In his reflection on the relation between earth and sun, Nietzsche thinks of the location of the sun in Plato's allegory of the cave.[5]

In *The Republic,* Plato says that we, in addition to things visible in themselves and our ability to perceive things, need a third instance in order to grasp things: light, through which we can first see the visible things across from us. In order to clarify this approach, Plato raises the double meaning of the sun. The sun is in the first instance a heavenly body that I see and about which I can make various statements. For example, I can say: the sun nourishes plants and helps them grow. Plato, however, sees that I myself have to stand in the light of the sun in order to be able to look at this heavenly body in the sky. The sun is the light through which I can see the heavenly body. On the one hand, the sunlight is according to that a heavenly body (Being) to which I can ascribe different characteristics, and at the same time, the very instance through which I can first see this heavenly body at all (Being). Plato calls this light of the sun the *zugon*, the yoke that holds together our *seeing* the sun and the sun itself as the *seen*.[6] I always have to be standing in this light of Being in order to be able to see a visible being.

Plato understands this light of the sun as the idea, or appearance, in whose light things can appear as themselves. Our wiping away of the horizon, as discussed by Nietzsche, points to the destruction of the Platonic horizon of the transcendental idea or essence of things, in which everything in the world has its fixed orientation and meaning. In the metaphysical tradition, the transcendental idea or essence of things counts as the truth and real world. Contrary to this transcendental and therefore *meta-physical* world of the idea (Being), our *physical world on planet* earth is unreal because it is permeated by contingency and change. Metaphysics distinguishes between the physical world we can see, hear and feel—Nietzsche calls this the earth or the world of becoming—and the metaphysical world of the idea; this metaphysical world of the idea is the measure for our earthly existence. The separation of the earth from the sun then means that there is no metaphysical measure anymore for our contingent existence on earth. According to Nietzsche, we wander through an "infinite nothingness."[7] The death of God therefore points to the experience of nihilism.

Since when does nihilism reign according to Nietzsche? In a note from 1887, Nietzsche says what nihilism means: "that the highest values devalue themselves."[8] This definition makes clear that Nietzsche understands the Platonic horizon of the idea as a domain of highest *values*. Nihilism concerns the experience that there are no values anymore—the devaluation of the values and in that sense the "nihil" of any given measure for our earthly existence—and with this that the Platonic *idea* has lost its value. This definition also makes clear that Nietzsche understands nihilism as a historical event, in which the highest values lose their binding force for our earthly existence. Although the word "nihilism" became prevalent in the nineteenth century, this historic event did not only occur in Nietzsche's lifetime.[9] According to Nietzsche, nihilism has reigned in the history of the West since Plato. We do not only speak of nihilism in the case of the devaluation of the Platonic horizon of the transcendental idea or essence of things.

In what sense can the metaphysical tradition be called nihilistic? The metaphysical *affirmation* of the transcendental-metaphysical world of Being is, according to Nietzsche, basically the negation of the world of becoming. The nihilistic character of metaphysics lies in the fact that the transcendental is represented as true Being, and all other beings are reduced to non-Being.[10] Metaphysics itself is nihilistic, because the prevalence of the "higher" or "better" world of the transcendental *idea* or essence of things involves the devaluation or the "nihil" of earthly existence.[11] This nihilism dominates the whole metaphysical tradition from Plato on. And that is why Nietzsche says that nihilism concerns the history of the West, in which it increasingly becomes clear that the transcendental and highest values are actually *nothing*.

Nietzsche tries to overcome this nihilism—the devaluation of the highest values—by a "revaluation of all values."[12] This response to the devaluation does not concern the destruction of their content. Such a destruction would maintain the metaphysical distinction between the transcendental world of Being and the world of becoming we live in, and only replace its content. Nietzsche calls this form of nihilism weak or *incomplete*.[13] Nietzsche criticizes this incomplete form of nihilism not because it represents the highest values, but because it places these values in a transcendental realm of Being, while our earthly existence in the world of becoming is devaluated.

The *complete* form of nihilism, on the contrary, does not merely replace old values for new ones, but rejects the transcendental realm of values as a measure for our earthly existence as such. Where then does Nietzsche find the principle of valuation? Nietzsche's revaluation of values is opposed to the transcendental world of Being and affirms the earthly world of becoming as the principle of valuation.[14] This reversal of Platonism includes an "inversion" of the concept of value: values are no longer estimated on the basis of a given measure, but values themselves are estimated by life itself. In conjunction with the question of "life" as a principle of valuation, we will now reflect on the will to power as a fundamental characteristic of life and, in the end, of the universe itself.[15]

In a note from winter 1887–1888, Nietzsche presents a concise formulation of his doctrine of the will to power:

> All "purposes," "goals," "meanings" are only modes of expression and metamorphoses of the single will that inheres in all that happens, the will to power; . . . having purposes, goals, intentions, *willing in general*, amounts to willing more strength, willing growth, and also willing the *means to this*; . . . All valuations are only consequences and narrower perspectives *in the service of this one will*: valuation itself is only this will to power.[16]

Life's valuation estimates values that are able to promote life (power-enhancement and growth) and shows with this its desire or *will* to become stronger and more powerful.[17] This estimation of values—what was once the given measure or *idea* of the things in the world—can be understood in terms of perspectivism. Perspectival valuation estimates values in which light reality appears and is explained as favorable or not favorable for life: a forest for example appears as a potential producer of wood or as a site for recreation after work. This perspectival valuation decides what we can and what we cannot encounter; a turtle hears the softest rustle in the grass but not the gun shot fired near her.[18]

If we want to know what the favorability for life consists of, we have to ask about the nature of life itself. According to Nietzsche, self-preservation and self-enhancement belong together as fundamental features of life. Each self-preservation of life serves the growth of strength and power, because a life that is purely focused on self-preservation would already imply its demise according to Nietzsche. Therefore, the self-preservation is never the "goal" or "destination" of life as such, but always and only as a means for the goal of self-enhancement. This self-enhancement is in turn dependent on the self-preservation of life; any transgression of life leads again to its preservation, which in turn is the starting point for each and every new self-enhancement (we will show this in a moment concretely based on the two interrelated appearances of the will to power). Because life, according to Nietzsche, is characterized by both self-preservation *and* self-enhancement, he characterizes life not in terms of "Being" but in terms of "becoming." The will to power as the nature of life itself is, according to Nietzsche, the principle of the "devaluation of all values."

According to Nietzsche, the will to power is the fundamental feature of life and ultimately of the universe itself, i.e., it is Nietzsche's answer to the metaphysical question of what Being as such is. As Martin Heidegger has shown, the perspectival estimation of values is an expression of the will to power, but this valuation cannot be interpreted in a psychological way. It belongs in Nietzsche's philosophical thought and with this in the philosophical tradition;[19] the will to power points to the appearance of reality *as* favorable or not favorable for one's own life, that is to say, as potential energy for self-preservation (*Machterhaltung*) and self-enhancement (*Machtsteigerung*). With this, we receive an indication of the two appearances of the will to power—the will to power as truth and the will to power as art—which can now be discussed in more detail.

Nietzsche takes the true world of the idea back in life's perspectival valuation and unmasks with this the metaphysical question about the transcendental idea or essence of things as a *will to truth*. There is, according to Nietzsche, no such thing as a transcendental world of eternal "Being," but only the perspectival estimation of values which is led by the will to power of life.[20] The will to truth aims at the stabilization (Being) of the world of becoming by the perspectival estimation of values—*idea*, category, scheme—in which reality appears as order.[21] Nietzsche unmasks the metaphysical question about the transcendent essence of things as will to truth, because this truth as stable presence (Being) in fact is only apparent (*Schein*); there is only the world of becoming, which is characterized by contingency and change. The truth as the stable presence of the essence of things does therefore not originate in a transcendental world of the *idea*, but in the will to power, that is, the will to stabilize.[22] The will to truth is according to Nietzsche only appearance (*Schein*), but nevertheless favorable for life. The stabilization of the contingent and the transitory is appearance and at the same time prerequisite for life, because life (becoming) would evaporate in constant variability and contingency without any stabilization.[23]

Although the idea of a transcendental world of the idea is an error according to Nietzsche, it is at the same time a necessary condition for the preservation of life amidst the world of becoming.

First of all, it becomes clear here why Nietzsche understands the transcendental world of the *idea* as a world of values. The *idea* as stabilization of the world of becoming with a view to "Being" is indeed favorable for life and in this sense a precondition for the self-preservation of life amidst the world of becoming. Secondly, it becomes clear here why self-enhancement and self-preservation are mutually dependent. The will to truth is a necessary condition for life, i.e., for the continuation and preservation of life amidst contingency and change. At the same time, this stabilized and permanent being appears amidst the world of becoming as the point of departure of life's self-enhancement.

The aspiration of the will to truth is to consolidate and stabilize the world of becoming and as such, to destroy this *becoming* aspect of life which aspires the enhancement and growth of power. The will to truth is, in other words, a necessary but not a sufficient condition for life, because it is insufficient for the enhancement and growth of power. Nietzsche therefore says that we are in need of art in order not to be destroyed by the truth.[24] This brings us to the other side of the will to power, namely the will to power as art.

Art does not primarily indicate works of fine art, but the creative or founding character that is the origin of each and every perspectival estimation of values. Perspectivism does not only estimate values in order to stabilize the world of becoming with a view to Being (will to truth), but also creates *opportunities* in which nascent life can transcend itself into a new necessary order. The latter is called the will to power as art according to Nietzsche. Because the will to power as art is the essence of life according to Nietzsche, the creation of works of fine art is only a special case of the will to power as art, which is "inherent in every event." Art is life-enhancing, because life itself creates opportunities in which the world of *becoming* is transcended (power-enhancement). Art wants to bring life itself to power by the perspectival estimation of *possibilities* in which the *becoming* of life (*das werdende Leben*) can transcend itself into a new necessary order.

It is against the background of Nietzsche's doctrine of the will to power, which can be outlined only briefly here, that Jünger develops his idea of the will to power as art to transcend total mobilization into a new necessary order in *The Worker*, the type of the worker as representation of the gestalt of the worker. We will postpone the description of a concrete example of the will to power as art in this section, since we will extensively return to this in the next chapter.

Notes

1. For the influence of various philosophical movements like platonism, spiritism and pantheism on Jünger's thought, cf. Schwarz, *Der konservative Anarchist*, 26–29 (Because of his concentration on the "political ideology" of Jünger, Schwarz overlooks the essential meaning of Nietzsche's doctrine of the will to

power for Jünger's thought and on the contrary emphasizes the influence of *Preußentum und Sozialismus* by Oswald Spengler on Jünger's thought in *The Worker* [Schwarz, *Der konservative Anarchist*, 79–83]). In the first edition of *Copse 125 (Das Wäldchen*, 125), Jünger says that he nearly owes all his thought to Nietzsche (cited in: Wilczek, R., *Nihilistische Lektüre des Zeitalters. Ernst Jüngers Nietzsche-Rezeption* [Trier: Wissenschaftlicher Verlag Trier, 1999] 18). For Nietzsche's influence on Jünger's thought, cf. the study by Wilczek (1999) and Ipema, J., "Pessimismus der Stärke. Ernst Jünger & Nietzsche," *Zur Wirkung Nietzsches*, eds. H. Ester and M. Evers (Würzburg: Königshausen & Neumann, 2001) 13–30; cf. Bohrer, K.H., *Die Ästhetik des Schreckens. Die pessimistische Romantik und Ernst Jüngers Frühwerk* (Frankfurt am Main/Berlin/ Wien: Ullstein, 1983) 118.

2. In this section, we confine ourselves to a brief elaboration of Nietzsche's thought. Besides Nietzsche's work itself, we mainly used Heidegger, Martin, "Nietzsches Wort 'Gott ist tot'," *Holzwege*, Gesamtausgabe, vol. 5 (Frankfurt am Main: Vittorio Klostermann, 1977) 209–267 and Visser, G., *Nietzsche en Heidegger. Een confrontatie* (Nijmegen: SUN, 1989). For a critical evaluation of Heidegger's Nietzsche interpretation, cf. Müller-Lauter, W., "Heideggers Nietzsche Lekture: zum Problem des Nihilismus," *Synthesis Philosophica* 11 1996: 123–130; Haar, M. "Critical Remarks on the Heideggerian Reading of Nietzsche," *Martin Heidegger: Critical Assessments*, ed. C. Macann (London: Routledge, 1992) 290–302. Ibáñez-Noé even argues that Heidegger's Nietzsche interpretation is mediated by his reading of the works of Jünger (Ibáñez-Noé, J.A., "Heidegger, Nietzsche, Jünger, and the Interpretation of the Contemporary Age," *The Southern Journal of Philosophy* 33 1995: 57).

3. Nietzsche, Friedrich, *Die fröhliche Wissenschaft*, Kritische Studienausgabe, vol. 3 (Munchen/Berlin: DTV de Gruyter, 1988) 480–482 (tr. 182–183).

4. Nietzsche, Friedrich, *Die fröhliche Wissenschaft*, 481 (tr. 182–183).

5. Heidegger, Martin, *Holzwege*, 261 (tr. 195).

6. Plato, *Republic* (Oxford: Clarendon Press, 1944) 508a–509b.

7. Cf. Heidegger, Martin, *Holzwege*, 217 (tr. 163).

8. Nietzsche, Friedrich, *Kritische Studienausgabe*, vol. 12 (Munchen/Berlin: DTV de Gruyter, 1980) 350.

9. Cf. Heidegger, Martin, *Holzwege*, 218–219 (tr. 163–164).

10. Cf. Heidegger, Martin, *Nietzsche*, Gesamtausgabe, vol. 6.1 (Frankfurt am Main: Vittorio Klostermann, 1996) 143.

11. The principle of this prevalence is the *spirit of revenge*, that is against the unavailable and perishable, and reduces the world of "becoming" in favor of an ideal world of "Being" (Nietzsche, F., *Also Sprach Zarathustra*, Kritische Studienausgabe, vol. 3 (Munchen/Berlin: DTV/De Gruyter, 1993) 128–131; cf. 146–149.

12. Nietzsche, Friedrich, *Kritische Studienausgabe*, vol. 12, 246.

13. Nietzsche, Friedrich, *Kritische Studienausgabe*, vol. 12, 476; Heidegger, *Holzwege*, 225–226; "Metaphysics is still needed by some; but so is that impetuous *demand for certainty* that today discharges itself among large numbers of people in a scientific-positive form. The demand that one *wants* by all means that something should be firm (while on account of the ardor of this demand one is easier and more negligent about the demonstration of this certainty)—this too, is still the demand for a support, a prop, in short, that *instinct of weakness* which, to be sure, does not create religious, metaphysical systems, and convictions of all kinds but—conserves them" (Nietzsche, *Die Fröhliche Wissenschaft*, 581–582). Cf. "I found that all of the supreme value judgments—all that have come to dominate mankind, at least that part that has become restrained—can be derived from the judgments of the exhausted" (Nietzsche, *Kritische Studienausgabe*, vol. 13, 412).

14. Cf. Nietzsche, Friedrich, *Also Sprach Zarathustra*, 99–100; Visser, *Nietzsche en Heidegger. Een confrontatie*, 49–50.
15. Nietzsche, Friedrich, *Jenseits von Gut und Böse. Vorspiel einer Philosophie der Zukunft*, Kritische Studienausgabe, vol. 5 (Munchen/Berlin: DTV de Gruyter, 1993) 55.
16. Nietzsche, Friedrich, *Kritische Studienausgabe*, vol. 13, 44–45.
17. "Final result: all the values by means of which up to now we first tried to make the world estimable to us and with which, once they proved inapplicable, we then *devaluated* it—all these values are, calculated psychologically, the results of particular perspectives of usefulness for the preservation and enhancement of human formations of rule, and only falsely *projected* into the essence of things" (Nietzsche, *Kritische Studienausgabe*, vol. 13, 49).
18. Cf. *Heidegger*, Nietzsche I, 214.
19. Heidegger, Martin, *Holzwege*, 228–240 (tr. 170–171).
20. Nietzsche, Friedrich, *Kritische Studienausgabe*, vol. 12, 354.
21. Nietzsche, Friedrich, *Also Sprach Zarathustra*, 146–149.
22. Cf. Nietzsche, Friedrich, *Die fröhliche Wissenschaft*, 395, 439, 477–478.
23. "Truth is the kind of error without which a certain species of life could not live. The value for life is ultimately decisive" (Nietzsche, *Kritische Studienausgabe*, vol. 11, 506).
24. Nietzsche, Friedrich, *Kritische Studienausgabe*, vol. 13, 500.

3 The Transformation of the Type of the Worker as Representative of the Gestalt of the Worker

The previous examples and references regarding the gestalt must not in any way create the impression that Jünger believes that the gestalt *is*.[1] It was argued in Chapter 1 that total mobilization "is far from that unity that can guarantee a new security and rank order of life,"[2] that is, the way reality is structured by the gestalt, and our human responsiveness. A new stamp of the gestalt does not immediately follow the dwindling of a type, and exactly this vacuum of power is called *nihilism*.[3]

In total mobilization, the gestalt can only be *adumbrated*. The *seeing* of total mobilization must not be confused for the *seeing* of the *gestalt-switch*. "We live in a state . . . in which one must first learn to *see*"[4] that total mobilization is an order influenced by the gestalt in a completely different way. "The past is created in such a way that one cannot cling to it, and the future in such a way that one cannot establish himself in it. . . . What can be seen is not the final order, rather the change of disorder, under which a great law is to be guessed."[5] It is precisely the issue of *The Worker*, of becoming transitive to a world that is no longer characterized by total mobilization, but in which the type of the worker represents the gestalt and in this sense corresponds to the "new turning of Being."

With Nietzsche's theory of the will to power serving as a foundation, Jünger develops the will to power of art in *The Worker*, in order to elevate total mobilization to a new necessary rank order; the representation of the gestalt of the worker through the will to power as art. This chapter asks after the specific nature of the concept of the gestalt, which is raised in *The Worker*. Because this responsiveness to the gestalt of the worker is understood from the will to power as *art*, we call Jünger's way of writing not thinking but *poetry*. First, we will examine the "elemental" in conjunction with the weak or incomplete nihilism of the *animal rationale* and the strong or complete nihilism of the type of the warrior (Section 3.1). Then, the overcoming of total mobilization and the transition toward a new and necessary arrangement of the world order—the dominion of the type of the worker as representation of the gestalt of the worker—will be discussed (Section 3.2).

3.1 Elementary Space: Incomplete versus Complete Nihilism

If reality and human responsiveness to the world appear as totally mobilized, the world can no longer be thought of in the light of the unchanging categories of the *animal rationale;* rather nihilism reigns. Jünger reveals that one cannot avoid total mobilization and with it the demise of the nature of man as *animal rationale*—that is, of man who understands himself and the world in the light of the transcendental essence of things. Rather, he must overcome it. We should even contribute to the destruction of its categories. Why? "First, the complete splintering, the loss of meaning makes it possible for reality to appear in other force fields."[6] As we saw in the first section, Jünger, because of the law of conservation of energy, did not believe that nihilism would last forever, that is, that "every abandoned space [. . .] [will be] filled by new forces."[7] Jünger calls the other force field that shows itself first after the destruction of the categories of the *animal rationale* "elemental life."[8]

What is the meaning of this elemental? Jünger experiences the "abandonment of man in a new unexplored *world.*"[9] The elemental concerns the earth as a principle of valuation which Jünger experienced for the first time through the destructive and cathartic effect of the foremost firing lines; the earth is saved from the demise of predetermined hierarchies because it is completely plowed up, and at the same time appears as a new energy or force field, filled with anarchy and variation. The elemental designates the earth as a fruitful domain of possibilities (*"typenträchtigen Fülle"*), on which the hope of a new determination of man and the world is placed.[10]

With that, the difference between total mobilization and the elemental becomes clear. Total mobilization describes the growing conversion of life into energy, in which man and the world appear *as function, as* work. The elemental refers to the force field that first appears with the total demise of the *animal rationale;* that which remains after this demise is elemental life and its motifs. The task of total mobilization is thus not only *destructive,* but also *preparatory,* for the conversion of life into energy remains at the same time related to elemental life as a fruitful domain of *possibilities.*

In that the complete or active nihilism of the new warrior (*Kriegerschlag*) of total mobilization can be survived, this warrior has a relationship with the elemental. "In the jubilations of the volunteers that greet it, there is more than the redemption of hearts that have been shown a new, dangerous life overnight. The revolutionary protest against the old values, whose validity has irrevocably expired, also hides itself in it. From here on, a new, elemental color flows into the stream of thoughts, feelings, facts,"[11] *earthly* existence as a principle of valuation that serves the active nihilism of the new type of warriors. Why does the *animal rationale* have no relationship to the elemental?

Despite the destruction of its categories, it appears that not the soldier on the front, who invokes the totally mobilized world, but rather the *animal rationale* will continue to exist after the First World War; the *animal rationale* appears as "the man who seeks to remove himself from a thoroughly dangerous reality through flight into security that has become utopian."[12] This flight is incomplete nihilism, which is ruled by the will to truth (security). Jünger understands the will to truth as the *will* that lets the world appear as a moral and rational order. Wherein does the illusory nature of this maneuver lie, and why does the *animal rationale* have no relationship with the elemental?

The *animal rationale* considers security its highest good, and he sees the "highest power" to guarantee it in rationality.[13] The rational design of reality *guarantees* the ordered appearance of the world, for it is led by the will to truth. This will, which allows the world to appear as moral and rational, becomes concrete through the outbreak of the First World War; total mobilization can no longer be overlooked. Since the war can no longer be denied, the *animal rationale* attempts to excuse it or interpret it as a mistake. "This happens in that it puts the ideology of progress over war-like processes, in that armed force appears as a regrettable exception, as a means of restraining backwards-minded barbarians."[14] The abandonment of man in the meaningless world is thus excused. Education or enlightenment can help avoid repeating these mistakes, "whose result [will] be the population of the globe with a unified, from scratch good and from scratch rational and therefore also from scratch secured humanity."[15] For the *animal rationale,* the world can never be anything but rational, because the opposite of reason—war or "danger' " in general—appears in the light of reason as a mistake.[16]

It becomes clear here that the *animal rationale* attempts to withstand the elemental through "the flight into security that has become utopian," whereby its categories remain restored and in the end preserved. In its will to truth (security), the incomplete nihilism of the *animal rationale* avoids the elemental, and attempts to remove itself from the completely dangerous world. "The effort of the citizen to hermetically insulate the living space from the incursion of the elemental is the especially successful expression of an ancient striving for security that can be followed in natural and intellectual history, in every individual life everywhere."[17] The will, which allows things to appear moral and rational, reveals itself as a will that the world of total mobilization does not want as it is, and is therefore a non-empirical will. The *animal rationale* flees into security that has become utopian, in which it can see its categories restored and preserved.[18]

The *animal rationale* removes itself from total mobilization and therefore also has no relationship to the elemental. The becoming-visible of the elemental requires that total mobilization and with it the destruction of the categories of the *animal rationale* open the possibility to experience the earth as a fruitful domain of new earthly-based categories. The hope for such a new determination of mankind—the type of the worker—is placed on elemental space or the earth as a fruitful domain. According to Jünger it is appropriate to recognize this new force field and to engage with it. "Whoever still believes that this process will let itself be restrained by old hierarchies belongs to the race of the conquered, which is condemned to destruction. New hierarchies have become far more necessary."[19]

In contrast to the *animal rationale,* the new type of warrior has a relationship to the elemental according to Jünger. We will now explain the relationship of the new type of warrior to the elemental, which is conceptualized as "spiritualization of the earth" (*Erdvergeistigung*) and is understood in light of the will to power.

As we have seen in Chapter 1, total mobilization concerns the growing conversion of life into energy; people and things have a functional or tactical value as potential energy for the "strategic will."[20] The fact that Jünger speaks of a "tactical value" for the "strategic will" means that he understands total mobilization from Nietzsche's metaphysics of the will to power (Chapter 2). The functional or tactical value of things and people in the world as "potential energy" refers to their favorability or non-favorability for the self-preservation and self-enhancement of the will, i.e., that they are the means to an end of the strategic will. The example of the double face of technology in Section 1.2 made clear that this tactical value can both consist of the production of perfume as well as in the production of poison gas. The transformation of life into potential energy (total mobilization) therefore means that people and things are ultimately understood and explained in terms of their favorability for the will to power.

Which indication of the relation between the new type of warrior and the will to power is implied in the expression "will to power"? Will to power does not primarily refer to people who are power-hungry, but is "inherent in every event" (see Chapter 2). It relates to the way reality appears *as* favorable or non-favorable for the will to power, i.e., as potential energy. Where there is a *human* will to power of the new type of warrior, this will has to be understood as *responsive* to the will to power as the nature of *life* itself. This is called the spiritualization of the earth by Jünger.[21] We must beware of directly identifying or opposing words like "elemental" and "earth" to "spirit" to "reason" as the main characteristic of the *animal rationale.*[22] In the case of a shaking of the world order, reality and our human responsiveness appear in an *incomparable* other way. Earthly existence therefore does not indicate any kind of *ir-rationality* that is bound to the physical and plunges into lower passions.[23]

The *animal rationale* is characterized by its incompatibility with the elemental. The relationship of the new type of warrior to the elemental is not irrational, but has its own reason.[24] The reason of the new type of warrior consists of the estimation of the tactical value of the potential energy for the strategic will, which is *responsive* to the will to power as the nature of life itself. In the same way, the word "spirit" no longer indicates an "isolated" and "subjective" position of the *animal rationale,*[25] but the *will* as the nature of life.

With this, the spiritualization of the earth becomes concrete, because both reality and the human response to reality is will to power. The earth itself is considered reasonable, as far as its *ratio* is found in its favorability for life (self-preservation and self-enhancing). At the same time, thinking has become *earthly*, when the estimation of the tactical value is responsive to the will to power as the nature of life, and with this, the earth or the elemental is seen as the principle of valuation. In the responsiveness of the new type of the warrior, Jünger sees a new emerging feeling for the earth and the vanguard of a new type of earth power, i.e., the son of the earth;[26] the "active nihilism" of the new type of warrior relies indeed on the total mobilized world and takes earthly existence or the elemental as the principle of valuation. We speak of a spiritualization of the earth when the rationality of the earth (will to power) is reproduced in the earthliness of thinking (will to power), being and thinking permeate each other completely[27] and eventually seamlessly coincide with each other, become identical.

That the elemental space becomes fertile ground for a new destination of man and world by the spiritualization of the earth means for Jünger that the elemental space is stamped by the gestalt; a stamping in which the elemental turns into a stamped form.[28] The reason for this assumption lies in his experience of the gestalt-switch during the Battle of Langemarck. This was the transition of the structure in which reality and the human response to it as a unity is at stake (Chapter 1). In the next subsection, the specific nature of the responsiveness to the will to power as the nature of life is discussed, i.e., the transition from the total mobilization to the type of worker, who is able to restrain the elemental.

3.2 Taming the Elemental: The Transition to the Type of the Worker

As stated, the gestalt *is* not in the middle of the total mobilization in which we currently live. "We must concede that we were born in a landscape of ice and fire. The past is created in such a way that one cannot cling to it, and the future, that one cannot establish himself in it."[29] The meaning of *The Worker* consists of leaving the essence of man as *animal rationale* and transitioning to the type of the worker as representative of the gestalt of the worker, in which we cannot yet establish ourselves. Since the race (type) of the worker is the embodiment of its gestalt, it has a relationship to the elemental.

Does a contradiction not reveal itself here? If Jünger on the one hand speaks of a gestalt, but on the other hand, one must still transition to the type of the worker as its representative, then the gestalt will be represented and not represented at the same time—it still counts as becoming transitive. Jünger points clearly to our situation, in which we first have *to learn* that the world of total mobilization can be seen still in a completely *different* way, namely as *order* stamped by the gestalt. With the stamping of the gestalt, the transition has already essentially taken place. *Our* transition to the type of the worker thus consists of a *becoming who you are*. "Time will ensure that he *recognizes* this relationship in increasing amounts and that he *sees* in himself the source of his own power."[30] The writing in *The Worker* is led by a type that *is* not yet, and is therefore transitioning to this type, that is, that the writing of the book recognizes itself as a representative of the gestalt of the worker. In this subsection, the specific nature of the responsiveness to the new turning of being will be discussed, which will turn out to consist of the transition to the new type of the worker as expression of the will to power as art.

Jünger calls the bearing necessary for the transition to the type of the worker heroic realism. The demise of the *animal rationale* and the senselessness of the world-views that attempt to restore their control, are observed by the heroic *realist*. He does not flee "into the security that has become more utopian," rather *affirms* the "abandonment of man in a new unexplored world." The heroic realist rejects the nature of man as *animal rationale* and transitions to the new type of the worker. The heroic aspect of realism thus does not consist of any heroic acts, rather describes precisely this transition, within which it is not clear yet *who we are*. How is the nature of man as *animal rationale* rejected by the heroic realist?

Jünger indicates that the heroic realist carries his own standard. The standard, which the heroic realist finds in himself, lies in its tactical value for the strategic will; man as potential energy or units of labor that, when necessary, can be employed functionally. But that does not mean the heroic realist is completely absorbed by it.

The heroic-realist affirmation of total mobilization does not describe a new form of quietism. His revolutionary act consists of the recognition of himself as a representative of the gestalt of the worker. When Jünger says that the heroic realist carries the standard in him and must use *himself* as a standard, then it seems this "self" is nothing more than that of the *animal rationale*. But with a stamp of the gestalt, every seeing and saying is already an expression of it. The revolutionary act of the heroic realist consists therefore of the recognition of itself as representative of the gestalt of the worker, that is, that the *self*, which is being used as a standard, is already an expression of the gestalt. "Seeing gestalts is insofar a revolutionary act as it recognizes a being in the whole and unified fullness of its life."[31] In other words, the gestalt is aroused in elemental space to live in the light of the gestalt, with which the gestalt *presents* itself in its *re*-presentation. In this sense, Jünger can also say that the heroic realist *as* representative "becomes an analogy to the gestalt."[32] The following will show that the revolutionary act of the heroic realist, just as his affirmation of total mobilization, must be understood from the perspective of the will to power.

Jünger calls the revolutionary act of the heroic realist the "secret will" to represent the gestalt of the worker. "An ever clearer will to power"[33] comes forward in that. This describes not the affirmation of total mobilization through the heroic realist, but the will to power as art, that is, the design of a standard—the type of the worker as representative of the gestalt of the worker—in which total mobilization is exceeded by a new order. The "highest art of living" points to these productive or creative aspects of the will to power.[34]

Wherein lies the necessity of surpassing total mobilization, the necessity of the will to power as art? According to Jünger, it is not possible for life to "tarry longer than a fleeting blink of an eye in this stronger and purer, but simultaneously deadly air of a pan-anarchic space."[35] Art is necessary in order to cope with the incursion of the elemental and exists in the design of orders that are unshakeable.[36] He understands this creation of order in accordance with the metaphysical tradition as a shaping of matter: "But it depends on giving a form to this material that is so willing and prepared."[37] These designs of *possibilities* (the will to power as art) to be able to surpass total mobilization will in practice have to prove their worth. That means that the designs must prove whether they are actually capable of creating orders that are unshakeable. The *legitimation* of the will to power as art is measured with the standard with which it restrains the elemental: "The identification of this legitimation exists in the mastering of things that have become overpowering—in the restraining of the absolute movement that can only be done through a new humanity."[38]

What relationship now exists between the gestalt of the worker and the will to power as art of the heroic realist? What does Jünger mean, when he indicates that only a new humanity is capable of restraining the elemental? Did we not just see that ultimately only the gestalt can restrain the elemental? The will to restrain the elemental is not primarily human. The standard that the heroic realist designs in the will to power as art is itself an *expression* of the gestalt, i.e., a presentation of the gestalt in the heroic-realistic *re*-presentation.

According to Jünger, however, the gestalt itself cannot be understood in terms of the will to power. It is not from this world, rather stamps *life* (will to power) and thus describes a "revision of life by Being":[39] "This Being is power in a completely different sense, is original capital that rushes into the State as into the world and stamps its own organizations, its own terms."[40] The power of the gestalt is an original force that stamps the appearance of the world and human responsiveness to the world. This power does not need to be willed anymore, because everything seen and spoken is already its *expression*.[41] In the design of the type of the worker through the will to power as art, the heroic realist recognizes himself as representative of the gestalt, that is, the will to power is led as a *magnet* by the gestalt as "original capital."[42]

Although up to this point the concern was the human responsiveness to the gestalt-switch, it is important to note that the unity of the gestalt is not limited to the human responsiveness to the world. The mobilization of the earth by the gestalt of the worker goes along with the mobilization of man by the same gestalt. From that ensues a reference to a specific kind of *restraint* of the elemental.

The last phase of mobilization exists, according to Jünger, in the realization of the total work-character, that is, the characteristic of the world *as* technological space and human responsiveness to the world through the type of the worker.[43] The restraint of elemental power through the gestalt exists therefore in the attunement of Being and thinking, through the stamping of the appearance of our work-world as technological space and human responsiveness to the world as type of the worker. The gestalt is represented not only by the type, but also by our technological world.[44] It is a question of an attunement of being and thought, because according to Jünger, technological space and the type of the worker depend on each other. On the one hand the type of the worker is a worker thanks to his relationship with the technological world. On the other hand, thanks to its relationship to technological space, the type is capable of restraining the elemental.

Technological space (the will to power as "the will to shape the world"[45]) *and* the type of worker (the will to power as art, as "the will to form the races" by the type[46]) are led as though by a magnet and grow towards each other.[47] Jünger calls this attunement an organic construction in which man and world permeate each other and he compares this merging of the type and the world with the unity of the claws with the crab, of a tusk with an elephant and a shell and a mussel.[48]

Only when the issue is one of such an attunement of the type of the worker *and* of technological space as representatives of the gestalt of the worker, is elemental-anarchic space restrained. Only then is the elemental-anarchic space of nihilism been overcome by a new order and can we talk about the dominion of the gestalt of the worker. This "epoch of the worker" is not our totally mobilized work-world. Our work-world has neither unity nor measure for order: it is excessive (ontological *in*difference). In the epoch of the worker, "work" would form the metaphysical measure of the world and men, in whose light the technological world appears as technological order and man finds his destination as the type of the worker. We can only speak of dominion in case of the representation of the gestalt of the worker—only this gestalt is the "unshakeable" that emerges from the chaos. Restraining the elemental thus requires a stamping by the gestalt—a stamping that grew "from the elemental to the stamped form."[49]

Jünger says this "'dominion' is already complete according to its essence," requires, "however, only a language (. . .), in order to emerge from its anonymous character."[50] With the gestalt-switch, the transition to the new order *essentially* already took place, but it will only emerge out of its anonymity when we transform ourselves to the type of the worker as representation of the gestalt of the worker. As we have seen in Chapter 1, the gestalt is not from this world and only *presents* itself in the *re*-presentation by the type of the worker.

The transition of the heroic realist in order to surpass total mobilization to a new necessary order, the revolutionary act as will, exists then also in the *recognition* of that which we already essentially were: the type of the worker as representative of the gestalt of the worker. Dominion means therefore the representation of the power of the gestalt, which presents itself in the will to power as art of the heroic realist. *As* expression of the gestalt, the heroic realist develops the value of the type in order to be able to overcome total mobilization to a new world order. When the heroic realist *recognizes* himself as the type of the worker, and consequently dominion emerges from its anonymous character, the heroic realist "has a share in a new humanity determined to reign by destiny."[51]

We have received now an answer to the question about the specific nature of the *concept* of the gestalt in *The Worker*, namely the representation of the gestalt of the worker by the will to power as art. With this artistic-ness of the gestalt, the *writing* and *reading* of *The Worker* places itself in another light. The *concept* of the gestalt of the worker is not an episode or narrative that *describes* the gestalt, rather it is *poetry*. The writing of *The Worker* is led by a gestalt that *is* not, and therefore transitions to the type of the worker as representative of the gestalt of the worker. The will to power is led as though by a magnet by the gestalt, which *is* not and only *is* in the will to power as art. When Jünger's way of writing transitions to the type of the worker in the will to power as art, then this transition is not *thought* but *poetry*.

Notes

1. *Arb*, 65–66.
2. *Arb*, 99.
3. "We live in a state . . . in which one must first learn to see" that total mobilization is an order influenced by the gestalt in a completely different way. "The past is created in such a way that one cannot cling to it, and the future, that one cannot establish himself in it. . . . What can be seen is not the final order, rather the change of disorder, under which a great law is to be discovered" (*Arb*, 100–101). The following proposition by Figal is therefore incorrect: "Thus the interim thought of nihilism, the disoriented relaxation between no-longer and not-yet, is completely foreign to him" (188).
4. *Arb*, 88.
5. *Arb*, 100–101; cf. 99.
6. *Arb*, 143.
7. *Arb*, 98; cf. *TNG*, 125–126.
8. *Arb*, 98.
9. *Arb*, 113–114.
10. *TNG*, 119; cf. *Arb*, 62–63, 75, 169–161.
11. *Arb*, 59; cf. 110; *Sta*, 355.
12. *Arb*, 61.
13. *Arb*, 54.
14. *Arb*, 167.
15. *Arb*, 56.
16. "The metaphor of 'danger' cloaks the exact specification of that which is dangerous, namely an 'encompassing transformation of the internal and external world'" (Bohrer, *Die Ästhetik des Schreckens*, 326; cf. 325–327).
17. *Arb*, 52.
18. Although the discussion of the non-empirical character of the *animal rationale* can arouse the appearance of a *critique* of its categories, the actual concerns of *The Worker* do not reside therein. In a later letter, Jünger recognizes that "topical

criticism, especially with a view to the 'citizen,' flowed in" (*Arb*, 390). However, this critique has little to do with the main *concern* in *The Worker*: the concept of the gestalt of the worker (*Arb*, 12).

19. *Arb*, 63.
20. *Arb*, 100–101; cf. 176–177.
21. *MM*, 332; cf. 334, 374.
22. Heidegger seems to suggest this, when he says that the elemental is "the *sensuous*, that which encounters the senses, the sense itself, 'sensuality.' As a counterphenomenon of the *reasonable, calculable*" (Heidegger, Martin, *Zu Ernst Jünger*, Gesamtausgabe, vol. 90 [Frankfurt am Main: Vittorio Klosterman, 2004] 22). Essential for the elemental is however, and this is recognized by Heidegger as well, that the world of becoming *(phusis)* concerns the chaotic and the unstable (Heidegger, *Zu Ernst Jünger*, 22; cf. 134, 137, 144).
23. "One of the chess moves of bourgeois thought namely tends to expose the attack of the cult of reason as the attack of reason and with that to dismiss it as unreasonable" (*Arb*, 53–54). It is therefore definitely untrue that Jünger's "theory of knowledge" distinguishes between "intellect" and "lived experience" and that he opts for this immediate experience, intuition or irrationalism, as Schwarz suggested (Schwarz, *Der konservative Anarchist*, 29–42). If the work of Jünger contains *Zeitkritik*—as the subtitle of *Der konservative Anarchist* suggests—this does not concern a critique of contemporary civilization or a protest against the world picture of the *animal rationale* (Schwarz, *Der konservative Anarchist*, 39). There is no lack of worldviews, "but what is suspicious about them is that they have become all too easy. Their numbers grow in the same dimension that the weakness of a doubtful security feels needy" (*Arb*, 99–100; cf. 134). "Once more we want to remember that our task is in seeing, but not in evaluating" (*Arb*, 140). If we already find critique in *The Worker*, then it concerns a metaphysical critique, i.e., a decision or delimitation of what nature as such is, when the era of the *animal rationale* has ended with the shaking of the world order (cf. *Arb*, 100, 208–210, 216–217).
24. Cf. *Arb*, 282.
25. *Arb*, 46.
26. Cf. *Arb*, 231, 21; *MM*, 333; *Sta*, 369.
27. *Arb*, 206; cf. *Arb*, 231; *KE*, 29; Schwarz, *Der konservative Anarchist*, 191, 224.
28. Cf. *Arb*, 182; in his later work, Jünger calls the elemental also the unseparated (cf. Chapter 3).
29. *Arb*, 100; cf. *UdS*, 190.
30. *Arb*, 217. Instead of recognition, Jünger speaks in this context also of a "memory" of the gestalt as an "undetachable inheritance" (cf. *Arb*, 41–42; *AH1*, 70–71, 75).
31. *Arb*, 46.
32. *Arb*, 42.
33. *Arb*, 70; cf. *Arb*, 51.
34. *Arb*, 41; cf. *Arb*, 214, 222.
35. *Arb*, 74.
36. In this we can also find an essential distinction between Jünger and Nietzsche. Contrary to the "unshakeable" order which is at stake in Jünger's will to power as art, in the case of Nietzsche, the will to power as art only produces "complex forms of relative duration of life within becoming" (Nietzsche, *Kritische Studienausgabe*, vol. 13, 36).
37. *Arb*, 214; cf. *Arb*, 187, 222.
38. *Arb*, 83; cf. *Arb*, 73, 287.
39. *Arb*, 46.

40. *Arb*, 77.
41. Jünger also compares the power of the gestalt, which does not need to be willed, but is related to the will to power, with the image of the rolling wheel and the unmoved axle. The original force of the gestalt reveals itself with that as related to the Aristotelian concept of an "unmoved mover" which itself is not subject to movement, but is nonetheless the origin of every movement (cf. Schwarz, *Der konservative Anarchist*, 24; *Arb*, 332).
42. *Arb*, 184; in this sense, the gestalt also lies beyond the values (cf. Part I). The gestalt itself has no value that is created in the will to power as art, but rather, an original force. The values are indeed designed with regard to the gestalt, for the design of the values by the will to power as art is led as a magnet by the gestalt. Therein also seems to exist one significant difference between Jünger and Nietzsche. Nietzsche at least gives the impression that the gestalt is the *product* of the will to power, while Jünger resolutely rejects this possibility (cf. *TNG*, 169). From here, it is understandable why Jünger says: "It has become unnecessary to occupy oneself with yet another revaluation of values—it suffices to see the new and engage with it" (*Arb*, 59–60). The gestalt is not the product of the will to power or the "devaluation of all values" of active nihilism, but "original power" that presupposes a "new glance" in order to be seen (cf. Part I). A further elaboration of Nietzsche's concept of gestalt and his relationship to Jünger is beyond the scope of this study.
43. *FB*, 116.
44. Cf. *Arb*, 244, 247, 288.
45. *Arb*, 222–226.
46. *Arb*, 111.
47. "In particular, in *The Worker* he speaks of an attunement or correspondence between the 'means' (i.e., technology) and the type of human being. This correspondence, he repeatedly warns, is not to be conceived in a causal manner, as though the new type of means would cause the new type of man, as Marx, for instance, thought. Nor is it to be conceived as causal in the other direction, with the new type of man causing the new type of means. Rather, these two dimensions (type of man and type of means) are functions of the domination of the *gestalt*—in our age, the *gestalt* of the Worker" (Ibáñez-Noé, "Heidegger, Nietzsche, Jünger, and the Interpretation of the Contemporary Age," 73).
48. *Arb*, 181, 206, 223, 231, 241; *PP*, 203; "For: the narrow and uncontradicted melding of man with the tools 'at his disposal' first attempted on the battlefield now as an 'organic construction' becomes the 'gestalt'—principle of a 'work' that in naturally using technological means achieves a certain degree of 'naturalness,' as accorded in 'organic' nature the use of 'animal or vegetable extremities'. . . . The 'revolutionary rank' of technological means is rooted therefore 'not in the extent of its dynamic energy,' rather in the quality of its 'representative character' for the respective 'achieved unity of man with his means'" (Segeberg, H., "Technikverwachsen Zur, organischen Konstruktion' des ,Arbeiters' bei Jünger," *Faszination des Organischen. Konjunktionen einer Kategorie der Moderne*, ed. H. Eggert, E. Schütz, P. Sprengel [München: Iudicium Verlag 1995] 220–221).
49. *Arb*, 99–100.
50. *Arb*, 98–99.
51. *Arb*, 72. Peter Koslowski has shown that Jünger's heroic realism is more familiar with French, rather than German romanticism (Koslowski, *Der Mythos der Moderne*, 24–25). For the influence of French Romanticism and Gnosticism on Jünger, cf. Koslowski, *Der Mythos der Moderne*, 23–31.

4 Stereoscopy and Trigonometry

Jünger's Method in the Light of the "Sicilian Letter to the Man in the Moon"

When we examine Ernst Jünger's main work *The Worker,* we are confronted with the fundamental problem of the interpretation of his concept of the gestalt. On the one hand, Jünger makes different statements about the gestalt in *The Worker*—he names it, for example, a general unity, a measure, within which the world appears as order—but on the other hand, he makes clear that the gestalt possesses no reality in our time: "the condition in which we find ourselves [is] far from that unity that can guarantee a new security and rank order of life. There is no visible unity here outside of rapid change."[1] Security and order need a unity or a measure for its order—a gestalt—and this unity is missing in our era of total mobilization: "What can be seen is not the final order, rather the change of the disorder, under which can be guessed a great law."[2] In times of total mobilization, the gestalt can only be surmised. The worker's task is to transform the work-world of total mobilization into a world in which the gestalt guarantees a new security and order of life.

The problem that we see in front of us is how Jünger can actually have access to a gestalt and speak about it, although it *is* not in our time. This question sharpens when we also consider that the gestalt in a further sense is *absent.* The gestalt is not only missing in our lifetime of total mobilization, but it is not at all from this world: "our view lies on this side of the prism, which breaks the colored stream into colorful light. We see the filings, but not the magnetic field whose reality determines it."[3] If this is the case, then a new, fundamental, methodological question precedes the question about the transition to the new era of the worker: how did Jünger have *any* access to this dark gestalt, which *is* not and cannot be placed before our eyes in any direct way? In the last chapter of this part, we concentrate on the question of methodology of Jünger's concept of the gestalt.

It is clear that Jünger made our nature and our way of looking responsible for the access to the gestalt. This manner has two aspects. On the one hand he makes clear that the gestalt does not spring from thought—an idea or a theory—rather, it is a matter of a new reality. "Since here . . . [it is a matter] of a new reality, everything depends on the sharpness of the discussion that eyes presume (*die Augen voraussetzt*), which have been gifted with full and impartial vision."[4] Our perception must regard the new reality *impartially*. On the other hand, the gestalt is not *something*—a thing or object in the world—that we have overlooked until now and to which Jünger is now drawing our attention. "The gestalt is thus no new magnitude that could be discovered just like the other things in the world which are already known to us, rather, from a new opening of the eyes on, the world appears as a theatre of gestalts and their relationships."[5] Thus, it is necessary to have another method of perception through which we can first *see* the unity of the gestalt.

In a letter to Walter Patt on February 6, 1980, Jünger says that his *Sicilian Letter to the Man in the Moon* from 1930 depicts the key to this new optics.[6] Therefore, in this chapter, we will take the *Sicilian Letter*, which can be understood as a preliminary draft of *The Worker*, as the point of departure, and we will ask about the methodology of Jünger's concept of the gestalt.

4.1 Sun- and Moonlight

When Jünger speaks about the man in the moon in the *Sicilian Letter*, it is not primarily about a heavenly body that appears as a human face. What is being discussed by Jünger is the *rays* or the *light* of the moon, in which things appear at night.[7] We see this at the beginning of the *Sicilian Letter*, in which Jünger speaks to the moon: "Your light fell into the room like that ghostly sword which freezes all motion when drawn. . . . Things stood silent and motionless, in a strange light, like the sea creatures one glimpses beneath a curtain of algae on the ocean floor. Did they not appear mysteriously changed?"[8] The things we encounter do not change in the light of the moon, but they do reveal another side. Wherein exists the changed characteristic of things? Normally, everything on this earth is subject to arising and decaying, things are changeable and moveable. In contrast, in the light of the moon, the world appears frozen and motionless. But not only things appear frozen in the light of the moon, for Jünger himself experiences a being absorbed "in the abyss of the sea," in other words, his own frozen-ness in the light of the moon.

Jünger's description of the moonlight hearkens back to Plato's image of the sun, which we introduced in Chapter 2, i.e., the sun as transcendental *idea*, category or view, in whose light things can appear as themselves. When Jünger speaks about the light of the moon in the *Sicilian Letter*, then Plato's approach is not far behind: in the light of the moon, the world appears *as* frozen and motionless. But at the same time it is clear that Jünger has something completely different in mind than Plato. That reveals itself in that Jünger does not speak about sunlight but about the moon—about the indirect light of the sun, which the moon reflects. Jünger's experience of nihilism speaks from there. Like Nietzsche, Jünger experiences the separation of earth and sun (cf. Chapter 2), thus of our world abandoned by the Platonic *idea*. "My small room, too, appeared submerged—the room where I had sat up in bed, immersed in a solitude too deep to be broken by men."[9] Jünger experiences a deep abandonment and loneliness of man on earth, and this "nihil" of the Platonic idea in our time is evidence of his basic experience of nihilism: there is no longer a metaphysical measure (unity) for our world, which has been pervaded with contingency and variability (multiplicity). "I felt no fear, only a feeling of inescapable loneliness in the middle of a mysterious, deserted world governed by silent powers."[10]

With this experience of nihilism, according to Jünger, we come to stand at a crossroads. Because of the abandonment of the Platonic idea, we can namely conclude that the metaphysical difference is actually nonsense and a mistake of the metaphysical tradition: there is no difference between the light and the things which, thanks to the light, can reveal themselves as they are. The only true light is the light of reason (*lumen naturale*). If we limit ourselves to the light of reason, then we prevent the same mistakes in the future. Then we limit ourselves to that which is self-evident for reason, that which can be grasped numerically, the countability of things on which and with which it will be calculated. For the countability and rationality, there is no *idea* and there are only beings, insofar that these beings are accessible to the counting and calculating: the moon as "light and shadow-play of levels, mountains, dried-out lakes and extinguished craters."[11]

On the other hand, it becomes apparent that Jünger first experiences the 'nihil' of the Platonic idea in the *indirect* light of the moon. This indirect light is not that of the Platonic *idea*, for this has irrevocably abandoned us. But this moonlight is also not nothing, for the world (multiplicity) appears first in the light of the moon *as* unity, namely as frozen, foreign and mysterious. The moonlight is not the bright light of the Platonic *idea,* rather a dark light, whose meaning we do not grasp. "But are you not yourself a master who knows how to artfully present his puzzles? Those puzzles, of which only the text, but not the solution is communicable?"[12] The indirect light of the moonlight is a dark light, in which things appear *foreign* and *mysterious*. Jünger understands this dark light not in terms of the astronomical moon, the object of our analytical-scientific view, but precisely in terms of the *man in the moon*.

The dark light of the man in the moon is important for Jünger in two respects. We saw before that Jünger first experienced the loneliness and abandonment of the world—nihilism—in the light of the moon. However, it is more important that the mysterious unity of moonlight indeed on the one hand does not concern the unity of the Platonic *idea*, but on the other hand is also not *nothing* (nihil); one recognizes a puzzle:

> We all know these moments of uncertain expectation when one feels the voice of the unknown near, and listens for it to resound, and when the hidden conceals itself only with difficulty in every form. A crackling in the woodwork, the vibration of a glass, over which an invisible hand seems to brush—just as space itself is charged around the exertions of a being who hungers for sense, and who can catch its signals![13]

Jünger brings the dark light of the moon into the context of *silent* powers, *nameless* forms and *signals* that then desire to be absorbed with symbols, runes and languages. "Here, light is called sound, is called life, which is hidden in the words."[14] Here, language is not an instrument that man *possesses* in his encounter with reality. In *The Worker* one reads: "The issue centers much more on a new language that is suddenly spoken, and man answers or he remains silent—and this decides its reality.[15] Man is not the subject of this language, for it translates itself into everything that can be thought, felt, wanted."[16] Language or the language of signs refers to the light within which we *see* the disparate *as* the same; in the dark light of the man in the moon, the landscape appears *as* unity, namely *as* frozen, motionless and abandoned. The dark light of the man in the moon is such a sign; the man in the moon in contrast to the moon as an astronomical heavenly body.[17]

4.2 Methodological Considerations: Ahasverian Thought

How do we see the language of signs of the man in the moon, which method do we have at our disposal? In the *Sicilian Letter,* Jünger says: "Symbols are scratched into decaying fences and signs at crossroads, and the citizen carelessly walks past them. But the wanderer has eyes for them, he is studied in them, they are for him keys in which the essence of an entire landscape reveals itself."[18] According to Jünger, we normally go carelessly past these symbols. He speaks of the "citizen," that is of the *animal rationale,* which merges into the inebriation of rationality and limits itself to counting and calculating (see Section 1.1). The inebriation of rationality is such that the counting merges with the countable and calculation only encounters the calculable. Thereby the *animal rationale* on the one hand has no access to the language of signs of the man in the moon and on the other hand is always *at home* in the world; the foreign or mysterious appears to him at most as not-yet-calculated—a problem in the sciences, that for example is still waiting for its solution—but that is principally calculable and comprehensible.

Jünger inserts the wanderer in contrast to the *animal rationale*. The wanderer is never at home and always underway. The methodological relevance of the wanderer is the following: As long as one feels at home in the world, the distance and space we need in order to see the *appearance* of the world, that is the ray or the light within which things appear, will always be missing. This becomes concrete in *The Worker,* when he names the wanderer Ahasver, the wandering Jew from the Book of Esther: "For Ahasver . . . human society and its activity present a *curious appearance*. . . . Which appearance presents a *homeless consciousness* that deviously sees itself in the middle of one of our largest cities and as though in a dream seeks to guess the laws of the processes? It is the *appearance* of an increased movement that takes place with clinical precision":[19] total mobilization. The homeless consciousness of Ahasverian thought stands thus in contrast to the native consciousness of the *animal rationale*. Precisely because Ahasverian thought is never at home and instead always underway, it has the necessary distance to see the appearance of the world, that is, the language of signs of the man in the moon.

The crossroads before which Jünger thus sees us placed—astronomical moon or the man in the moon—hearkens to a crossroads before which our consciousness sees itself placed: are we *animal rationale* (native consciousness) or Ahasverian thought (homeless consciousness)? "Whether anyone can see in the infinite a number or a symbol—this question is the only and last touchstone on which the kind of a spirit answers."[20] If we wish to see this language of signs, then we must give up counting and calculating—the nature of man as *animal rationale*—and become *Ahasverian,* a wanderer who has an eye for the language of signs.

That is easier said than done. We ourselves *are* the *animal rationale* that merges into inebriation of rationality. How do we then depart from this inebriation of rationality? Jünger asks. How do we see the language of signs with other words, if the inebriation of rationality depicts *our* essence?

In the preface to *The Worker,* Jünger also says that an "important collaboration" is expected from the *reader; he teaches* us to see the language of signs in *The Worker.* Jünger calls his own manner of writing wanderings,[21] that is, wanderings that offer access to the *appearance* of the world. We must *follow* him, if we wish to gain access to the man in the moon and so become the wanderer ourselves. It is with this in mind that Jünger speaks about the necessity of a new opening of the eyes (see Section 1.5).

That *The Worker* is a textbook that teaches us how to see the language of signs is also revealed in the text itself. It is organized according to the rules of military exercises: "It will be attempted to support this important collaboration through the methodology of the lecture, which strives to proceed according to the rules of military exercises, which serves a manifold material as opportunity for practice and the same access."[22] Jünger then also says that another activity besides *reading* will be expected from the *reader* (*Arb,* 89), and that we can only follow him if we depart from man as *animal rationale* and become ourselves the wanderer: "Whoever has ears for it has also experienced it, the 'out, up!', when the hand has turned the last page and the freer momentum of an ideal landscape, whose afterimage has hardly disappeared from the retina, is still fresh and alive. The literature comes from heroic songs whose fundamental value corresponds to their battle value and whose effect is sensed by male dispositions as a call to battle."[23]

In the end it is not *our* decision whether we are capable of departing from the *animal rationale* and becoming Ahasverian. Because we normally merge with the inebriation of rationality of the *animal rationale,* Jünger asserts an opposing force is necessary, one that detaches us from the entanglements in the world and so enables the transition from *native* to *non-native* consciousness. This opposing force is the dark light of the moon itself that "robs" us "of gravity, and sucks irresistibly into empty space. "Sometimes I dreamt I let my caution slip, and saw myself in a long, white shirt, devoid of will, like a cork on a sinister flood tide, driven high above a landscape in whose depths lurked nightshade forests, and where the roofs of villages, castles, and churches glimmered like black silver—the language of signs of a threatening geometry, directly apprehensible to the soul."[24] First through the magnetic effect of the man in the moon do we receive the necessary distance to see the language of signs of the man in the moon. "Are there not hours when one is beloved by everything, like a flower who blossoms in wild innocence? Hours when from sheer excess we are shot like a projectile along the paths of habit? Only then do we begin to fly, and only in uncertainty is there a high goal."[25] This *flying* is the transition from the native consciousness of the *animal rationale* to the homeless consciousness of Ahasverian thought, whereby we not only have access to uncertainty—rather this uncertainty itself is elevated to the highest goal (we will return to this presently).

What is the particular nature of the homeless consciousness of Ahasverian thought? Although Jünger says in the previously mentioned quote, "no more thoughts," embracing the nameless life has not abandoned thought in itself. How then can Ahasverian thought be characterized? We have already seen that Ahasver is the wanderer who never is at home in the world and therefore is first of all capable of seeing the language of signs of the man in the moon: "The warm air that is laden with the pollen of the grasses as though with narcotic gunpowder, creates a wild eruption that drives him screaming and blind across the silent landscape. . . . No more thoughts that darkly merge characteristics. The nameless life is embraced with jubilation."[26] The adventuresome heart of Ahasver thus has an eye for the language of signs, without the urge to immediately understand it and to provide a concise name or meaning for it. With that we embrace a first negative characteristic of the nature of Ahasver. His wanderings are not marked by the *law of homecoming*, not by the tendency of thought to appropriate the anonymous by giving it a distinct name.

In a hidden manner, this also becomes clear in the *Sicilian Letter*, when Jünger's description of the silent landscape describes "the bitter fume of the wild carrots and the mottled hemlock."[27] The crop of mottled hemlock is a component of the poison that killed Socrates.

According to the Platonic Socrates, the origin of philosophical contemplation lies in an *aporia*. That is no uncertainty with regard to mysterious things or events. The *aporia* exists in relation to the identity or essence of things that had remained hidden in our daily dealings with the things around us. Through his specific type and manner of questioning, Socrates moves the questioned into an *aporia* with respect to the identity of these things. By moving him into *aporia*, man was ejected from his accustomed contact with things and *thinking* about the essence of things developed. The implicit permeability of "Being" or of the identity of things for thought is broken through and presents the impetus for the philosophical question about the *Being* of these things. Through the question of Being, metaphysical thought attempts to find a way out of this *aporia* (literally: impasse), which means that the beginning of philosophy is rooted in the search for ways out. As we have seen, the Greeks find this way out in the Platonic *idea*.

What is significant about Socratic thought, however, is not that the way out is found in the concept of the *idea;* rather, we must recognize the *nihil* of the *idea* and therefore nihilism. If the impetus for philosophical thinking is found in an *aporia* and thought seeks ways out through the concept of the *idea* or the being of things, then this search is in advance focused on the *restoration* of the permeability (porousness) of being and thought. The *alfa-privans* of the word "a-poria" refers to a *privatio,* to the *brokenness* of this permeability (see also Section 8.1). This *brokenness* remains related just to this permeability: the *a-poria* is understood from the porousness (*poros* originally means "passage, "bridge," "fordable location"). Thought seeks a *way out* and is in advance invested in the *restoration* of this brokenness in a new permeability, in the "homecoming" of being in thought and vice versa. Socrates's a-poretic thought is thus characterized by the *law of homecoming.*

This native consciousness characterizes not only the metaphysical tradition, but also the *animal rationale:* for counting and calculating rationality (thought) *is* in the actual sense only the countable and the calculable (being). Because the native consciousness of the metaphysical tradition and the *animal rationale* is always invested in homecoming, it has no access to the *silent* powers and *nameless* forms; it is not capable of receiving the *nameless* life.

In contrast, the homeless consciousness of Ahasverian thought has departed from the law of homecoming. This thought is and remains homeless and only so has access to the *silent* powers and nameless forms. Without comprehending this again directly, it nonetheless is capable of receiving the nameless life *as such.*

But is it not so that Ahasverian thought in the end flows into nihilism? Ultimately there is for Jünger namely not only no highest goal such as the idea for which we can live or die (nihilism)—every possible goal is doubted by him. It elevates only uncertainty to the highest goal. Is the path not cleared here for the excess of the present, hedonistic life oriented towards the satisfaction of demand and pleasure? We will follow the *Sicilian Letter* for a moment and with it articulate a second characteristic of Ahasverian thought.

As though led by a magnet, Ahasver wanders around and embraces the nameless life. "In the distance a barrage is booming and the ear, which has come near the primeval language, feels dangerously tempted. The stars shimmer up from bottomless depths and begin to dance when the water swirls."[28] Jünger sees in the reflective water the language of signs of the man in the moon. What is significant here is not the indirect manner of the access to the primeval language through the reflection of the surface of the water. It occurs to him that the language of signs of the man in the moon shines *from bottomless depths.* With that, Jünger learns that the language of signs, in whose light the landscape appears frozen and motionless, remains surrounded by darkness:

> The clearing breaks open, and your light falls into the *darkness* like an excommunication of the law. . . . Every tiny branch and the last tendrils

of the blackberries are touched by your light, opened and interpreted, and at the same time surrounded—struck by a great moment, in which everything becomes significant and in which chance surprises on its secret paths. They are included in an equation whose *unknown* symbols are written with glowing ink.[29]

The landscape is included in an equation but the sign in which the night landscape appears is unknown; it is a dark sign. With that it becomes clear that the homeless consciousness does not deny the possibility of home and does not flow so much into nihilism: "How in even the most muddled landscape are the simple lines of home hidden! Exhilarating allegory in which a deeper allegory is embedded."[30] In contrast, Jünger brings to our attention the bottomless depths or darkness that surrounds the light of every home. The homeless consciousness of Ahasverian thought recognizes that every home has a dark origin and remains surrounded by this darkness:

> But so, too, do we speak a language whose significance is incomprehensible to us ourselves—a language of which every syllable is both transitory and non-transitory. Symbols are signs, which nevertheless give us consciousness of our values. They are first of all projections of forms from a hidden dimension, then, too, searchlights through which we hurl our signals into the unknown in a language pleasing to the gods.[31]

If a home for the homeless consciousness is the concern, then it is this hidden dimension, this homeless home of the gestalt.

4.3 The Concept of Gestalt: The Stereoscopic View

With reference to this hidden dimension, we encounter first the term *gestalt* in the *Sicilian Letter*. We are now sufficiently prepared to scrutinize this gestalt. As we saw in the previous section, the gestalt is characterized in *The Worker* as a summarizing unity; as a measure within which the world appears as order. However, it becomes clear in the *Sicilian Letter* that this summarizing unity of the gestalt cannot be identified with the unity of the language of signs. Signs are projections of the gestalt from a hidden dimension, that is, the unity of the gestalt reaches further than the unity of the language of signs.

The first question is how we can characterize the gestalt in a positive manner. The answer is complicated, since the gestalt is called a *hidden* dimension. The second question is how we then can find any access to the gestalt at all. And this is where the stereoscopic view that Jünger introduces in the *Sicilian Letter* becomes important. In this section we concentrate on the stereoscopic view in order to be able to answer the two related questions with its help.

A stereoscope is a device in which one looks with both eyes. Each eye sees a different photo, and together the the pair of eyes build a stereo-photo. The effect that emerges from the seeing of two photos (multiplicity) is that we perceive *one* picture or image with depth (unity). The stereoscope thus has two functions. It first allows the unity of two images (multiplicity) to be recognized, and second, allows depth to be seen (the dimensional). Jünger says in the *Sicilian Letter* that he wishes to attain a stereoscopic view, a view that *sees* the unity of multiplicity. We will concentrate first on the first function of the stereoscopic view, and then we will come back to its second function.

In the first version of *The Adventurous Heart* from 1929, Jünger explains what he intends with the stereoscope. If the color of a painting calls forth delight, it touches on a perception that encompasses more than the pure color. "In this case something comes up, which one could call the tactile value of the color, a sensation of the skin that allows the thought of the touching to appear pleasant."[32] Jünger calls this perception of the color stereoscopic, for one and the same object is simultaneously reproduced through a single sensory organ in two sensory qualities. In the case of *intellectual* stereoscopy, it is exactly the reverse, and the issue is the perception that sees the unity of different things. Jünger gives a letter with corrections as an example. "Intellectual stereoscopy captures the unity in internal contradiction," in this case between a word that has been crossed out and the word that has been written above it.[33] The significance of the stereoscopic view is that it sees the unity of multiplicity.

If we regard the first function of the stereoscopic view in the light of the analysis of the last section, then we can draw a first conclusion. In Section 4.1 we saw that the multiplicity of things, thanks to the language of signs of the man in the moon, appears as unity. In Section 4.2, we saw that the homeless consciousness of Ahasverian thought has access to this language of signs. The first function of the stereoscopic view, thus, is that it enables us to see the unity of language of signs.

But now, according to Jünger, there is a crossroads between the astronomical moon and the man in the moon (cf. Section 4.2). Is it possible that the unity to which the stereoscopic view provides us access in addition also pertains to the unity of the moon *as* man *and as* astronomical heavenly body? Exactly this possibility is the point on which Jünger sets. He ends the *Sicilian Letter* with the perception that the moon appears to him *simultaneously as* heavenly body *and as* the man in the moon: "But the unheard-of part for me in this moment was to see these two masks merge inseparably into one another as one and the same Being. Then for the first time, an agonizing rift opened up here, that which I, great-grandson of an idealistic, grandson of a romantic, and son of a materialistic race, had hitherto regarded as irreconcilable. It did not happen that an either-or transformed into an as-well-as. No, the real is just as magical as the magical is real."[34] The second function of the stereoscopic view is that it sees the moon *as* man and *as* heavenly body merge together into a unity thanks to the stereoscopic view.

Here, however, we must insert a critical question. Does Jünger not lapse into the law of homecoming of the metaphysical tradition, if the stereoscopic view allows the moon *as* heavenly body and *as* man to merge? Does this merging then not extend so far that the most disparate—the real and the magical—be *annulled* in the unification of every contradiction? With that is not every significant darkness and strangeness annulled and with that is not the stereoscopic view itself not evidence of the law of homecoming?

This critique is superficial, for the actual meaning of the second function of the stereoscopic view is misunderstood here: "That is what we found so tempting about the doubled images that we saw as children through the stereoscope: In the same moment in which they merged together into one image, the new dimension of depth in them also broke forth."[35] The second function of the stereoscopic view is that it enables the perception of depth. But if we want to be able to see the depth in a stereo-photo, then we need two *different* photos. The merging of the moon *as* heavenly body and *as* man thus does not extend so far that both are identified.[36] Only when we hold onto their principle difference does the stereoscopic view have access in an *indirect* manner to the dimension of depth revealed therein.

With that it is revealed why the unity of the gestalt extends further than the unity of the language of signs. The gestalt is not only a sign of the moon, but also the unity of the different signs or views of the moon that only show themselves in indirect ways when we simultaneously—stereoscopically—see the different views or identities of the moon—the moon *as* heavenly body and at the same time *as* man,[37] the dimensional.

How can we more closely characterize this dimensional of the gestalt? The comparison with a magnetic field indeed made clear that the gestalt is only accessible in an indirect manner through its effects—its projections, rays, and signs—he does not, however, make clear how we are to understand the dimensional of the gestalt itself and its relationship to the language of signs.

The difference between the man in the moon and the astronomical moon is not related as we have seen to the moon itself, rather to different views, identities or meanings of the moon. That the language of signs of the moon has *different* meanings gives nuance first to the implicitness of the common concept of the moon as an astronomical heavenly body, and second subverts the absolutizing of this characteristic of the moon through the *animal rationale*. As naturally perhaps as the moon is also for us an astronomical heavenly body, *it could also have been different*. And it *is* also different, for at the same time with the moon as a heavenly body, Ahasverian thought sees the moon as man. Through this split in the meaning of the moon, we not only see that no individual attempt at interpretation can claim absolute validity and is always characterized by finiteness.[38]

Even more important is that this split creates a *distance* between the different meanings of the moon. Through this distance, our attention shifts from an articulate meaning with which thought merges to its *horizon of meaning*.

The horizon of meaning of the language of signs is the fertile ground of possibilities that not only encompasses the two meanings discussed, but also includes every possible and future meaning of the moon. This horizon of meaning is the origin of the different meanings of the moon, and always extends beyond the articulated meaning. "But we also speak a language whose significance is incomprehensible to us ourselves—a language of which every syllable is both transitory and non-transitory."[39] No single articulated meaning of the moon is capable of coming equally to the horizon of meaning and bringing it home. In this sense, the horizon of meaning of the language of signs, is incomprehensible to us, that is, silent, nameless and hidden. "We live in it but are only capable of beholding its projection in significant beings. There are signs, allegories, and keys of various kinds. We resemble the blind man, who indeed cannot see, but senses the light because of its muffled characteristic of warmth."[40] The hidden horizon of meaning of the language of signs *is* the hidden dimension of the gestalt.[41] It is an empty place, an "open window" that can only be framed through the language of signs.[42]

With that we receive an answer to the first question we posed in this section. The gestalt is a summarizing unity, a measure within which the world appears as order. But this unity for the orderly appearance of the world extends further than the unity of the language of signs. In the light of the man in the moon, reality already appears as unity. Namely, frozen and motionless. The summarizing unity of the gestalt relates not only to the articulated meanings of the moon, but also to the horizon of meaning of the language of signs, whereby the *different* meanings of the moon are led as though by a magnet, and in whose light the moon harmonizes *as* heavenly body or *as* man, and so appear as order. The summarizing unity of the gestalt can only be seen in an *indirect way* and only approximately, when we look— stereoscopically—at the different meanings within the language of signs at the same time. That means that the gestalt only emerges *as* inaccessible and hidden *in* this cleavage.[43]

With that, our task also becomes apparent if we wish to gain access to this hidden dimension of the gestalt. We have no *direct* access to the gestalt, for by *naming* the *nameless* gestalt, we would immediately disguise and mask its dimensional character in favor of an articulated meaning. The gestalt is only accessible in an *indirect* manner. How can we concretely understand our access to the gestalt?

Jünger also calls the stereoscopic view "a kind of higher trigonometry that deals with the measurement of invisible fixed stars."[44] Trigonometry is originally the study of corners in flat planes and focuses on the origin of trigonometric functions such as sine and cosine. Spherical trigonometry deals with triangles on the surfaces of spheres. With the help of spherical trigonometry, *depth* can be measured. On the basis of two fixed points on a sphere, a third, hidden corner can be measured. So transferring higher trigonometry to our question about our access to the gestalt can be a method to fathom in an indirect manner the hidden horizon of meaning, that is the depth of the gestalt, using two fixed points as its basis—the moon *as* man and *as* heavenly body.[45]

When we give voice *at the same time* to different meanings of the same moon, our speaking is trigonometric. Ahasverian thought is capable of conducting this higher trigonometry, for its wandering movements are constantly roaming between the moon *as* heavenly body and *as* man, wandering constantly back and forth between the different articulated meanings of the language of signs. Wandering and never at home, Ahasverian thought experiences in passing by and in an indirect manner the hidden horizon of meaning of the language of signs, the hidden dimension of the gestalt: "Every word is related to the axle that itself can carry no words."[46]

But what next if in our era the *animal rationale* is ubiquitous and only one meaning is absolutized; the dominion of the astronomical—calculable—moon for calculating thought. If indirect access to the gestalt necessitates wandering between *different* meanings while the division of these meanings in our times is reduced to a unity—the man in the moon is not in the actual sense—then something different preceded Ahasverian *thought*.

And with that we hit in the end upon the actual task of the Ahasverian wanderings in our time. The concept of the gestalt demands then namely the *poetry* of the language of signs with respect to a *different* direction of meaning; the *poetry* of the man in the moon. Underway, the poet listens to the language of signs, to the "voice of the unknown," "the silent powers," the "nameless gestalt" and the "signals" that the senses crave that can perceive them, that is, to the *possible* meanings that the language of signs reveals: "The service of the poet counts among the highest of this world. When he transforms the word, the spirits surround him; they sniff the blood that is given. There, the future is not only seen; it is conjured and also banished."[47] The poetry of the language of signs unfolds, points to a different meaning that the language of signs reveals.

The poetic articulation of the language of signs is not merged with this newly articulated meaning: the man in the moon. The poetry is and remains stereoscopic and therefore holds primarily the *division* between the different meanings open and so has in an indirect manner access to the horizon of meaning of the language of signs, to the hidden dimension of the gestalt: "The true language, the language of the poet, reveals itself in words and images that are so taken, words that, although they have been known to us for a long time, unfold like blossoms and from which an untouched brilliance, a colored music appears to flow. It is the hidden harmony of things that ring here."[48] Because the poetic wanderings call on the horizon of meaning of the language of signs, the poetic unfolding of the language articulates not only a different meaning—the moon *as* man—but also with that becomes one and raises in an indirect manner the *untouched* brilliance and the *hidden* harmony of the gestalt. The language of signs alone allows, according to Jünger, this dichotomy between the articulated meaning of a word and the horizon of meaning of the language of signs, the hidden dimension of the gestalt.[49] And with this Ahasverian poetry alone is capable of the concept of the gestalt in our lifetime.

Notes

1. *Arb*, 99.
2. *Arb*, 101.
3. *Arb*, 89.
4. *Arb*, 13.
5. *Arb*, 38.
6. *MM*, 393.
7. That Jünger never speaks of things, but rather of the light in which things appear, reveals itself already in the title of his collected journals from the Second World War: *Rays*. There, the primary issue is not the "impression that the world and its objects call forth for the author," rather "the fine bars of light and shade that is built by them," thus the light, within which the events of this period stand (Jünger, Ernst, *Strahlungen. Sämtliche Werke*, vol. 1 (Stuttgart: Klett-Cotta, 1981) 14 (hereafter cited as *Strl* 14). "Rays—the author ropes in light that is reflected onto the reader. In that sense, he is conducting preliminary work. The abundance of images is to be harmonized and then valued all at once—that is: to equip it with light that corresponds to its rank, according to a secret key" (*Strl*, 16).
8. Jünger, Ernst, "Sizilischer Brief an den Mann im Mond," *Sämtliche Werke*, vol. 9 (Stuttgart: Klett-Cotta, 1981) 11 (hereafter cited as *SBr*, 11).
9. *SBr*, 11.
10. *SBr*, 13.
11. *SBr*, 14.
12. *SBr*, 15.
13. *SBr*, 11–12.
14. *Strl*, 16.
15. *Arb*, 141.
16. *Arb*, 104.
17. For a further elaboration of Jünger's concept of language, cf. Chapter 9 and Part III.
18. *SBr*, 12.
19. *Arb*, 102 (my emphasis).
20. *SBr*, 14.
21. *Arb*, 112.
22. *Arb*, 13.
23. *AH1*, 56.
24. *SBr*, 12 (modified).
25. *SBr*, 16.
26. *SBr*, 16–17 (modified).
27. *SBr*, 16.
28. *SBr*, 17.
29. *SBr*, 17 (my emphasis).
30. *SBr*, 18.
31. *SBr*, 20.
32. *AH1*, 83.
33. *AH1*, 86.
34. *SBr*, 22.
35. *SBr*, 22.
36. Cf. "Things should reveal their true Being together with their dreamlike-magical side and at the same time be recognizable in the framework in a world-immanent prudence. But, as becomes clear in later work, Jünger is not thinking here about an encompassing synthesis of the nature of speculative natural philosophy. . . . Also there [in earlier works, VB] the conviction is already presented that the

third dimension of things, the depth, does not reveal itself in philosophical contemplation in the classic sense once again revived by idealism and romanticism (Figal, Günter, "Flugträume und höhere Trigonometrie," *Les Carnets Ernst Jünger* 4 1999: 180–181).

37. The unity that the stereoscopic view produces is thus more typically understood as unity of harmony: "Rhyme also belongs to stereoscopically affected appearance. Two of its conceptual meanings according to completely different words, 'bread' and 'death,' are set in a deeper harmony—they resonate from one tuning fork. Here, the secret relationship of all things becomes direct to the heart" (*AH1*, 89).

38. With this it also becomes clear that Jünger does not like to oppose the calculating thought of the *animal rationale*, for which the astronomical moon only *is*, rather, he only opposes the absolutizing of this way of thinking.

39. *SBr*, 20.

40. *SBr*, 20.

41. In *The Worker*, the gestalt is brought explicitly together with language. Cf. Chapter 9.

42. *Arb*, 89.

43. In this sense, the stereoscopic view cannot be equated "with the Latin *perpiscuitas*, which means the transparency of things, clarity of depiction and apparentness," as Gorgone asserts (Gorgone, Sandro, "Naturphilosophie und stereoskopische Sicht bei Ernst Jünger," *Jünger Studien* 5 2011: 21–39). In *Maxima—Minima* Jünger then says later: "In order to perceive gestalts, or as Goethe calls it 'experiences,' more is needed than basic equipment such as excellent optics, for seeing, or describing or even painting is only the signature of the gestalt and not its essence. If the eye has perceived the symbol in its vastness, it must close in order to receive an idea of its unity that can only ever get nearer: a veiled and dormant counterpart of the restlessly orbiting world" (*MM*, 333).

44. *SBr*, 21.

45. That Jünger has such a thing in mind is shown in *The Adventurous Heart*. Here, the stereoscopic view is laid out in military terms. On the basis of two outmost ends of the field of fire, the hidden gun position of the artillery cuts with the greatest sharpness. (*AH1*, 87).

46. *SBr*, 15.

47. *Strl*, 16.

48. Jünger, Ernst, *Das Abenteuerliche Herz (Zweite Fassung). Sämtliche Werke*, vol. 9 (Stuttgart: Klett-Cotta, 1979) 198–199 (hereafter cited as *AH2*, 198–199).

49. Through the reference to the relationship between Jünger's term of language and the crystals, Sandro Gorgone further worked out this function of language: "Only such a significant word can enable the insight that at the same time comprehends the depth and the surface of the real, just as it happens when considering the crystals that Ernst Jünger so especially cherished, because they possess the characteristic of building inner surfaces as well as being able to turn their own depth outwards" (Gorgone, "Naturphilosophie und stereoskopische Sicht bei Ernst Jünger," 29).

Part II

Heidegger's Reception of Jünger

Work, Gestalt and Poetry

"Resolve always to be a beginner."

(Rilke)

Introduction

If Jünger's evocation of the gestalt of the worker has had an influence on someone, then it is Martin Heidegger, and his reflections about technology. Heidegger remarks that because of his reading of Jünger, he had seen very early on what the dreadful events of the Second World War would confirm much later: "The universal dominion of the will to power within planetary history."[1] Moreover, he says that Jünger's description of the technological era in *The Worker* had a great influence on his line of thought in *The Question Concerning Technology*, which Heidegger acknowledged "is indebted to the enduring stimulus·provided by the descriptions of *The Worker*."[2] The question arises: what exactly could this enduring stimulus in Jünger's work be?

In *Across the Line*, which was first published in a *liber amicorum* occasioned by Heidegger's sixtieth birthday in 1949, Jünger discusses the question of whether we live in the age of fulfilled nihilism and, if so, whether we can overcome such nihilism. Because the true causes of our situation are unknown and cannot be discerned by hasty explanations, it is our task to first give a key definition of nihilism, that is, an assessment of our life situation. He also compares the experience of nihilism with a movement towards a zero point or zero line. The zero line or the zero meridian corresponds to the nihil of the transcendental measure of things and the dominance of the work-character in our totally mobilized world, which we saw in Part I.

Although Junger remarks that our ability to *heal* nihilism is limited, because we do not know its causes, he adopts no definitive position in *Across the Line*. On the one hand, he says that the definition or assessment of the situation of nihilism does not immediately imply its healing and yields only "practical hints regarding the movement *in* the area of nihilism."[3] On the other hand, the essay undoubtedly comes from a medical perspective—the classification into prognosis, diagnosis and therapy—as Heidegger remarks. The title of the essay, which thematizes our *crossing over* the zero point or zero line, also reflects this. With that, Jünger also asserts that this crossing over the line is well underway. It is a matter of a "new turning of Being," that is, the realization of the gestalt that stamps a meaningful order on the world. In other words, Jünger wants to *cross the line* of nihilism into a new era where "a new turning of Being"[4] takes place and puts an end to the age of fulfilled nihilism. This new turning of Being involves an *overcoming* of nihilism. Six years later, in 1955, in a *liber amicorum* occasioned on Jünger's own sixtieth birthday, Heidegger responded with an "open letter": *Concerning "The Line,"* later published as *On the Question of Being*. In this essay, Heidegger insists on the prior question about the *essence* of nihilism. He explains the specific manner with which, according to Jünger, nihilism can be overcome. Contrary to Jünger's *crossing the line*, Heidegger's main concern is the line itself: "In the title of your essay *Über die Linie,* the *über* means as much as: across, *trans, meta.* By contrast, the following remarks understand the *über* only in the sense of *de, peri.* They deal 'with' the line itself, with the zone of self-consummating nihilism."[5] In the end, Heidegger argues against Jünger that nihilism cannot be overcome at all and that the question of nihilism must be brought back to the question of Being. He calls his own way of thinking the discussion of the zero line with regards to the *essence* of nihilism. He engages with the horizon of metaphysical thinking, which has always structured our encounter with the world, and in a way that for the most part goes unobserved (see Chapter 6).

What could the enduring stimulus of Jünger be, considering that according to Heidegger, he asked the wrong question? Does Heidegger in *The Question of Being* merely speak kindly of a colleague, when he speaks of an *enduring stimulus*? Heidegger states that the essence of technology has depths that are hidden from Jünger's view.[6] If one thing becomes clear in Heidegger's annotations and remarks regarding Jünger in the 1930s, it is that, according to Heidegger, Jünger pays full tribute to Nietzsche's metaphysics of the will to power and nowhere surpasses Nietzsche's line of thought.[7] But if Jünger's work stands in such a relationship to Nietzsche's, why should a critical analysis of Nietzsche's concept of the will to power not be sufficient?

According to Heidegger, the confrontation with Nietzsche is tainted because of positivistic and romantic interpretations of his work. Jünger's achievement is that he is the only real follower of Nietzsche.[8] Jünger shows our world of the will to power, free from positivistic and romantic connotations. As opposed to the positivists, he has a nose for the metaphysical question about the essence of beings: "It is a bringing back of metaphysics to the 'Volk.'"[9]—As opposed to romanticism, "[he] does not copy the real out for a tentative demonstration; instead, the description inscribes us in the belongingness of the real."[10] Heidegger's observation needs some modification. Whereas he says here that Jünger's only achievement is that he portrayed the will to power free of positivism and romanticism, he elsewhere explicitly calls Jünger's position *romantic positivism:* "Heroic realism is romantic positivism that deviates beyond itself into unrecognized positivisms, but in the process also campaigns heavily *against* all positivisms, *against* all 'romanticism.' For what is that, when one only knows *beings* and takes these as the real and these as that which determines time, even if one sees that which exists most eminently the *gestalt*?"[11] Jünger affirms our world of the will to power without searching for exclusion or excuses. His singularity is, in other words, that he is in *our* time the gateway to Nietzsche's metaphysics of the will to power, according to Heidegger. But when Jünger pays full tribute to Nietzsche, it is not clear why Heidegger should speak of an enduring stimulus.

Several interpreters have examined this question. Günter Figal, for example, has shown that Heidegger became the "diagnostician of modernity" because of his confrontation with Jünger.[12] According to Figal, his diagnosis of the technological era, which figures prominently in his later work, is inspired by Jünger's analysis. Michael Zimmermann has shown that Jünger influenced not only Heidegger's diagnosis of modernity, but also his philosophical-political reaction to it:

> Jünger's view that this will to power mobilized humanity in terms of the *gestalt* of the technological worker influenced Heidegger in two crucial ways. First, it helped convince him that only a radical new beginning, like that proposed by National Socialism, could help Germany to escape Jünger's technological forecast. Second, it led Heidegger to look for the essence of that new beginning not so much in philosophy, but in art, especially art as understood by Nietzsche and Hölderlin.[13]

He thus discerns a second level of—negative—influence, namely the stimulus to furnish an alternative to, and escape the technological future forecasted by Jünger. In other words, it was his response to the thought of Jünger that drove Heidegger into the arms of the National Socialists.[14]

However true Zimmermann's analysis of Jünger's influence on the political thinking of Heidegger may be, we discern a third and positive level of influence, i.e., an *enduring stimulus* which is *philosophically* motivated. We discern three moments of a philosophically motivated influence of Jünger on Heidegger's work, which will be explored in this part: (1) We will first argue that Jünger's descriptions of the work-world are to a large extent *consistent* with Heidegger's concept of being-in-the-world in *Being and Time,* and that his ontology of work in the 1930s is explicitly influenced by Jünger (Chapter 6). (2) Around 1934, Heidegger started to see the negative implications of his ontology of work. In this, Jünger played a decisive role as Heidegger later on admitted; in *Facts and Thoughts,* Heidegger says about the importance of Jünger that he showed the universal dominion of the will to power within planetary history.[15] We will argue that Jünger has this importance for Heidegger in the 1930s, because the confrontation with Jünger's way of thinking showed him that the other beginning of philosophical thinking presupposes the irrevocable release of work and willing and a *gelassen,* or nonwilling, way of philosophical thinking. (3) From that moment on, the main theme of Heidegger's philosophical thinking was overcoming the metaphysics of the will to power, which consisted of his turn to the work of art and to the poetry of Hölderlin (Chapter 7).[16] But, notwithstanding Heidegger's rejection of Jünger's metaphysics of the will to power, it will become clear that Heidegger's concept of the gestalt in *The Origin of the Work of Art* is in fact inspired by Jünger (Chapter 8). We will finish this part of the book with a critical reflection on Heidegger's confrontation with Jünger. It will become clear that Heidegger's reception of Jünger is biased. Because he takes Jünger's writings a priori as *philosophical* reflections in light of Nietzsche's metaphysics of the will to power, Heidegger does not see that Jünger is underway to a non-metaphysical method to envision the turning of Being, and to a non-metaphysical concept of language that is much closer to Heidegger's than he would admit. We begin this part of the book, however, with Heidegger's reception of Jünger in the 1930s.

Notes

1. Heidegger, Martin, *Reden und andere Zeugnisse eines Lebensweges, Gesamtausgabe*, vol. 16 (Frankfurt am Main: Vittorio Klostermann, 2000) 375.
2. Heidegger, Martin, "Zur Seinsfrage," 391 (tr. 295).
3. *ÜdL*, 264.
4. *ÜdL*, 264
5. Heidegger, Martin "Zur Seinsfrage," 386 (tr. 292).
6. Heidegger, Martin, *Zu Ernst Jünger*, 6; What then is the essence of technology according to Heidegger? "Technology is not the way of mobilization, rather the foundation of truth." (Heidegger, *Zu Ernst Jünger*, 80).
7. We agree with Günter Figal, that Heidegger seeks to pin Jünger to his early position in *The Worker*, while Jünger's later work is much closer to Heidegger than he would admit: "Heidegger would like Jünger to clarify the continuity of his writing and fix him to his earlier position. That is most important to Heidegger, because it gives him the opportunity to examine Jünger's earlier position—in all likelihood his paramount interest lies therein. Jünger also examines his earlier position; but in order to be really able, he must have changed his perspective and with that, Heidegger is no longer fair with his answer. Then it could be aside from that that Heidegger evades the point on which Jünger approaches the Heideggerian perspective and eventually even opens possibilities to understand this more precisely or to relativize it to their advantage" (Figal, "Der metaphysische Charaktere der Moderne," 184–185).
8. Heidegger, Martin, *Zu Ernst Jünger*, 227; cf. 239, 255, 277.
9. Heidegger, Martin, *Zu Ernst Jünger*, 76; cf. 254.
10. Heidegger, Martin, *Zu Ernst Jünger*, 255.
11. Heidegger, Martin, *Zu Ernst Jünger*, 90, 177, 181–183.
12. Figal, Günther, "Erörterung des Nihilismus. Ernst Jünger und Martin Heidegger," *Etudes Germanistiques*, 51, 1996: 718; cf. Herrman, Friedrich-Wilhelm von, "Topologie und Topographie des Nihilismus aus dem Gespräch zwischen Ernst Jünger und Martin Heidegger," *Heidegger Studies* 24 2008, 21–39.
13. Zimmermann, M., *Heidegger's Confrontation with Modernity: Technology, Politics, Art* (Bloomington, Indianapolis: Indiana University Press, 1990) XX.

14. "Although he employs the masculine rhetoric of Jünger's 'heroic realism,' Heidegger hoped that National Socialism would allow the German people to take care of themselves and not get lost in the wasteland of technological nihilism. This is why Heidegger sought an alternative to Jünger" (Zimmermann, M., "Die Entwicklung von Heideggers Nietzsche-Interpretation," *Heidegger Jahrbuch* 2 2005: 111). Cf. for Heidegger's National Socialism, Blok, Vincent, "Naming Being: Or the Philosophical Content of Heidegger's National Socialism," *Heidegger Studies* 28 2012: 101–122.
15. Heidegger, Martin. *Reden und andere Zeugnisse eines Lebensweges*, 375.
16. Heidegger, Martin. *Reden und andere Zeugnisse eines Lebensweges*, 376; cf. Zimmermann, *Heidegger's Confrontation with Modernity*, 94–135.

5 Jünger's Fundamental Metaphysical Position

In the previous chapter, we encountered Jünger's understanding of concepts such as total mobilization and the gestalt of the worker and their conceptualization in light of Nietzsche's idea of the will to power. In his annotations from the 1930s, Heidegger states that Jünger "sharpens, hardens and articulates" Nietzsche's metaphysical design of the world, out of his essential experiences of the First World War.[1] Will to power means that reality is grasped in terms of its benefit for life (power-preservation—*Machterhaltung*—and power-enhancement—*Machtsteigerung*); a forest appears for instance *as a* potential producer of wood or *as* recreation after work. Accordingly, the increasing conversion of life into energy (total mobilization) (cf. Chapter 1) means that man and things emerge as *potential energy* for power-preservation and power-enhancement, that they have a functional value. Therefore, Heidegger concludes that in his description of total mobilization, Jünger, more than anybody else, shows our current world of the will to power.[2] Heidegger draws two conclusions from Jünger's metaphysics: Jünger's Platonism (Section 5.1) and the modern character of Jünger's Platonism (Section 5.2).

5.1 Jünger's Platonism

Within the metaphysical tradition, the gestalt is conceived in various ways. The first way is that of Platonism. In Platonism, the gestalt (*idea, eidos* or form) is the ideal and transcendental form (Being) which is the measure for all beings on earth, the world of becoming. The chasm—opened up by Platonism—between the merely apparent beings here below and the real Being somewhere up there is not neutral. In respect of the transcendental realm of Being above, the world of becoming down here is a non-being, which thus has to be denied. Here the gestalt (Being) is conceived in the *turning away* from our worldly existence, and this implies the negation (*nihil*) of the world of becoming in Platonism. In the Platonic concept of the gestalt, the transcendental realm of Being prevails over the world of becoming.

The second way is that of Nietzsche, who sees the nihilistic character of Platonism, the denial of life in its concept of the gestalt. His reversal of

Platonism takes its point of departure precisely from within the world of becoming and conceives the gestalt as the *product* of the will to power of life (cf. Chapter 2). The gestalt is a form of domination amidst the world of becoming, which serves the power-preservation and power-enhancement of life. The gestalt is a necessary condition for the power-preservation of life, which would otherwise evaporate in the face of relentless variability (becoming). Nevertheless, this gestalt is not stable and everlasting, because all stabilization destroys becoming, the principal character of life. Thus the gestalt has relative duration and in this way serves the power-enhancement of life. In Nietzsche's concept of the gestalt, the world of becoming prevails over Being.

According to Heidegger, the same reversal of Platonism is at stake in Jünger's thought. Like Nietzsche, Jünger sees the possibility of overcoming nihilism in the will to power. The gestalt of the worker is represented by the will to power of life, and should not be confused with the Platonic idea. Nevertheless, Heidegger says that in the reversal of Platonism "all the props of Platonism return."[3] Why? According to Jünger, there is no home base (*Heimat*) to be found in the world of becoming—he calls this the "elementary world" (see Chapter 3). The gestalt is necessary to regulate the elementary world of becoming. The representation of the gestalt means a stable order that is unshakeable and guarantees as such "a new security and rank order of life."[4] He finds this security in the gestalt of the worker.

The gestalt (Being) is necessary in order to regulate the elementary (becoming). Jünger understands this regulation in line with the metaphysical tradition so that a "substance" is given a "form."[5] The emphasis on the elementary points to "the primacy of the *hule*," according to Heidegger, which is brought in order by the gestalt (*eidos*).[6] On the one hand, the gestalt is the result of the reversal of Platonism, which represents something stable in the world of becoming. On the other hand, Jünger's elementarism is Platonic. Only the gestalt—the everlasting and eternal Being—is able to regulate the elementary. Thus, according to Heidegger, this attempt to reverse Platonism remains unsuccessful: "Out of the necessity of the revaluation of all values, which is a reversal of Platonism—which has to remove Platonism but isn't able to do it! The idea remains in force as *Platonic perception*."[7] All properties of Platonism return: once again Platonism, "*everlasting being*."[8]

5.2 The Modern Character of Jünger's Platonism

That Jünger is focusing on the regulation of the elementary or the *mastery of chaos* brings Heidegger to a second conclusion: although his "Platonic metaphysics of the gestalt" represents the gestalt as everlasting and transcendental, it is at the same time essentially *modern*.[9] What does the modern character of Jünger's metaphysics consist of? For Heidegger, modernity is marked by the thinking of René Descartes. Descartes sought after indubitable and certain knowledge and he found the unshakeable foundation (*fundamentum inconcussum*) for this in the *ego cogito;* human being is the *subjectum,* which is the basis for certain knowledge. Like Descartes, Jünger also seeks certainty. He finds this *fundamentum inconcussum* of certainty in the gestalt of the worker.

According to Heidegger, the gestalt is the product of the will to power, which projects a perspectival *picture* to regulate the elementary.[10] Such a world picture is not a *painting* of the world, but means rather that the world is grasped *as* picture. The world *is,* "insofar as it is set in place by representing-producing humanity."[11] Only what is represented in accordance with this picture *is* in the proper sense of the word. Jünger's "gestalt" is such a world picture, according to Heidegger. In representing the world as picture, the elementary is filtered out in favor of the presence of the world as representative of the gestalt of the worker. Heidegger calls this representation of the world as picture the "mastering of the earth" in the "fight for the domination of the earth (*Erdherrschaft*)."[12] These gestalts or world pictures are not needed in all times according to Heidegger. They are only necessary "in reality as will to power, in chaos, and that means in modernity."[13] That is to say, only when truth is understood as certainty does reality appear as chaos that must be regulated.

It is important to be clear that Jünger does not speak about the gestalt of *work,* but about the gestalt of the *worker.* Like Descartes, Jünger connects the question about the subject with the question about human being, namely the worker type which represents the gestalt of the worker. According to Heidegger, the reason for this connection is "modern metaphysics, which understands human being as subject."[14] For Heidegger, Jünger's representation of the gestalt is grounded in the "determination of the animal man."[15] The worker type as representative of the gestalt of the worker is the "determinate animal," which founds the regulation of the elementary in a world picture.

However, that the grounds for certainty are found in the gestalt of the worker does not, according to Heidegger, mean that the worker type (Jünger) is identical with the *ego cogito* of Descartes. It means only that since modernity all philosophy is anthropological and every representation anthropomorphic.[16] Ever since Descartes, the question about the *fundamentum inconcussum* has been connected to human being *as* subjectum. Therefore, Heidegger characterizes Jünger's fundamental metaphysical position in the following way: "the unconditional anthropomorphism of absolute subjectivity of the *homo natura* as *homo faber militans.*"[17]

The fundamental metaphysical position of Jünger's Platonism is modern because it remains trapped in the gestalt of human being as subject. "*The self-assertion in the gestalt* is *then* the only form of *certainty* and *security,* because exactly this represents the highest subjectivity in the domain of modern freedom anyway."[18] This subject is the foundation for the modern understanding of truth *as* certainty. The certainty of the gestalt is therefore the certainty of the subject, where the objectivity of the object is reduced to and guaranteed by the representation of the subject. The regulation of the elementary through the projection of the gestalt aims at the domination of the earth and so is an indication of the *battle for the domination of the world*,[19] whereas the gestalt of the worker is the concealed *meaning (Sinn)* of our world, the human being is the subject which *gives* this meaning to the meaningless by regulating the elementary.

Notes

1. Heidegger, Martin, *Zu Ernst Jünger*, 227.
2. Heidegger, Martin, *Zu Ernst Jünger*, 263; cf. 53.
3. Heidegger, Martin, *Zu Ernst Jünger*, 82.
4. *Arb*, 99.
5. *Arb*, 214.
6. Heidegger, Martin, *Zu Ernst Jünger*, 124; cf. 94, 96.
7. Heidegger, Martin, *Zu Ernst Jünger*, 23.
8. Heidegger, Martin, *Zu Ernst Jünger*, 81; cf. 22f, 28, 74, 81f, 93f, 100, 131, 167. Although Heidegger points to Jünger's Platonism, what is at stake is the relation between Platonism and the reversal of Platonism. He does not draw from this the conclusion that something else that matters in Jünger can be found in Nietzsche or Plato, but only that Jünger thinks everything unclearly, mixes up and levels out everything (Heidegger, *Zu Ernst Jünger*, 131). In fact, there is a *fusion* between Nietzscheanism and Platonism happening in the work of Jünger, which cannot be elaborated upon here.
9. Heidegger, Martin, *Zu Ernst Jünger*, 93f.
10. Heidegger, Martin, *Zu Ernst Jünger*, 21, 133–137.
11. Heidegger, Martin, *Zu Ernst Jünger*, 133–137; Heidegger, Martin, "Die Zeit des Weltbildes," *Holzwege*, Gesamtausgabe, vol. 5 (Frankfurt am Main: Vittorio Klostermann, 1977) 89 (tr. 67).
12. Heidegger, Martin, *Zu Ernst Jünger*, 53, 59, 80; Heidegger, "Die Zeit des Weltbildes," 111.
13. Heidegger, Martin, *Zu Ernst Jünger*, 134.
14. Heidegger, Martin, *Zu Ernst Jünger*, 132f.
15. Heidegger, Martin, *Zu Ernst Jünger*, 23.
16. Heidegger, Martin, *Zu Ernst Jünger*, 99; Heidegger, "Die Zeit des Weltbildes," 99ff. (tr. 74ff).
17. Heidegger, Martin, *Zu Ernst Jünger*, 45; cf. 5.
18. Heidegger, Martin, *Zu Ernst Jünger*, 134.
19. Heidegger, Martin, *Zu Ernst Jünger*, 20f, 39, 53, 59, 80, 151; Heidegger, "Die Zeit des Weltbildes," 111 (tr. 84); Heidegger, Martin, *Die Geschichte des Seins*, Gesamtausgabe, vol. 69 (Frankfurt am Main: Vittorio Klostermann, 1998) 74.

6 Heidegger's Ontology of Work

Despite Heidegger's criticism of Jünger's metaphysical position in the period of 1934–1940, a more nuanced picture shows itself if we look at Heidegger's concept of work in the beginning of the 1930s. In *The German Student as Worker* from 1933 for instance, Heidegger argues that work "confronts us with beings in a whole."[1] "Work displaces and inserts the people in the radius of action of all essential powers of being. The structure of *völkisch* existence, which is shaped and constituted *in* its work and *as* work, is the state. The National Socialist state is the work-state."[2] Work seems to be the fundamental category of human existence in the 1930s, which, as we will see, is inspired by the work of Jünger.

In this chapter, we will first show that Heidegger's ontology of work in the 1930s is already prefigured in *Being and Time* (Section 6.1 and Section 6.2). With this, the question arises how this prefiguration of the "total" work-character in *Being and Time* is related to the ontology of work in the 1930s (Section 6.3). Our hypothesis is that Heidegger's concept of work in *Being and Time prevents* access to Being, while the concept of work in the 1930s provides exactly access to Being. It will turn out that precisely because Heidegger returns to his previous position in *Being and Time* in his later work, he later on rejects the concept of work categorically (Section 6.4).

6.1 The Work-Character of being-in-the-World in *Being and Time*

In *Being and Time*, Heidegger argues that we first and mostly exist in association with inner-worldly beings which we use and take care of. In our dealings *in* the world and *with* entities within the world—writing, hammering, opening, building, etc.—things become accessible as useful things or equipment; they encounter our "practical" behavior in dealing with the world as equipment "in-order-to" hammer, write, etc.[3]

A first distinction between equipment and mere things is that pieces of equipment are not autonomous or independent, but have to be understood out of a context or world of equipment. Pencil, table, lamp, room, etc., form a context *in-order-to* write, and the meaning of the pencil as equipment is dependent on this context for writing; without a table and a paper, for instance, the pencil is not equipment, i.e., not *in-order-to* write.[4] The meaning of equipment has to be understood in a contextual way, i.e., as dependent on a world of interrelated equipment.

A second distinction between equipment and mere things is that useful things never stand in front of us like objects. On the contrary, our being is primarily *involved* in this world of practice and reciprocal to it. Heidegger speaks for instance about our "dealing geared to equipment," which shows that *Dasein* is primarily adaptive to the world of practice: "In dealings such as this, where something is put to use, our concern subordinates itself to the 'in-order-to,' which is constitutive for the equipment we are employing at the time; . . . The hammering itself uncovers the specific 'manipulability' of the hammer. The kind of being which equipment possesses—in which it manifests itself in its own right—we call '*readiness-to-hand*.'"[5] Items of equipment are only useful in reference to our dealings with them. Our involvement in or reciprocity to this world of practice shows that *Dasein* is not a subject in front of an object, but being-in-the-world. This means, that the readiness-to-hand of equipment is understood in a relational way, as the way the world appears *as* ready-to-hand for handling or manipulatory people.[6] "*Da-sein* is initially and for the most part *together with* the 'world' that it takes care of."[7]

Our involvement in the world of practice shows that Heidegger's concept of the ready-to-hand world of practice cannot be understood as an early concept of pragmatism.[8] The meaning of the world of practice is not primarily derived from its usefulness for us, because "we" are involved in this world of practice as well; our involvement with the world of practice discloses it as meaningful from the beginning, i.e., as a world of interrelated pieces of equipment in which we are at home. "This is what makes up the structure of the world—the structure of that wherein *Dasein* as such already is."[9]

A third distinction between equipment and mere things is that what is ready-to-hand—equipment—*withdraws* in its character of readiness-to-hand in order to enable us to focus on the *work* of our everyday dealings; writing a letter for instance. Our concernful dealings do not focus on the writing materials in writing for instance, but primarily concern the work itself; the letter I have in mind. Equipment withdraws in our bringing forth of the work they are used for. But insofar each work—in *Being and Time* at least[10]—can be understood again as equipment (the letter is the work of writing on the one hand and on the other itself equipment *in-order-to* apply for a job for instance), all works are characterized by this double movement of their withdrawal as equipment in favor of their presence as work. This withdrawal of equipment in favor of its presence as work, which withdraws itself again in favor of the next work, etc., is characteristic for the world of practice we are dealing with.

The scope of the world of practice becomes clear if we take an example. The work of a shoemaker—new work boots for instance—is itself a useful thing *in-order-to* wear it, which withdraws itself in plowing and sowing for instance. First of all, that *what* the work is useful *for* belongs to the world of practice; the plowed land is useful for a rich harvest, the harvest is useful for the animals, the animals are useful for their hides, their hides are useful for the bringing forth of work boots, etc. All these items of equipment/work belong to the world of practice we are associated with. Secondly, the materials the works are produced from belong to the world of practice; work boots are dependent on leather, leather is produced from hides, hides are taken from animals, animals are raised by farmers, farmers are dependent on footgear and so on. All these items of equipment/work belong to the world of practice we are associated with. Also human beings belong to the world of practice, as the one who wears and uses these works. According to Heidegger, this world of practice even includes the whole of nature, i.e., beings in the whole:

> Any work with which one concerns oneself is ready-to-hand not only in the domestic world of the workshop but also in the *public world*. Along with the public world, the *environing nature* is discovered and is accessible to everyone. In roads, streets, bridges, buildings, our concern discovers *nature* as having some definite direction. A covered railway platform takes account of bad weather; an installation for public lighting takes account of the darkness, or rather of specific changes in the presence or absence of daylight—the "position of the sun."[11]

Nature appears here in its serviceability and usability, just as the world of practice; it is part of the meaningful world which we have always already understood and in which we are always already intentionally involved. Can we conclude, then, that the ontology of work shows itself already in Heidegger's description of the work-world in *Being and Time*?

In a lecture about the *Basic Concepts of Aristotelian Philosophy* in the same period (1924), this world of equipment and work is explicitly connected with the concept of work. In his productive appropriation[12] of Aristotle's basic concepts, Heidegger explores what primarily encounters us in the world: "A being thus in the world is there and can, as *dunamis*, at the same time be something usable. *Dunamis*, 'not yet,' can mean: is usable for . . ., transformable into. . . . This being that is there thus, as there completed and usable for . . . is characterized by the *dichoos* as a being."[13] We encounter here not only Heidegger's interpretation of Aristotle's concept of *dunamis*, but also an early formulation of his own analysis of equipment in *Being and Time*: the leather is usable for shoes, it *can* become a shoe, like timber can become a table. On the one hand, we encounter the *readiness-to-hand* of equipment in this ability-to-be of timber; timber is usable to make a table or—in terms of *Being and Time*—a useful piece of equipment in order to make such a table. On the other hand, precisely this ability-to-be is understood as being-in-work (*in-Arbeit-Sein*) of the table; the *being-serviceable for . . .* or *usable for . . .*[14] of ready-to-hand equipment is thus understood here as *being-in-work* of equipment. This being-in-work is according to Heidegger not only "thought" by us but also *a way of being,* namely the way the timber primarily encounters us in the environment in its usefulness for or serviceability as a table.[15]

As in *Being and Time,* Heidegger argues in this lecture as well that the being-in-work of ready-to-hand equipment does not only concern instruments and handicrafts, but is extended to the whole of nature: "The hermeneutic fact of the matter: I and you, we are not concerned with it [the being-in-work of beings], and yet it is there, it happens, is concerned with itself, is there arising, and the like—to come from itself into presence and, e.g. to rest therein—reality. *Phusis* characterizes a being that is: *to be in itself the worker of itself.*"[16] Here we encounter therefore the work-character of the ready-to-hand world in which we are at home *as* worker. As in *Being and Time,* this work-character is extended to the whole of the world of practice, i.e., this work-character determines beings in the whole.

As our dealing geared to equipment in *Being and Time* is included in the work-world, so is the work-character of the world also in this lecture understood in relation to human being as worker. As equipment only *is* in our dealing geared to equipment and in our focus on its work, so is the relation with timber here characterized in the following way: the timber is originary *at work,* provided that the carpenter has it in hand. "What is able-to-be (the wood lying before in the workshop), that is in work, is there as able-to-be precisely when it is taken up into work."[17] The whole of nature is therefore being-at-work—the *phusis* is "worker of itself"—but *originary* being-at-work is nature precisely in our dealing with it: "In work, one has the surrounding world (also that which is of interest, and the like). We are concerned with the surrounding world in hand."[18] Work is thus understood in a relational way, as the unity of the being-at-work of the work-world and human work with regard to this world, and concerns therefore the appearance of the world as being-at-work and our human responsiveness to the world of work as worker.

Also in *Being and Time,* our dealing geared by equipment is explicitly called "work"; the work-world "is found when one is at work,"[19] we meet other people "at work," etc.[20] It is precisely this handling or working with equipment with regard to the works of labor, which is called being-in-the-world by Heidegger.

6.2 Heidegger's Ontology of Work in the 1930s

When being in the whole is already characterized by its work-character in the period of *Being and Time,* then we have to reject Lacoue-Labarthe's suggestion that "the ontology of work" is developed at the beginning of the 1930s.[21] On the contrary, we have to conclude that Heidegger's ontology of work is at least prefigured in *Being and Time.* With this, the question arises how this prefiguration of the "total work-character" in *Being and Time* is related to Heidegger's ontology of work in the 1930s. In order to answer this question, we first compare Jünger's description of the work-world in Part I with Heidegger's description of the work-world in the previous section.

When we compare Jünger's description of the total mobilization in the First World War with Heidegger's description of the work-world in *Being and Time*, we encounter one similarity and one difference between the two. Jünger's description of the total mobilization, in which man and things appear as function or operative, is comparable with Heidegger's description of the ready-to-hand world, which is extended to the whole of being. Also for Heidegger, the whole of nature appears as ready-at-hand equipment or work, which derives its meaning from its productivity (serviceability, usability): "The wood is a forest of timber, the mountain a quarry of rock; the river is water-power, the wind is wind 'in the sails.' "[22]

Contrary to Jünger's description of the worker as a *functionary* within the total mobilization, however, it is clear that for Heidegger, human existence is excluded from this work-character. Human work is indeed *included* in the ready-to-hand work-world according to Heidegger and can in this sense be understood as worker, as we have seen in the previous section. Never, however, is human existence itself conceivable as ready-to-hand or as a functionary in the sense of Jünger. Why not? "What belongs to the being of *Dasein* is not being within the world but being-in-the-world. Intraworldliness cannot even devolve upon the *Dasein*."[23]

According to Heidegger, the inter-relation of the ready-to-hand work-world goes back to a "towards-which": "this 'towards-which' is not an entity with the kind of being that belongs to what is ready-to-hand within a world; it is rather an entity whose being is defined as being-in-the-world, and to whose state of being worldhood itself belongs."[24] The work-character of the world goes back to a towards-which—*Dasein*—that itself cannot be understood anymore as work or equipment in-order-to . . .: "But that for which something environmentally ready-to-hand has thus been freed (and indeed in such a manner that it becomes accessible *as* an entity within-the-world first of all), cannot itself be conceived as an entity with this discovered kind of being,"[25] i.e., not as a ready-to-hand equipment. This for-the-sake-of-which is on the contrary the relational point for the signification of the specific in-order-to:

> The "for-the-sake-of-which" signifies an "in-order-to"; this in turn, a "towards-this"; the latter, an "in-which" of letting something be involved; and that in turn, the "with-which" of an involvement. These relationships are bound up with one another as a primordial totality; they are what they are as this signifying in which *Dasein* gives itself beforehand its being-in-the-world as something to be understood.[26]

To the extent that *Dasein* cannot be understood in terms of its serviceability or usability, but has to be understood as indeterminate—while mortal—relational point for the work-character of the world, human existence is no longer to be understood out of this in-order-to relation, i.e., as functionary or worker in the sense of Jünger.

With this, it becomes first of all clear that contrary to Jünger, the work-character of the world is not total in case of Heidegger. Heidegger characterizes human dealing with the world indeed as being-at-work in the work-world, but this inclusiveness of our being-in-the-world is not total. In the end, he distinguishes clearly between human responsiveness to equipment and work (being-at-work) and *Dasein* itself (the for-the-sake-of-which of *Dasein*). With this, it becomes secondly clear that *Dasein* is ambiguous in *Being and Time;* on the one hand, *Dasein* can be characterized as being-at-work of the worker, as we have seen in Chapter 1—but on the other hand, *Dasein* is precisely excluded from this work-character: "this primary 'towards-which' is a 'for-the-sake-of-which.' But the 'for-the-sake-of' always pertains to the being of *Dasein,* for which, in its being, that very being is essentially an *issue."*[27] The work-character of the world is not total in the case of Heidegger, because notwithstanding the appearance of the world as work-world and our human responsiveness to this work-world as worker, it is precisely *Dasein* (the for-the-sake-of-which) which is excluded from this work-character; in the end, *Dasein* is concerned about its own being. In a formal way therefore, we can conclude that this care for the being of *Dasein,* respectively the meaning of being, is excluded from the work-character of our being-at-work.

We speak with intention of a *formal* distinction between the work-character of our human dealings in the work-world and our care for being. The world of work is not in front of us like a thing or object, as we have seen in Section 6.1. We are included in the work-world, which is precisely *at work* in our responsiveness to it. As we have explained elsewhere, Heidegger's basic experience in *Being and Time* is that the being of *Dasein,* respectively the meaning of being, is *not* discussed by thinking, because *Dasein* is primarily absorbed as worker by the ready-to-hand world of work.[28] Heidegger introduces this basic experience right at the beginning of *Being and Time.* He claims here "that we live already in an understanding of being and that the meaning of being is at the same time shrouded in darkness."[29] In Section 6.1, we have seen how work determines our understanding of the world: the appearance of the work-character of the world and our human responsiveness to this work-world as worker. According to Heidegger, in our self-evident understanding of the work-world, the *meaning* of being remains hidden.

This concealment cannot be projected in a projection of thinking, nor can it be understood. Heidegger calls the meaning of being the projection-domain, "wherein the intelligibility of something maintains itself."[30] This domain is the space *between* being and thinking, the openness I have to stride through to reach things in the world. Our understanding of the work-world presupposes this projection-domain, which cannot be projected in a projection of thinking. Heidegger experiences, in other words, an incommensurability or twofold between the brightness of our understanding of the work-world (unconcealment) and the darkness of the meaning of being (concealment), something *beyond* thinking and *beyond* work which cannot be reached by thought. This twofold of the unconcealment of the world of work and the concealment of the meaning of being, is in his later work called the truth of being (see Chapter 8 for Heidegger's concept of the truth of being).

Why is it impossible to understand the meaning of being? Human existence primarily consists of our being-at-work, which is absorbed by the work-world, as we have seen. The question regarding the meaning of being remains forgotten in our being-at-work, which means that the forgottenness of being reigns. When Heidegger thus argues in *Being and Time* that *Dasein* is essentially concerned about being, what is at stake is not human existence as the meaning of work, but the meaning of being, which remains forgotten and concealed in the work-character of the world and in our human responsiveness to this work-character as worker. With this, it becomes clear why the difference between the work-character of our human existence in-the-world and our concern for being is *formal*, because there is no way from my being-at-work to my care for being. In case I am really concerned about being, I have to reject my being-at-work. But because the work-world is omnipresent and is inescapable for us, our being-at-work cannot easily be replaced by a new way of philosophical thinking. We are always already absorbed by the omnipresence of the work-character of our being-in-the-world.

For this reason, Heidegger later on argues that *Being and Time* "points to a completely different domain of questioning."[31] The question regarding the meaning of being is not answered in *Being and Time*.[32] Its attempt is, on the contrary, to "reawaken an understanding for the meaning of this question."[33] In *Being and Time,* it becomes clear therefore that the question regarding the meaning of being implies our farewell to work. Work provides access to entities or beings—presupposing a pre-ontological understanding of being—and prevents therefore our access to the meaning of being.

To conclude this chapter: on the one hand, the total work-character of Jünger's description of the work-world is comparable with Heidegger's description of our being-at-work in *Being and Time*. On the other hand, this work-character is not total as in Jünger's description of the world of work, because the essence of human existence is precisely excluded from this work-character. For Heidegger, the essence of human existence consists of its concern about its being itself, respectively the meaning of being. Because of the work-character of our being-in-the-world, Heidegger's main concern in *Being and Time* is the transition toward a way of human existence that has *access* to the question concerning the meaning of being.

6.3 Total Work-Character in the 1930s

Also in the beginning of the 1930s, Heidegger saw the mission of thought in the destruction of philosophy, i.e., "*the end of metaphysics* out of a more originary question regarding the 'meaning' (truth) of being."[34] But when he discusses the concept of work at the beginning of the 1930s, the worker is no longer the one who is absorbed by the ready-to-hand world of work. Contrary to *Being and Time*, the worker is precisely the one who is transitory toward a way of human existence that is concerned about the meaning of being. In *The German Student as Worker* from 1932, he argues for instance that the German student has to be understood out of a "complete transformation" of the German reality. He is no longer an academic civilian, but "becomes a worker."[35]

And here we see the positive influence of Jünger on Heidegger's conceptualization of the worker. Following Jünger, Heidegger rejects economic conceptualizations of work and worker, just as conceptualizations of the worker as a class. Heidegger conceptualizes work in the following way: "The word work is ambiguous. It means on the one hand work as enactment of specific behavior. On the other hand, it means work as a product, the result or success of this enactment. According to this broad and doubled meaning, all human behavior, provided that it is *about* something, is *work* and *care*."[36] In terms of *Being and Time*, work means our being-at-work in the ready-to-hand world, as well as this world of work with equipment and work itself. This statement from the early 1930s is not only consistent with *Being and Time*, but the fundamental category of human existence—care—is here explicitly understood in terms of work.

Heidegger continues, however: "But, the substance of the essence of work is not to be found in the *enactment* of this behavior nor in the *result* of this enactment, but in *that, what essentially happens in this,* and that is: Man presents himself *as worker* in the confrontation with beings in the whole. In this confrontation, the authorization, enforcement, compliance, and taming of the listed earth-shaping powers happens."[37] Contrary to *Being and Time*, the essence of work is no longer found in our being absorbed in the world of work, nor in the results of this work in the beginning of the 1930s, but in the confrontation with the meaning or the truth of being. In this confrontation, work "puts being to work in a being (*er-wirkt, erwirken*). To put to work here means to bring into the work—a work within which as what appears, the emerging that holds sway, *phusis,* comes to seem. . . . Setting-to-work is putting being to work *in* beings, a putting-to-work that opens up."[38] While Heidegger seems to reserve this setting-to-work exclusively for the work of art in his *Introduction to Metaphysics* from 1935, this setting-to-work is unconditionally used to characterize our care for being in the notes and lectures of the early 1930s.[39]

Here, precisely work puts being to work in a being, i.e., constitutes the identity of the German state; precisely "work displaces and inserts the people in the radius of action of all essential powers of being. The structure of the national existence, which is shaped and constituted *in* its work and *as* its work, is the *state*. The National Socialist state is the work-state."[40]

The big difference with *Being and Time* is therefore not that the for-the-sake-of-which of *Dasein* at the outset of the 1930s is no longer found in the singularity of *Dasein* but in the people or the state.[41] The big difference with

Being and Time is precisely that the essence of work consists of our care for the meaning or truth of being. Work is here understood namely in the light of the authorization, enforcement, compliance, and taming of the earth-shaping powers of being (nature, history, art, technology and the state),[42] whereby the people conquered and realized their rootedness in the state.

In the "advancement" and "insistence" of the German student as worker, Heidegger sees an indication that our *Dasein* begins to shift toward another way of being,[43] i.e., to a way of being of the people that exposes itself to the meaning or truth of being. Work therefore no longer *prevents* access to the meaning of being, but arises out of, and provides access to the experience of being. The essence of work consists here in the care for being. And as Jünger saw the harbingers of the new worker type in the soldiers of the Great War, Heidegger saw the harbingers of *Dasein,* which is characterized by the exposure to the meaning of being, in the German students: "This type of student doesn't 'study' anymore, i.e., he does not *sit* somehow secure and 'strive' towards something from out of this sitting position. This new type of those who want to know are always on the way. This student becomes a *worker*."[44] At this moment, we find "at every university half a dozen" of these workers. "The new student advances however in the new order of the state's existence and his national knowledge, and this in such a way that he from his side helps to shape this new order."[45]

It is clear that Heidegger initially saw in the rise of Hitler the moment at which this shift towards another way of being could take place.[46] Heidegger speaks in this respect about "world-shaping powers," i.e., the shaping of the world and of the human habitation of this world in the light of the meaning of being,[47] which can only be fulfilled by the German,[48] and this work puts being to work in a being. It is precisely this world-shaping power, which is called work.[49] For Heidegger, the National Socialist Revolution was exemplary for the shift towards another way of being, and the university should also contribute to the "pedagogical will"[50] of the National Socialists and the "construction of a new spiritual world for the German people, i.e., to the shift toward human existence as worker who is exposed to the meaning of being."[51]

To conclude this subsection: While Heidegger in *Being and Time* claims that the essence of human existence is excluded from the work-character of our being-in-the-world and is concerned about the meaning of being, in the 1930s he claims precisely that the essence of work directs *Dasein* to its care for being. Human existence is here characterized by work, and precisely work provides access to our experience of the meaning of being.

6.4 The Positive Inspiration of Jünger's Concept of Work on Heidegger

It is clear that the transition from the position in *Being and Time*—work prevents access to the meaning of being—to Heidegger's thought at the outset of the 1930s—work precisely provides access to being—is inspired by the work of Jünger. As we have seen, Heidegger remarks that because of his reading of Jünger, he had, very early, already seen "the universal dominion of the will to power within planetary history."[52] And in *The German Student as Worker* from 1933, he directly refers to the work of Ernst Jünger:

> The so-understood nature of work determines now *in a fundamental way* the *Dasein* of human being. Our *Dasein* begins to shift into a different mode of being, whose character I pointed out to be *care* already years ago, and what is rejected unanimously by academic philosophy. *Ernst Jünger* has recently interpreted this upcoming mode of being of the human being of the next age *by* the *Gestalt* of the Worker, from a creative understanding of Nietzsche and based on his experience of mechanized warfare in World War one.[53]

Heidegger's conceptualization of care in terms of work makes clear that Jünger initially did not have a negative influence on Heidegger's thought at the beginning of the 1930s, as suggested by Michael Zimmermann, namely the stimulus to develop an *alternative* for the technological future forecasted by Jünger.[54] Heidegger's use of the concept of work in the period 1930–1934 is definitely positively inspired by Jünger, although not necessarily completely the same as Jünger's.[55]

Notes

1. Heidegger, Martin, *Reden und andere Zeugnisse eines Lebensweges*, 113.
2. Heidegger, Martin, *Reden und andere Zeugnisse eines Lebensweges*, 205–206.
3. Heidegger, Martin, *Sein und Zeit*, Gesamtausgabe, vol. 2 (Frankfurt am Main: Vittorio Klostermann, 1977) 89–94 (tr. 122–128). According to Dreyfus, Heidegger's practical account of being-in-the-world shows that *Being and Time* bears witness to a proto-technological metaphysics, of which he was so critical in his later work (Dreyfus, H., *Being-in-the-World: A Commentary on Heidegger's Being and Time, Division I* [Cambridge: MIT Press, 1991] 175; cf. Ihde, D., *Heidegger's Technologies: Postphenomenological Perspectives* [New York: Fordham University Press, 2010] 47–48; Blok, Vincent. "Being-in-the-World as Being-in-Nature: An Ecological Perspective on *Being and Time*," *Studia Phaenomenologica* 14 2014: 215–236).
4. Cf. "Rather, technologies are contextual, or field involved; the hammer 'is' what it is in reference to the context of nails, project, and so on. It belongs to a reference system that always includes more than a mere hammer. Thus, while the hammer is always 'thingly,' it is never a *mere* thing and is, in use, transformed into a world-related and world-revealing way in which humans are involved with their environments" (Ihde, *Heidegger's Technologies*, 78).
5. Heidegger, *Sein und Zeit*, 93 (tr. 125–126).
6. Weberman has shown that for Heidegger, exactly this *relational* aspect of the *Sachverhalt* is the reason to reject the ontology of objective precense: "An important and perhaps primary reason for Heidegger's rejection of *Vorhandenheit* is that it contradicts what I call the relationality thesis. The relationality thesis holds that, contrary to first impressions and to much of the philosophical tradition,

entities are not self-contained. They are not self-contained because entities are what they are partly in virtue of their relations to entities outside of themselves, whether spatially or temporally" (Weberman, D. "Heidegger's Relationalism," *British Journal for the History of Philosophy* 1 2001: 109).

7. Heidegger, Martin, *Sein und Zeit*, 232 (tr. 274–275).
8. Cf. Gehtmann, C.F., "Heideggers Konzeption des Handelns in Sein und Zeit," *Heidegger und die praktische Philosophie*, ed. A. Gehtmann-Siefert and O. Pöggeler (Frankfurt am Main: Suhrkamp, 1989) 140–176.
9. Heidegger, Martin, *Sein und Zeit*, 116–117 (tr. 152–153).
10. While Heidegger in *Being and Time* argues that every work as such can be understood as ready-to-hand (Heidegger, *Sein und Zeit*, 94), this is no longer the case in his *Origin of the Work of Art* from 1935–36. For this, cf. Chapter 8.
11. Heidegger, Martin, *Sein und Zeit*, 95–96 (tr. 128–129).
12. For the concept of Heidegger's productive appropriation as characteristic of his philosophical method, cf. Blok, Vincent, "Communication or Confrontation: Heidegger and Philosophical Method," *Empedocles* 1 2009: 43–57.
13. Heidegger, Martin, *Grundbegriffe der aristotelische Philosophie*, Gesamtausgabe, vol. 18 (Frankfurt am Main: Vittorio Klostermann, 2002) 313 (tr. 143–144).
14. Heidegger, Martin, *Grundbegriffe der aristotelische Philosophie*, 300 (tr. 203).
15. Heidegger, Martin, *Grundbegriffe der aristotelische Philosophie*, 378 (tr. 255–256).
16. Heidegger, Martin, *Grundbegriffe der aristotelische Philosophie*, 380 (tr. 257).
17. Heidegger, Martin, *Grundbegriffe der aristotelische Philosophie*, 321 (tr. 217).
18. Heidegger, Martin, *Grundbegriffe der aristotelische Philosophie*, 378 (tr. 255–256). Also in the case the carpenter is gone from the workshop, the table that was begun lies there, this table *in rest* is still *at-work*, to the extent that for Heidegger, rest is an extreme case of movement, i.e., of being-at-work (Heidegger, *Grundbegriffe der aristotelische Philosophie*, 314; cf. 378–380 [tr. 256–257]).
19. Heidegger, Martin, *Sein und Zeit*, 94 (tr. 127); cf. 156–157.
20. Heidegger, Martin, *Sein und Zeit*, 160 (tr. 203).
21. Lacoue-Labarthe, P., *Heidegger, Art and Politics*, trans. Chris Turner (Oxford: Blackwell, 1990) 109.
22. Heidegger, Martin, *Sein und Zeit*, 95 (tr. 128).
23. Heidegger, Martin, *Grundbegriffe der Phänomenologie*, Gesamtausgabe, vol. 24 (Frankfurt am Main: Vittorio Klostermann, 1975) 240 (tr. 168–169 modified).
24. Heidegger, Martin, *Sein und Zeit*, 113 (tr. 149).
25. Heidegger, Martin, *Sein und Zeit*, 114–115 (tr. 149–151).
26. Heidegger, Martin, *Sein und Zeit*, 116 (tr. 151–152).
27. Heidegger, *Sein und Zeit*, 113 (tr. 147–148).
28. Cf. Blok, Vincent, "Naming Being," 101–122.
29. Heidegger, Martin, *Sein und Zeit*, 6 (tr. 25–26).
30. Heidegger, Martin, *Sein und Zeit*, 201 (tr. 245).
31. Heidegger, Martin, *Einführung in die Metaphysik*, Gesamtausgabe, vol. 40 (Frankfurt am Main: Vittorio Klostermann, 1976) 214 (tr. 119–120).
32. Cf. Oudemans, Wouter, *Ernüchterung des Denkens oder der Abschied der Onto-Theologie* (Berlin: Dunckler & Humblot 2008) 78–95.
33. Heidegger, Martin, *Sein und Zeit*, 1 (tr. 1).
34. Heidegger, Martin, *Der Anfang der abendländischen Philosophie. Auslegung des Anaximander und Parmenides*, Gesamtausgabe, vol. 35 (Frankfurt am Main: Vittorio Klostermann, 2012) 1.
35. Heidegger, Martin, *Reden und andere Zeugnisse eines Lebensweges*, 204.
36. Heidegger, Martin, *Reden und andere Zeugnisse eines Lebensweges*, 205.
37. Heidegger, Martin, *Reden und andere Zeugnisse eines Lebensweges*, 205.
38. Heidegger, Martin, *Einführung in die Metaphysik*, 168 (tr. 169–170).

39. Even the freedom of *Dasein* is found in work. Contrary to animals, human existence has a *free* determinability and endurance to work (Heidegger, *Reden und andere Zeugnisse eines Lebensweges*, 236). "The animal and that what is just vegetating cannot work. They lack the basic experience which enables them to work: the decisive commitment to a task, the ability to be disclosed to and to stand firm in an accepted mission, in short freedom i.e.: the spirit" (Heidegger, *Reden und andere Zeugnisse eines Lebensweges*, 239).
40. Heidegger, Martin, *Reden und andere Zeugnisse eines Lebensweges*, 205–206. Cf.: "The will to self-responsibility is however not only the fundamental law of being of our *Volk*, rather also the fundamental event of realizing the National Socialist state. Every job of every status, large or small, in every location and of every rank in their equal necessity moves from this will to self-responsibility. The work of the classes carries and secures the living structure of the state; work allows the Volk to recover its rootedness, moves the state as the actuality of the Volk into the field of influence of all essential powers of human being." (Heidegger, *Reden und andere Zeugnisse eines Lebensweges*, 190).
41. Lacoue-Labarthe, Philippe, *Heidegger, Art, and Politics*, 78; cf. 109.
42. Heidegger, Martin, *Reden und andere Zeugnisse eines Lebensweges*, 201.
43. Heidegger, Martin, *Reden und andere Zeugnisse eines Lebensweges*, 205.
44. Heidegger, Martin, *Reden und andere Zeugnisse eines Lebensweges*, 204.
45. Heidegger, Martin, *Reden und andere Zeugnisse eines Lebensweges*, 207.
46. Cf. Blok, Vincent, "Naming Being," 101–122; Trawny, Peter, *Heidegger und der Mythos der jüdischen Weltverschwörung* (Frankfurt am Main: Vittorio Klostermann, 2014) 20. In *The German Student as Worker*, the new type of student is explicitly connected to the group of people who started the National Socialist movement, with the few people, "with whom the Führer once began *his* work, the Führer, who today is already far beyond the year 1933 and beyond us all and is putting the states of the earth in a new motion" (Heidegger, *Reden und andere Zeugnisse eines Lebensweges*, 206; cf. 327–328).
47. Heidegger, Martin, *Reden und andere Zeugnisse eines Lebensweges*, 113.
48. In the black notes from 1931–1938, Heidegger argues: "The German alone can originally newly compose being and say—he alone will conquer the essence of *theoria* anew and finally achieve *logic*" (cited in Trawny, *Heidegger und der Mythos der jüdischen Weltverschwörung*, 25).
49. Cf. Heidegger, Martin, *Reden und andere Zeugnisse eines Lebensweges*, 82, 232.
50. Heidegger, Martin, *Reden und andere Zeugnisse eines Lebensweges*, 224; cf. 221.
51. Heidegger, Martin, *Reden und andere Zeugnisse eines Lebensweges*, 136; cf. 233; 790–791.
52. Heidegger, Martin, *Reden und andere Zeugnisse eines Lebensweges*, 375.
53. Heidegger, Martin, *Reden und andere Zeugnisse eines Lebensweges*, 205.
54. Zimmermann, *Heidegger's Confrontation with Modernity*, XX.
55. Cf. Section 6.3. In a recent study, Peter Trawny argued that Heidegger's concept of work cannot be compared with Jünger's. Heidegger distinguishes between three services—*Arbeitsdienst, Wehrdienst* and *Wissensdienst* (Heidegger, *Reden und andere Zeugnisse eines Lebensweges*, 113)—which means that Heidegger's concept of work as one of the three services cannot be reduced to Jünger's *total* work-character (Trawny, Peter, "'Was ist Deutschland?' Ernst Jüngers Bedeutung für Martin Heideggers Stellung zum Nationalsozialismus," *Heidegger Jahrbuch* 5 2009: 209–234). At the same time, we have to nuance this position. On the one hand, it became clear that work is understood as care, which is the fundamental category of *Dasein* in Heidegger's thought. On the other hand, Heidegger seems to reject the difference between *Arbeitsdienst* and *Wissensdienst* in his

notes from the early 1930s: "Farmers and craftsmen, miners and engineers, scholars and soldiers stand *each* in their own rank and class through their circle of co-workers. And all ranks are borne and led by the care for the historical designation of the people" (Heidegger, *Reden und andere Zeugnisse eines Lebensweges*, 303; cf. 234). In fact, work is understood as a "fundamental relationship of man" (Heidegger, Martin, *Logik als die Frage nach dem Wesen der Sprache*, Gesamtausgabe, vol. 21 [Frankfurt am Main: Vittorio Klostermann, 1998] 156 [tr. 133]).

7 Jünger's Concept of the Gestalt of the Worker as the Consummation of Modernity

From 1934–1935 on, Heidegger does not see this positive relation with Jünger's concept of work anymore.[1] Heidegger also calls the epoch of the worker "the epoch of the consummation of modernity."[2] To what extent can Jünger's thinking be called the consummation of modern metaphysics? As we saw in Part I, Jünger's basic experience is the collapse or the end of metaphysics (nihilism). In this context "consummation" thus means the end of a specific concept of philosophy, namely of the philosophical orientation toward a transcendental world of "Being." In his thinking, Jünger is working on overcoming this end.

Yet this is not Heidegger's concept of consummation. For him it does not mean the end of the modern view of human being as *animal rationale* and the rise of a new type of man, the worker. In his *Introduction to Metaphysics* from 1935, Heidegger explains that *Ende* does not mean that something ends, can go no further and can be followed by something else. *Ende* can also be called a limit, namely that which surrounds and limits our field of vision (*Gesichtskreis*). Considered thus, consummation means that something—in this case the *modern* way of philosophical thinking—comes to its *limit* and so—in its limit—will show itself *as such*.

To what extent can Jünger's thought be called the consummation of modern metaphysics in this second sense of the word? According to Heidegger, Jünger is the only real follower of Nietzsche, because he does not speak *about* Nietzsche and his doctrine of the will to power. He *sees* beings as will to power without *describing* them: "his way of thinking is itself a *gestalt* of the will to power; in Jünger's language: thinking itself has 'work-character.'"[3] Jünger calls his own way of thinking heroic realism as we have seen in Chapter 3, because he not only sees the reality of the work-character of people and things in the world, but also affirms this in such a way that his own way of thinking has work-character itself.

In *The Worker,* this becomes concrete when Jünger comments on the status of his own statements: "Please note, that all these terms are ready to be understood. They are not what really matters for us. They can be forgotten or put aside right away, after they are used as working values (*Arbeitsgrößen*) to understand a fixed reality, which exists in spite of and beyond these concepts."[4] Jünger is saying here that his own terms have to be understood as *work,* just as other things in the world are, which means that these terms are working hypotheses which have to be fruitful for the power-preservation and power-enhancement in different situations. Thus the descriptions in *The Worker,* which show the work-character of our world, also have this work-character themselves. As such, Jünger understands his own method of writing in *The Worker* just as he understands the totally mobilized world, namely out of Nietzsche's metaphysics of the will to power.

Heidegger concentrates on this identification of the subject of *The Worker* (worker) and the way this subject is being discussed in Jünger's book (work). "Is the essence of the worker determined out of the *essence of work*? . . . Or is the essence of work put forward out of the essence of the worker? . . . how does Jünger decide? Does he see this question at all, does he notice its weight?"[5] On the one hand, the subject (worker) is the basis for the work character of the world as its object. On the other hand, the essence of the worker is determined by work as its object. According to Heidegger, Jünger's descriptions of our work-world move around in a flat circle *(flachen Zirkel).*[6] These move unnoticed over from *what* is described ("Being" as work) to *how* it is described (thinking as work) and so mutually define one another. "The actual motion is not in reality as work ('Being') nor in the way we grasp the world (thinking), but in the capacity to move back and forth between 'Being' as work and thinking as work."[7] Jünger's descriptions are caught up in the continuing circle of the work-character of thought (will to power) to the work-character of reality (will to power) and vice versa.

We understand why Heidegger says that Jünger is the consummation of modern metaphysics when we take the "flat circle" of Jünger's descriptions literally. The circular course of Jünger's descriptions of reality as work for human being as worker *encircles* and *delimits* not only Jünger's field of vision, but the *horizon* of modern metaphysics as such. The consummation of modern metaphysics as *end* (limit) consists of its being delimited and this delimiting *is* the encircling, which shows itself in the circular course of the descriptions in *The Worker.* The circular course is delimiting reality as work as the object for the worker as the thinking subject, which means that *The Worker* as such *is* the end *(Ende)* or *Vollendung* of modernity.

In a note, Heidegger writes: "Jünger's descriptions (and explanations) achieve only this: indicating being by showing beings (in the character of the will to power), without questioning this being."[8] He does not only argue here that Jünger's concept of work can be reduced to Nietzsche's concept of the will to power. More important, he argues that Jünger's concept of work indicates being without questioning it.[9]

If we remember Heidegger's analysis of the work-world in *Being and Time,* we can understand this distinction. During our discussion of *Being and Time* in Section 6.1, we made a formal distinction between the work-character of the world and the meaning of being. We spoke with intention of a formal distinction, because we normally subordinate to the work-world that is precisely *at work* in our responsiveness to the work-world. Our responsiveness to the work-world can be understood as an *indication* of the appearance of the world *as* work-world and our human responsiveness to this work-world *as* worker, i.e., an indication of beings in the whole in the technological era we live in. But because we are normally *absorbed* by the work-world, our responsiveness is not only an indication of this work-character of beings in the whole, but the question of being remains forgotten in our being-at-work (see Section 6.2).

The same is at stake in Jünger's concept of work according to Heidegger. While Jünger's ambition in *Across the Line* is to *cross the line* into a new era where "a new turning of being" takes place and puts an end to the age of fulfilled nihilism (*trans linea*), Heidegger's response in *On the Question of Being* concentrates on the specific way in which, according to Jünger, nihilism (*de linea*) can be overcome (see the introduction of this chapter). Here, Heidegger argues: "Yet the attempt to say something *de linea* in a dialogue with you by letter confronts a peculiar difficulty. The reason for this difficulty lies in the fact that in your 'crossing' over the line, i.e., in the space on this and on the other side of the line, you speak the same language."[10] What is indicated in the descriptions of *The Worker* is a continuous transition of the work-character of the world (will to power) to the work-character of the way human being is dealing with it (will to power), to the work-character of Jünger's way of speaking about all this (will to power). This circular course, which is the consummation of modern metaphysics, confronts us with the work-character of the *whole* of beings, with "Being." It is in this way that the descriptions of *The Worker* indicate "Being." At the same time, this circular course shows that Jünger speaks the same language on this and the other side of the zero line of nihilism. Both the *description* of the work-world of the total mobilization on this side of the line and the *description* of the worker type that is able to overcome the total mobilization (nihilism) on the other side of the zero line, have work-character. Jünger's thinking of the gestalt beyond the zero line of nihilism remains according to Heidegger domiciled in the work-character. This shows that, with the crossing of the zero line, the position of nihilism already appears abandoned; but according to Heidegger, his language has remained the same. According to Heidegger, this work-character of Jünger's speaking "on this and on the other side of the line" is the result of Jünger's modern-metaphysical basic position. In the end, Heidegger argues against Jünger that nihilism cannot be overcome at all and that the question of nihilism must be brought back to the question of being.

For Heidegger, the question of being is no longer the metaphysical question of *what* beings *as such* are and does not end up in a metaphysical description of the being of beings—will to power or the total mobilization as the beingness of beings—as we have seen. Heidegger's question of being asks after "being" itself, the *meaning* of Being, as we have seen in Section 6.2. According to Heidegger, Jünger only indicates "Being" by showing the will to power of beings (work and workers), but because his descriptions move unnoticed over from *what* is described ("being" as work) to *how* it is described ("thinking" as work), he ignores the relation between the *essence* of the subjectivity of human being and the *essence* of the will to power:[11] machination and lived experience. To what extent is this the case? With the development of our answer to this question, the real controversy between Heidegger and Jünger comes to light.

For Heidegger, "being" cannot be associated with work and workers. Work and workers designate in the first instance (human) beings in the world, and so concern in this way metaphysically understood *beings*, whereas "Being" concerns the way reality appears together with the way people deal with it. In the epoch of the worker, reality appears as produced and represented (will to power) for representing-producing humanity (will to power). According to Heidegger, this means that the essence of the work-world (*totale* Mobilmachung) has to be found in the machination of beings (*totale Mobil*machung).[12] Machination indicates the makeability of beings, which consists of the: "interpretation of beings as re-presentable and re-presented. In one respect re-presentable means 'accessible to intention and calculation'; in another respect it means 'advanceable through pro-duction and execution.' But thought in a fundamental manner, all of this means that being as such is the re-presented and only that which is represented *is*."[13] This makeability does not primarily depend on an act of the worker. The making (*poiêsis, technê*) as human comportment of the worker toward beings is on the contrary only possible on the basis of the appearance of the world *as* represented work (*Machenschaft*) for human dealings with it, i.e., for the worker who represents and experiences this work (*Erlebnis*).[14] To what extent can we call machination and lived experience the essence of the work-world?

In Chapter 6, we have seen that the work-world appears in its serviceability and usability, for instance a forest *as* potential producer of wood or *as* recreation after work in our being-at-work. From 1934–1935 on, Heidegger stresses that the appearance of the work-world in its usability presupposes the *representation* of beings as potential energy and the *calculation* of their possible functionality (see Chapter 6). This calculation is not necessarily carried out in figures but has to be understood as an accounting—a taking into account—that proceeds in a calculating way; it counts *on* something and calculates *with* something in order to calculate the beneficiality of the work for the worker. The work-world is "the re-presented by calculating and calculation, where all depends on securing the operational effectiveness of the power, and whose essence (machination) pervades everything."[15] From 1934 on, Heidegger concentrates on machination as the origin of our being-at-work; the work-world appears as re-presented (*machination*) for human experience as representation (*lived experience*). Lived experience is the center of reference on which the makeability of beings depends, which means that beings (*machination*) count as being to the extent that they are experienced in life, i.e., to the degree and extent that they become life-experience. With this, it becomes clear that machination and lived experience is the essence of the work-world and of the worker as the subject of our being-at-work in the work-world.

But because Jünger is absorbed by his responsiveness to the work-character of beings in the whole *as* worker, he only indicates this essence of the work-world while the question of being itself remains forgotten and concealed. As Heidegger in *Being and Time* says, the question of being remains forgotten as long as we are absorbed by the work-world. From 1934–1935 on, he argues again that our responsiveness to the work-world is absorbed by this work-world and is therefore blind for the essence of work. Heidegger learned from the confrontation with Jünger that it is exactly the will to power of representation itself which blocks access to this "Being." Why? Jünger's thinking is bound up with the will to power of representation and for that very reason remains dependent on the representation of work and workers as metaphysically understood *beings*. His thinking is absorbed in the circular course like a snake biting its own tail—moving from the work-character of the world to the work-character of human being and so on—without questioning whether the worker is determined by work or *vice versa;* because of this circular course, "the modern freedom of subjectivity is completely absorbed into the corresponding objectivity."[16] And because the will to power of representation is absorbed in and by the circular course, it encounters only the re-presented (beings) and remains blind for "Being."[17] So the will to power of representation characterizes the thinking in *The Worker* in such a way that the will to power is its end or limit, but is not accessible by this very concept of the will to power.[18] And this is the reason why Jünger's writings are said to *indicate* Being without asking after it.

Jünger's absorption by the work-world is however not primarily his mistake or fault. According to Heidegger, it belongs to the inner logic of machination that it conceals itself all the more as it unfolds itself.[19] We can understand this self-concealment of machination if we remember Heidegger's analysis of the movement of work in *Being and Time* (see Section 6.1); all works are characterized by a double movement of their withdrawal as equipment in favor of their presence as work. In 1934–1935, Heidegger conceptualizes this double movement in terms of the concealment of machination as the essence of the work-world in favor of its presence as work for the worker. The dominion of machination and lived experience thus reigns in such a way that it demarcates the way in which the world appears *as* work (*machination*) for our human responsiveness as worker (*lived experience*), without ever being accessible for work itself.[20] Heidegger's criticism of Jünger's concept of work can therefore be understood as self-criticism regarding his own use of the term in the early 1930s. Our being-at-work has an origin—the meaning or truth of being—which is itself inaccessible for work and therefore remains forgotten.[21] This forgetfulness, and in this sense the "nihil" of the horizon of being—the meaning of being—within the work-world of machination and lived experience, is what Heidegger calls the forgottenness of being as the *essence* of Nihilism.[22]

In that Jünger's writing loses itself in representation, his description of the total mobilization, or the "power of technology over being," is blind for the horizon of the total mobilization and the gestalt of the worker, and he can "never set technicity as its ground," as the ground of representation, namely as machination and lived experience.[23] If the forgetfulness of being is the essence of nihilism, then Jünger's attempt to overcome nihilism is inadequate. Every idea in order to overcome nihilism is then already tributary and surrounded by it. For this reason, Heidegger says, Jünger's attempt to overcome nihilism would fail.[24] Regarding Jünger's "heroic realism," Heidegger argues: the heroic realist "has all the markings of 'capitulating' before the extant as such, that is, before the machinationally determined beings that are abandoned by being. . . . 'Heroic realism'—seemingly the highest form of knowing of, and attitude towards beings—amounts only to the most covert way of evading being; but by pretending that it has the sharpest insight into what 'is,' this 'realism' explicitly seals off the forgottenness of being."[25]

Although Jünger is important because he *indicates* being, his attempts to overcome nihilism remained arrested by representation and with this, by the forgottenness of Being.[26] That means that, despite his efforts to overcome nihilism, he is himself overcome precisely by this.

That also explains what urges Heidegger to take a "step back." If the work-character of representation builds in itself the barriers to overcoming nihilism, then the question arises as to whether we must abandon representation for the benefit of another way of speaking. "If this were the case, would not crossing the line then necessarily have to become a transformation of our saying and demand a transformed relation to the essence of language?"[27] The transformed relationship to the essence of language exists for Heidegger in that language relates to the delineation of the appearance of the world and human responsiveness; "Essence and Being speak in language."[28] His transformation of saying exists in the response "to the essence of being" (We will come back to this in Chapter 8).[29]

We can conclude that Heidegger, at the beginning of the 1930s, seemed to be quite revolutionary in heralding the other beginning of philosophy. Inspired by Jünger, he developed a destructed concept of work and will to characterize his own way of philosophical thinking, and was *willing* the overcoming of the metaphysics of the will to power.[30] But from the confrontation with Jünger, Heidegger learned that every "overcoming of the metaphysics of the will to power" is doomed, as long as it is characterized by work and will.[31] Working and willing is absorbed in the circular course from the work-character of the world to the work-character of the way human being is dealing with it, the circular course which indicates the end of metaphysics. To put it differently, Heidegger learned from Jünger that the overcoming of the metaphysics of the will to power is the *circumambulation within* metaphysics and not the *transition* to another beginning of philosophical thinking, as long as it is characterized by will and work. As soon as Heidegger realized again, as in *Being and Time*, that our being-at-work is absorbed by the work-character of the world, he realized again that there is no way from our working responsiveness to the work-world to our care for the meaning of being, and that we have to release ourselves from work, will and technicity in order to enhance our ability to reflect on the meaning of being. When he realized this, he began to advocate the release from the willful way of thinking. In his later work, Heidegger speaks about the willing of the nonwilling, about a *gelassen* or non-willing way of philosophical thinking—because the will itself is the main barrier for the experience of "Being."[32] In light of the findings of the previous section, we can understand this free relation as the *de-formalization* of the distinction between the work-character of beings in the whole and the question regarding the meaning of being.

The experience of "Being" demands our bidding farewell to the concept of work and will, and demands a radically different other beginning of philosophical reflection (*Besinnung*). "Why a beginning at all? . . . Because only the greatest occurrence, the innermost knowing, can still save us from being lost in the bustle of mere events and machinations. What must take place is enopening being for us and putting us back into this [Being] and thus bringing us to ourselves and before the work and the sacrifice."[33] This *saving* consists of the transition to a way of human existence that is exposed to the experience of "Being" (*Dasein*).

That Heidegger bids farewell to work and will does not mean that he is attempting to break out of the circular course, for doing so would equally lead us to lose contact with "being." As such, Heidegger is concerned with the right way to attain and to *enter* the circular course, to move in the circular course of the will to power of the work-world and at the same time to hold back, to experience "Being" in its center.[34]

Heidegger calls this new beginning of philosophical reflection a decision. This *Ent-scheidung* does not concern any division between two eras, for instance between the era of the worker and a new era, in which we reflect on the sense of being. In fact, "Being" shows itself only *in* the circular course of representation. As becomes clear with the end of modern metaphysics, the decision concerns the unbridgeable division or twofoldedness between the omnipresence of work and workers on the one hand and "Being" on the other hand.[35]

And here culminates Heidegger's critique of Jünger. Heidegger speaks about the "great indecisiveness and undecidability of this whole fundamental metaphysical position."[36] Because Jünger is absorbed in the circular course of representation, he does not see this realm of the decision and so continues to understand every decision as an act of rationality of man as subject. According to Heidegger, the work of Jünger is rather that of settling thinking into indecisiveness. In this, "Being" sinks into oblivion and thinking is absorbed by the hegemony of beings.[37] In this respect, Jünger is not only the end of modern metaphysics for Heidegger, but also the perishing (*Ver-endung*) of this end (*Ende*),[38] the oblivion of this end in the circular course of representation. And here Heidegger sees the greatest danger of our time: "And the danger is now that the oblivion of Being . . . will certainly solidify and all that will be sought after and operated with is the real, is beings. That the ground and the truth of this reality become more and more inaccessible. And in that, the book [*The Worker*] has 'work-character.'"[39] Can we allow that this danger is the greatest danger of *our* time? Then, Jünger could be in fact a "passage, an encouragement of the transition"[40] to Heidegger's radical new beginning of philosophy.

Notes

1. This shift in Heidegger's appreciation of Ernst Jünger may be related to the shift in Heidegger's appreciation of the National Socialist movement (Trawny, *Heidegger und der Mythos der jüdische Weltverschwörung*, 29–30).
2. Heidegger, Martin, *Zu Ernst Jünger*, 96; cf. 78, 139.
3. Heidegger, Martin, *Zu Ernst Jünger*, 227; cf. 287, 247, 263.
4. *Arb*, 313.
5. Heidegger, Martin, *Zu Ernst Jünger*, 52f.
6. Heidegger, Martin, *Zu Ernst Jünger*, 6; cf. Heidegger, Martin, *Besinnung*, Gesamtausgabe, vol. 66 (Frankfurt am Main: Vittorio Klostermann, 1997) 16 (tr. 12).
7. Oudemans, Wouter, "The Man of the Crowd. Of: Wat heet informatisering?," *Ergo Cogito V. Pleidooi voor de filosofie*, ed. F. Geraedts and L. de Jong (Groningen: Historische uitgeverij, 1996) 176; cf. Heidegger, *Zu Ernst Jünger*, 173.
8. Heidegger, Martin, *Zu Ernst Jünger*, 73.
9. Cf.: "Ernst Jünger is the first and only person to perform a reflection—*but* the question remains: whether this reflection also co-founds its very own field and ground for truth or not, or just lapses into an increase of the already existing (technology—worker) (the total mobilization)—which changed the formerly particular into the total—that still remains a part of the modern way of thought and does not achieve an initial questionableness—is still metaphysics (Heidegger, Martin, *Überlegungen VII–XI (Schwarzen Hefte 1938–1939)*, Gesamtausgabe, Band 95 [Frankfurt am Main: Vittorio Klostermann, 2014] 370).
10. Heidegger, Martin, "Zur Seinsfrage," 394 (tr. 298).
11. Heidegger, Martin, *Zu Ernst Jünger*, 13, 14, 100–101, 264.
12. Cf. Heidegger, Martin, *Zu Ernst Jünger*, 173.
13. Heidegger, Martin, *Beiträge zur Philosophie (vom Ereignis)*, Gesamtausgabe, vol. 65 (Frankfurt am Main: Vittorio Klostermann, 1989) 108–109 (tr. 76); cf. Heidegger, *Besinnung*, 16 (tr. 12).
14. Heidegger, Martin, *Beiträge zur Philosophie*, 126 (tr. 88–89); cf. 131 (tr. 93–94); Heidegger, *Besinnung*, 173 (tr. 151). Machination is already implied—but not yet fully manifest in its essence—in the Greek distinction between natural beings (something which *makes* itself by itself) and technical beings (something *made* by something else). The machination of beings becomes explicit in the Middle Ages, where beings are understood as *ens creatum*. And even when the idea of a creator is abandoned in the following ages, being's being-caused becomes essential and all-dominating: "that is an essential distancing from *phusis* and at the same time the crossing toward the emergence of machination as what is essential to beingness in modern thinking (Heidegger, *Beiträge zur Philosophie*, 127 (tr. 88 modified).
15. Heidegger, Martin, *Metaphysik und Nihilismus*, Gesamtausgabe, vol. 67 (Frankfurt am Main: Vittorio Klostermann, 1999) 116. It is precisely this calculation (machination) which is connected with the "world Judaism" according to Heidegger and

is the root cause of his being-historical anti-Semitism (Heidegger, *Überlegungen VII–XI*, 97; cf. Heidegger, Martin, *Überlegungen XII–XV*, Gesamtausgabe, vol. 96 [Frankfurt am Main: Vittorio Klostermann, 2014] 56).

16. Heidegger, Martin, "Die Zeit des Weltbildes," 111 (tr. 84); cf. Heidegger, *Zu Ernst Jünger*, 14, 59, 78, 100f, 154, 264.

17. "Metaphysical representation owes this sight to the light of Being. The light itself, i.e., that which such thinking experiences as light, no longer comes within the range of metaphysical thinking; for metaphysics always represents beings only as beings" (Heidegger, Martin, "Einleitung zu 'Was ist Metaphysik'," *Wegmarken*, Gesamtausgabe, vol. 9 [Frankfurt am Main: Vittorio Klostermann, 1976] 365 [tr. 276]).

18. Heidegger, Martin, *Besinnung*, 16 (tr. 12); Heidegger, *Zu Ernst Jünger*, 100f.

19. Gorgone, Sandro, "Machenschaft und totale Mobilmachung: Heideggers Besinnung als Phänomenologie der Moderne," *Heidegger Studies* 22 2006: 52.

20. Cf. Heidegger, Martin, *Besinnung*, 16 (tr. 12); Heidegger, *Zu Ernst Jünger*, 100–101. We can call this the *deceptive* character of the machination. Radloff shows that this deceptive character of machination lies in the word *Machenschaft* itself: "The common meaning of '*Machenschaft*,' as of the English word 'machination,' is intrigue and plotting, the unfolding of deceptive appearances to further hidden ends. While we have, in the first instance, focused on *machen* (to make, effectuate, to do) as the root of *Machenschaft*, the meaning of 'deception' is equally significant, for the primacy of beings arises out of a fundamental concealment of being *(Seyn)*" (Radloff, Bernard, "Self-Overpowering Power and the Refusal of Being," *Existentia* 17 2007: 397).

21. Cf. "All working and achieving, all action and calculation, keep within an open region within which beings, with regard to what they are and how they are, can properly take their stand and become capable of being said" (Heidegger, Martin, "Von Wesen der Wahrheit," *Wegmarken*, Gesamtausgabe, vol. 9 [Frankfurt am Main: Vittorio Klostermann, 1976] 184 [tr. 141]).

22. Cf. Heidegger Martin,*Besinnung*, 19–20 (tr. 14–15).

23. Heidegger, Martin, *Besinnung*, 17 (tr. 12–13); cf. Heidegger, *Zu Ernst Jünger*, 13–15.

24. "In this connection, however, it is not sufficient, for example, to affirm technology or, out of a stance incomparably more essential, to set up 'the total mobilization' as an absolute, once it is recognized as being at hand" (Heidegger, "Die Zeit des Weltbildes," 97 [tr. 73]; cf. Heidegger, *Besinnung*, 59 [tr. 48]). "Present positions within fulfilled metaphysics, without meeting its essence anymore: . . . the adventure in the elementary and the decline into the indestructible (E. Jünger)" (Heidegger, *Metaphysik und Nihilismus*, 113–114; cf. 119).

25. Heidegger, Martin, *Besinnung*, 19–20 (tr. 14–15).

26. Cf. Heidegger, Martin, *Metaphysik und Nihilismus*, 133; Heidegger, *Besinnung*, 66 (tr. 54–55); Heidegger, *Zu Ernst Jünger*, 73.

27. Heidegger, Martin, "Zur Seinsfrage," 405 (tr. 306).

28. Heidegger, Martin, *Einführung in die Metaphysik*, 41 (tr. 40–41).

29. Heidegger, Martin, "Zur Seinsfrage," 409 (tr. 309).

30. "I am still undecided and believe to know only one thing, that we are preparing ourselves for a great spiritual transformation, i.e., to have to bring this about ourselves" (Heidegger, *Reden und andere Zeugnisse eines Lebensweges*, 169).

31. For the development of Heidegger's concept of the will, cf. Davis, Bret, *Heidegger and the Will: On the Way to Gelassenheit* (Evensten: Northwestern University Press, 2007) and Blok, Vincent, "'Massive Voluntarism' or Heidegger's Confrontation with the Will," *Studia Pheanomenologica* X111 2013: 449–465.

32. Cf. "For this will, which makes everything, has already subscribed to machination, that interpretation of beings as re-presentable and re-presented. In one

respect, re-presentable means 'accessible to intention and calculation'; in another respect it means 'advanceable through pro-duction and execution.' But thought in a fundamental manner, all of this means that beings as such are re-presentable and that only the representable *is*" (Heidegger, *Beiträge zur Philosophie*, 108 [tr. 76]). For Heidegger's criticism on the will, cf. Davis, *Heidegger and the Will*, 146–185.

33. Heidegger, Martin, *Beiträge zur Philosophie*, 57 (tr. 40).
34. "The only thing that ordinary understanding can cf. in this circling motion is the movement around the periphery which always returns to its original point of departure on the periphery. Thus it misses the decisive issue here, which is an insight into the *centre* of the circle as such, an insight made possible in such a circling movement and in this alone" (Heidegger, Martin, *Die Grundbegriffe der Metaphysik. Welt—Endlichkeit—Einsamkeit*, Gesamtausgabe, vol. 29/30 [Frankfurt am Main: Vittorio Klostermann, 1983] 267 [tr. 180]).
35. This decision cannot be understood as a decision *against* work and workers and *for* the whole of Being, because such a decision would neutralize the twofoldedness (cf. Heidegger, *Besinnung*, 15, 24, 46, 57 [tr. 11, 18, 38, 46–47]; Heidegger, *Zu Ernst Jünger*, 13–15).
36. Heidegger, Martin, *Zu Ernst Jünger*, 54.
37. Heidegger, Martin, *Zu Ernst Jünger*, 34, 13, 84
38. Heidegger, Martin, *Zu Ernst Jünger*, 74.
39. Heidegger, Martin, *Zu Ernst Jünger*, 75.
40. Heidegger, Martin, *Zu Ernst Jünger*, 15.

8   Establishing the Truth
Heidegger's Reflections on Gestalt

Although Heidegger started to criticize Jünger from 1934 onwards, there is at least one other aspect in which Jünger influenced the development of Heidegger's thought. In 1936 Heidegger introduced a concept of the gestalt into his own account of *The Origin of the Work of Art*. According to this account, the creation of a work of art concerns the bringing forth of the gestalt. At first sight this seems strange because the concept of the gestalt appears to be inherently metaphysical. Within the metaphysical tradition, the being of beings is found in a form, *idea* or the gestalt of beings—the beingness of beings—whereas Heidegger's question of being asks about being as such, about the truth of being. In other texts of the same period, for example in his *Contributions to Philosophy*, Heidegger explicitly rejects the concept of the gestalt: "this thinking [about the truth of being, VB] should never seek refuge in a gestalt of a being."[1] Why? Because the gestalt is "only in a being."[2] In Heidegger's "being-historical thinking," as developed in his *Contributions* and in *Mindfulness*, concepts like "gestalt" might prove helpful, but only when they are interpreted as signposts to being-historical thinking, rather than as a substitute.[3] What induced Heidegger to maintain a non-metaphysical concept of the gestalt in his essay on the origin of art, and why did he later reject the entire concept? What led him to change his mind? It is our hypothesis that the answers to these questions are to be sought in Heidegger's confrontation with Jünger's work. On the one hand, we have seen that Heidegger developed a strong critique of Jünger's metaphysical concept of the gestalt in the 1930s in Chapter 5. On the other hand, it seems likely that Heidegger developed his own non-metaphysical concept of the gestalt in the course of this confrontation.[4]

In this chapter, we shall first inquire into Heidegger's criticism of the concept of the gestalt, which governs the metaphysical tradition (Section 8.2). We shall then test the plausibility of Heidegger's destructed concept from *The Origin of the Work of Art* in light of his criticism of Jünger (Section 8.3). In Section 8.4, we close with a critical discussion of Heidegger in relation to his subsequent renunciation of the gestalt in favor of the name, of language. However, in preparation for this discussion, we begin with a short exposition of Heidegger's understanding of the essence of truth as un-concealment, because his concept of the gestalt grows out of his understanding of the essence of truth (Section 8.1).

8.1 The Essence of Truth in *The Origin of the Work of Art*

In *The Origin of the Work of Art*, Heidegger breaks with the traditional aesthetical categories and develops his own view of the origin of art. Heidegger does speak about the creative character of art and of its beauty, but these characteristics receive a new meaning because of their orientation to the essence of truth. According to Heidegger, the createdness of a work of art means that the truth is fixed in the work's gestalt.[5] What is the origin of this gestalt, that Heidegger should think about it in close relation with the essence of truth? In order to understand this, we must begin by inquiring into Heidegger's concept of the essence of truth.

Heidegger derives his concept of the essence of truth from the Greek ἀ-λήθεια, which, taken literally, means the un-concealment of beings. Unconcealment is not only another word for the traditional definition of truth, the agreement (*adaequatio*) of our knowledge with the facts. Our knowledge can only agree with the facts when they *show* themselves, when they stand unconcealed. "A statement is true by conforming to the unconcealed, i.e., to that which is true."[6] Heidegger wants to show us that the unconcealment of beings (truth) is a necessary condition for our knowledge of facts to be true (*adaequatio*, correctness). The unconcealment of beings is, however, not the only condition presupposed. For our knowledge of facts presupposes no less the unconcealment of human being, of *us*: "Rather, the unconcealment of beings (being) puts us into such an essence that all our representing remains set into, and in accordance with, unconcealment."[7] Moreover, the whole region in which my knowledge of facts can be true (*adaequatio*, correctness) must be unconcealed, at least when these facts have to occur to *me*: "We could never make the presupposition of there being something manifest to which we conform ourselves—if the unconcealment of beings had not already set us forth into that illuminated realm in which every being stands for us and from which it withdraws."[8]

According to Heidegger, this "illuminated realm," in which human beings can encounter other beings, is itself *beyond* beings. "In the midst of beings as a whole, an open place comes to presence."[9] He calls this open place a clearing (*Lichtung*): "Only this clearing grants us human beings access to those beings that we ourselves are not and admittance to the being that we ourselves are."[10]

This clearing is not however a fixed stage on which our knowledge is always in conformity with the beings we encounter. When Heidegger calls attention to the essence of truth as *aletheia*, he is primarily interested in the *alpha privative* in the word *a-letheia*, a *not* or a *un-* which takes place in the essence of truth: un-concealment. A *privatio* is not just a *negatio*, for instance the negation of concealment (*lethe*). The *privatio* un-concealment indicates the *brokenness* of concealment and stays, as such, always related to this concealment. Therefore, Heidegger turns toward the concealment (*lethe*) at the heart of unconcealment as the essence of truth: "The essence of truth, i.e., unconcealment, is ruled throughout by a denial. This denial is, however, neither a defect nor a fault—as if truth were a pure unconcealment that has rid itself of everything concealed. . . . *Denial . . . belongs to the essence of truth as unconcealment.*"[11]

How are we to understand this relation between concealment and uncon-cealment? It might seem that Heidegger, in *The Origin of the Work of Art,* is asking us to attend to the fact that every light is surrounded by darkness, but that would be a superficial reading of his essay on the origin of art. According to Heidegger, our questioning is only *really* philosophical when this questioning *recoils back* from what is asked, back upon itself.[12] We have an experience of this *recoil* when we ask: Does Heidegger's questioning about the essence of truth as unconcealment "unconceal" this concept itself? Our answer to this is unflinchingly negative. The essence of truth is most *concealed* in Greek philosophy: "for the hidden history of Greek philosophy consists since its beginning of this: that it does not measure up to the essence of truth that lit up in the word *aletheia,* and so, of necessity, has misdirected its knowing and saying about the essence of truth more and more into the discussion of the derivative essence of truth. In the thought of the Greeks and all the more completely so *in the philosophy that followed,* the essence of truth as *aletheia* remained unthought."[13] The essence of truth as unconceal-ment is concealed both for Greek existence and for the following tradition, and is therefore *concealed* from thinking as such.

Heidegger differentiates between two kinds of concealment of beings. The first kind is encountered when beings refuse themselves to us to the extent that all we can say of them is that they "are." In principle, this could be the kind of concealment pre-eminently at stake in discussions of the word *aletheia.* The essence of truth as unconcealment is not only refused to the Greeks, but to thinking at all: "No attempt to ground the essence of uncon-cealment in 'reason,' 'spirit,' 'thinking,' '*logos,*' or in any kind of 'subjec-tivity,' can ever rescue the essence of unconcealment. In all such attempts, what is to be grounded—the essence of unconcealment itself—is not yet adequately sought out. . . . What is first required is an appreciation of the 'positive' in the 'privative' essence of *aletheia.*"[14] We appreciate this positive in the privative when we see that the refusal of *aletheia* does not end in its disappearance; one can experience this refusal indirectly in the *alpha priva-tive* of the word *a-letheia.* It is precisely this refusal, indicated by the word *aletheia,* which gives rise to Heidegger's experience of "the opposition which exists within the essence of truth between clearing and concealment."[15]

The second kind of concealment has the character of an obstruction; a thing can show itself as something else and can therefore deceive us in this way. Again, in principle, this could be the kind of concealment pre-eminently at stake in discussions of the word *aletheia*. The Greeks and the following tradition did not measure up to the essence of truth that comes to light in the word *aletheia*; rather they understood it *as adaequatio, as* a property of facts or statements. Yet this is a *derivative* of the essence of truth and this *as* is actually an *as-if*: The correctness of facts or statements acts *as if* it is the essence of truth, but in this, the essence of truth *as* unconcealment is *concealed*.

According to Heidegger, we are never really certain as to which of the two kinds of concealment—refusal or obstructing—is at stake: "Conceal- ment conceals and obstructs itself. This means: the open place in the midst of beings, the clearing, is never a fixed stage with a permanently raised cur- tain on which the play of beings enacts itself. Rather, the clearing happens only as this twofold concealment. The unconcealment of beings—this is never a state that is merely present but rather a happening."[16] Precisely because the clearing happens only as this twofold concealment we conclude, first of all, that there is not a plain *opposition* between concealment and clearing within the essence of truth, but concealment (*lethe*) is the heart of uncon- cealment as the essence of truth.[17] Secondly, because of this *happening* of clearing *and* concealment, we conclude that *aletheia* is better understood by the participle *unconcealing-concealing*: the concealing of the essence of truth *as* un-concealment is the *origin* of the unconcealing of the derivative essence of truth *as* correctness. "Truth presences as itself only because the concealing denial, as refusal, is the continuing origin of all clearing but yet, as obstruc- ting, metes out to all clearing the rigorous severity of error."[18] The essence of truth is unconcealing-concealing and, according to Heidegger, the touchstone for philosophical thinking about the essence of truth is the extent to which we can accept and expose ourselves to this clearing of self-concealment.

8.2 Truth and the Creation of Art (τέχνη); Metaphysical Gestalt I

What are the consequences of this concept of the essence of truth for Heideg- ger's concept of the origin of art and that gestalt which it creates? A work of art is, at first sight, a created being such as a painting or building. Yet, as we said above, truth is not a property of beings. In what way, then, does Heideg- ger take the essence of truth to be related to the creation of works of art?

The creation of a work of art may be understood as the bringing forth of that work. Bringing forth, however, is not exclusive to art: the making of equipment is also a bringing forth as we have seen in Chapter 6 and this explains why the Greeks use the same word, *techne*, for handicraft and for art. Yet, according to Heidegger, this does not mean that we have to determine the nature of creation in terms of its craft aspect. Very early on, Heidegger saw that *techne* means neither craft nor art for the Greeks, but rather designates a way of knowing the truth: "As knowledge experienced in the Greek manner, *techne* is a bringing forth of beings in that it brings *forth* what is present, as such, *out of* concealment, specifically *into* the unconceal-ment of their appearance."[19] We pause for a moment to consult Plato's defi-nition of this bringing forth *(techne)* in his *Sophistes*, to better understand this relation between truth and creation *(techne)* in Greek thought.[20]

In the *Sophistes*, Plato differentiates between two kinds of *techne—techne poietike* and *techne ktetike*. The ground for this distinction is found in two domains of beings, in each of which *techne* is a way of knowing the truth. *Techne poietike* concerns, for instance, the cultivation of arable land or the production of artifacts. The main characteristic of *techne poietike* is that it brings forth into presence (unconcealment) what was not present (conceal-ment) before.

In contrast to *techne poietike, techne ktetike* concerns beings which are present by nature or brought-forth by *techne poietike*. The main charac-teristic of *techne ktetike* is the representation of the unconcealed being in *logos* (a judgment, for instance) or in *praxis* (hunting, for instance). What is present in *techne ktetike* is the *whatness, (essentia)* of a being, its form, *eidos* or gestalt (i.e., the beingness of beings).

Further, *techne poietike* is guided by the representation of the form or gestalt. For example, in order to produce shoes, we have to know *what* a shoe is. Even so, *techne poietike* is not primarily the production of shoes, but the representation of the *essence* of shoes (the form, *eidos* or gestalt of shoes) *in* actual shoes.

On the one hand, against this background, we can understand why Heideg-ger in *The Origin of the Work of Art* can say that the creation of a work of art is not primarily its physical production. "The artist is not a *technites* because he is also a craftsman but rather because both the setting-forth (*Her-stellen*) of works and the setting-forth of equipment happen in that bringing forth which allows beings, by assuming an appearance, to come forth into their presence."[21] On the other hand, the Greek-metaphysical *techne* showed us that the bringing forth of a gestalt concerns the representation of the *eidos* or gestalt, in which the beingness of beings is present. In representation, the essence of truth—the concealment at the heart of un-concealment, the hap-pening of unconcealing-concealing—is exactly concealed: "Unconcealment is, for thought, what is most concealed in Greek existence. At the same time, however, it is that which, from early times, has determined the presence of everything present."[22]

This becomes clear when we look again at the *alpha privative* in the Greek name for truth: *a-letheia*. The privative shows that *phusis*—i.e., what emerges from itself and is subject to generation and corruption—has the tendency to conceal itself,[23] to resist the representation of *techne*. *Techne* is *against phusis* and makes present the *whatness* or *essence* of beings (its *eidos* or gestalt), to prevent its regression to concealment. This *attack* of *techne* on *phusis* does not yet indicate the utilization or extortion ("the total mobilization") of nature in our time. The present form or gestalt is that by which each being is what it is and with a view to which separate beings can be brought-forth or cultivated (*techne poietike*), studied or hunted for (*techne ktetike*). As a consequence, the essence of truth as *aletheia* remained unthought in the thought of the Greeks and all the more so in the tradition of philosophy that followed.

When Heidegger states in *The Origin of the Work of Art* that the created-ness of a work of art means that the truth is fixed (*festgestellt*) in the work's gestalt, we can already draw the negative conclusion that the bringing forth of this gestalt cannot be understood in the Greek-metaphysical sense of the word.

8.3 Heidegger's Destructed Concept of the Gestalt in *The Origin of the Work of Art*

In his early and later writings on Jünger it becomes clear that Heidegger thinks of the gestalt as closely connected with metaphysics, as we have seen. Heidegger points first of all to the Platonic-metaphysical character of Jünger's concept of the gestalt: according to Jünger there is no home base to be found in the world of becoming, which he calls the "elementary" (see Chapter 3). To be at home in the world, we need a gestalt (being) to regu-late the elementary (becoming). Such a gestalt is a "resting being" which is *unchangeable* and *everlasting*[24] and as such guarantees a new certainty and rank order of life. Moreover, Jünger understands this regulation of "beco-ming" by the gestalt (being) in accordance with the metaphysical tradition, that is, as a *design* for matter. From all this, Heidegger concludes: "once again Platonism, '*everlasting being*'" (see Section 5.1).[25] Heidegger points second of all to the *modern*-metaphysical character of Jünger's concept of the gestalt: Jünger seeks certainty and finds the *subjectum* for this certainty in a gestalt of the Worker, which is a type of people. That Jünger's search for the *subjectum* for certainty is tied up with human being is, according to Heidegger, due to "modern metaphysics in the sense of the installation of human beings as *subjectum*."[26] According to Heidegger, Jünger's concept of the gestalt is therefore modernly metaphysical (see Section 5.2). He even asserts that the fact that Jünger is thinking in terms of a gestalt at all is a sign of his entanglement in metaphysics.[27] What then inspired Heidegger to maintain a non-metaphysical concept of the gestalt? Why did he not reject the concept of the gestalt as an inherently metaphysical concept?

Although Heidegger is very critical about Jünger's concept of the gestalt, it seems also to have inspired him to develop his own destructed concept of the gestalt. In an annotation on Jünger he remarks, he argues: "From where and how is the gestalt as such, gestalt-like? The gestalt-like as essential swaying of *being* (but *this* is *not* the way Jünger thinks)."[28] What, then, is the status of Heidegger's own concept of the gestalt? In this section, we distinguish Heidegger's non-metaphysical concept of the gestalt from the metaphysical tradition in three different ways. Afterwards, we finish this chapter with a critical discussion of Heidegger's later rejection of the gestalt in favor of language, in favor of naming.

The first characteristic of Heidegger's destructed concept of the gestalt shows itself when we elaborate the relation between the essence of truth and beings. Heidegger says: "The openness of this open, i.e., truth, can only be what it is, namely *this* open, when and as long as it establishes itself in its open. In this open, therefore, there must be a being in which the openness takes its stand and achieves constancy."[29] The truth is only what it is— namely this openness of unconcealing-concealing—when it establishes itself *in* a being. According to Heidegger, one of the essential ways in which truth establishes itself in beings is art, namely, the establishment of the truth in a work of art.[30] What is the nature of this establishment?

According to Heidegger, a work of art is indeed brought-forth, but the product of this bringing forth is not a present form or gestalt of beings (see Section 8.2). The happening of unconcealing-concealing is here not *neutralized* in favor of the presence of a gestalt *in* a created being, but on the contrary, it is, exactly, *opened* in this being. "Truth establishes itself as strife in a being that is to be brought-forth only in such a way that the strife opens up in this being the being itself, in other words, is brought into the rift-design."[31] *Riß* comes from *Reißen,* which means to rift, to write, to sketch. The bringing forth of the rift does not cut out a form as *opposed* to the formless (unconcealment as *opposed* to concealment). The rift of which Heidegger speaks is indeed a *distinction,* but it carries the contestants into the source of their *unity.* The rift cuts the contestants from each other in such a way that they can show themselves *as* they are. "It brings the contest between measure and limit into a shared outline (*Umriß*),"[32] i.e., the outline of the "as" or meaning of this being (unconcealment), which stays in touch with its surrounding and concealed horizon.

Thus far, this remains abstract. How are we to understand this establishment of the truth in a being, even leaving aside the question of whether this being is brought-forth in an artistic or another way? Let us return to our example of the word *aletheia,* whose essence was concealed for the Greeks.[33] The word *aletheia* is an example of a being which is inscribed with an outline (*Umriß*), by a rift (*Riß*). In this case, the outline with which we are dealing is the actual meaning of truth *as adaequatio* (unconcealment), but this remains surrounded by its self-concealing horizon of meaning (*aletheia*), namely, the two kinds of concealment (refusal, obstruction) at the heart of unconcealment. In this way, *aletheia* is brought into *relief as adaequatio* in the rift-design.

According to Heidegger, this rift-design, as it is established in a being, is said to be *the gestalt.* Such a gestalt is the crystallization point, in which the self-establishment of truth in a being and this being's occupation of the openness of truth meet each other. Understood in this way, Heidegger's gestalt has nothing to do with "giving form to an existence impacted by the threat of formlessness!"[34] As long as we think of the gestalt in terms of form and formlessness, we will not recognize the fundamental and irremovable openness of truth. Heidegger's concept of gestalt does not neutralize this openness in favor of the presence of the form, *eidos* or gestalt in the manner of the metaphysical tradition, rather the happening of clearing *and* conceal-ment establishes itself exactly in the gestalt. With this, we encounter our first difference between Heidegger's destructed concept of the gestalt and that of the metaphysical tradition.[35]

Our second such difference comes into view when we consider the fol-lowing observation, made by Heidegger in the *Introduction to Metaphysics* of 1935: "But from an *observer's* point of view, what stands-there-in-itself becomes what puts itself forth, what offers itself in how it looks. The Greeks call the look of a thing its *eidos* or *idea*" (my italics).[36] What is at stake in this passage? When we start with "observation," a being is not taken strictly in terms of itself, but rather in the way it *shows* itself, its *eidos* or form. That, in the metaphysical tradition, the theme of philosophy should be understood in terms of *eidos, idea* or form is thus not something obvious, nor directly comprehensible. It is orientated to the present-at-hand being *opposite* to me, and derives from this a *point of view,* out of which the *eidos* or form becomes accessible.[37] When the being of beings is grasped as *idea* or *eidos,* then the being of this being is not understood out of itself, but out of the way the Greeks have *access* to being. For the Greeks, pure seeing or *theoria* is the primary mode of access to being.[38] It is because the being of beings is accessed from a point of view *opposite to* the present-at-hand being and becomes accessible through pure seeing, that it comes to be called *idea* or "form."[39]

Contrary to the metaphysical tradition, Heidegger tries to draw his way of speaking from the *phenomenon* of which he is speaking, and this is the meaning of the maxim of Phenomenology: *to the things themselves!* To what extent, then, can we say that Heidegger's understanding of the gestalt is drawn from the *phenomena themselves*? Does the word "gestalt" itself give us, in other words, a single reason to bring it into connection with the strife or rift between clearing and concealment?

The word gestalt is originally the participle of *stellen*.[40] *Stellen* means *the-sis,* i.e., the bringing forth of a being. The reason for using exactly this word—gestalt—lies in its character as a participle; what is brought-forth in the gestalt is not a present form, but the *happening* of unconcealing-concealing: "The 'happen' in the 'letting happen of truth' is the prevailing movement in clearing *and* concealment or, more precisely, in their union; in other words it is the movement of the clearing of self-concealment as such, from which, in turn, all self-illumination arises."[41] That gestalt is thus not "ever-lasting being," but is understood as a participle, i.e., as the *happening* of unconcealing-concealing, is the second of our three differences between Heidegger's concept of the gestalt and the metaphysical tradition.

Now, one might object that Heidegger's destructed concept of the gestalt cannot escape degenerating into a present form because he also feels it urgent to speak about the *establishment* of truth in the gestalt. Does not every *establishment* ultimately lead to a stable and present form, and thus also the gestalt as conceived by Heidegger? It might seem so. However, this objection is anticipated and parried in the appendix to *The Origin of the Work of Art:* "But if, in the context of the artwork-essay, we keep in mind the Greek sense of *thesis*—to let lie forth in its radiance and presence—then the 'fixed' corresponding to 'fix in place' can never mean the stiff, motionless, and secure."[42] The establishment of truth in a gestalt exists in the outline of the *as* (or meaning) of a being, in order that it gives itself *as* itself free in the unconcealed, fulfills itself and begins to *be* in the proper sense of the word.

> Instead, "end" means completion in the sense of coming tofulfillment. Limit and end are that whereby beings first begin to *be*. This is the key to understanding the highest term that Aristotle used for being: *entelecheia,* something's holding—or maintaining)—itself-in-its-completion—or limit. . . . Whatever places itself into and thereby enacts its limit, and thus stands, has gestalt, *morphe.* The essence of the gestalt, as understood by the Greeks, comes from the emergent placing-itself-forth-into-the-limit.[43]

Yet, if we accept Heidegger's argument as to why his gestalt does not degenerate into a present form, a further fundamental question arises: Can we still speak of a *destruction* of the concept of the gestalt, when Heidegger here seems to *endorse* it as he refers to the Greek *entelecheia* and *morphe*? Does he not just take over the Greek concepts without destructing them? It might appear so, but consider the following passage. "Where beings are apprehended as beings, and distinguished from other beings, *in view of their outer appearance,* the demarcation and arrangement of beings in terms of outer and inner limits enters on the scene. But what limits is form, what is limited is matter" (emphasis added).[44] It is only when we understand the outline of a gestalt from the way we have access to it, that we understand it as limiting form. Further, it is only when we understand this outlining and establishing as representation, that the limiting form is then understood as the representation of the gestalt (presentness) of a being. But Heidegger's destruction of the gestalt is first and foremost the destruction of the sense of being as presentness in view of the truth of being—unconcealing-concealing—and therefore, the "fixation" of truth in the gestalt never runs counter to its happening-character. Heidegger finds only a *trace* of his destructed concept of the gestalt in the Greek *morphe* as fulfillment and limit: *to-bring-forth-the-delimitation-of-oneself.*

The term *aletheia* is an example of such a gestalt, and one which we already reviewed a couple of times. *Aletheia* is an example of a being which is inscribed with an outline (*Umriß*) or rift, namely, the outline of the actual meaning of truth as *adaequatio,* which stays surrounded by its concealed horizon of meaning. This outline of the meaning of truth is not a question of semantics, but rather regards the *horizon of our vision.* The outline of truth as *adaequatio* or correctness articulates the way beings appear to us and the way human being deals with them; our world appears *as* fitting (*rectus*) or uncanny (*sinister*), about which we can utter cor*rect* or incor*rect* statements.

Here we see that the established gestalt of truth *as* correctness does not outline *a* being but the *whole* of beings in which I am included. With this, we encounter the third and final of our three differences between Heidegger's destructed concept of the gestalt and the metaphysical tradition.

As we have seen, the metaphysical gestalt (*eidos,* form) is accessible only when we take up a point of view or standpoint opposite to the present-at-hand being. With the adoption of this point of view, the metaphysical gestalt becomes primarily the gestalt of beings and our pure seeing of this gestalt is *external* to it. Heidegger sees, by contrast, that the established gestalt of truth *as* correctness not only outlines the way the whole of beings appear to us, but, together with this, the way human being deals with them. This means that we are not after all *external* to this gestalt, because it concerns the relation *between* being and thinking, in which I know myself *included.* This inclusion of thinking in Heidegger's concept of the gestalt is the third characteristic difference at work in his destructed concept of the gestalt.

The first consequence of our inclusion is that the bringing forth of the gestalt concerns that which is our *own* (i.e., our own being), thus the gestalt is related to our *ownness* or identity. What is, in this sense, *our* own? That the essence of truth as unconcealment is *concealed* from thought as such! This means, first of all, that not only Jünger and the metaphysical tradition, but *all of us* are ruled by the desire for presence, that *none of us* is capable of accepting and exposing himself to the clearing of self-concealment. But it is precisely this experience of inaccessibility, which is indicated by the word *aletheia,* that gives rise to our indirect experience of the essence of truth as unconcealing-concealing (see Section 8.1).

Secondly, our inclusion in the bringing forth of the gestalt means that our experience of the gestalt requires that we drop our everyday way of life, including our metaphysically drawn understanding of the relation between being and thinking, and that we dwell by the happening of clearing and concealment.[45] "For a work only actually is as a work when we transport ourselves out of the habitual and into what is opened up by the work so as to bring our essence itself to take a stand within the truth of beings."[46] But this "transportation" is not primarily *our* achievement: the gestalt, as the self-establishment of truth, has the power to throw our metaphysical way of thinking off its balance and to invite us to be mindful of the essence of truth. This is, for Heidegger, the real achievement of the gestalt: "Preservation of the work does not individualize human beings down to their experiences but rather, brings them into a belonging to the truth that happens in the work. By so doing it founds their being-with-one-another as the historical standing out of human existence from out of the relation to unconcealment."[47]

Through this analysis of *The Origin of the Work of Art,* we have seen three characteristics of Heidegger's destructed concept of the gestalt; its openness, its happening character and its inclusiveness. *In the bringing forth*

*of Heidegger's gestalt, an unconcealing-concealing of being, in which I am
included, is happening.*

8.4 Gestalt and Name

The question remains: why did Heidegger change his mind and resolutely
reject the concept of the gestalt—not only the metaphysical concept of the
gestalt but also his own destructed concept—in other texts from the same
period? As a way into this question, we focus once more on the nature of
the creation of the gestalt.

In *The Origin of the Work of Art,* Heidegger quotes a known utterance of
Albrecht Dürer: "For in truth, art is found in nature; whoever can wrest it from
her has it."[48] In the previous section, we learned how we have to understand
this wresting, namely, as the bringing forth of the unconcealing-concealing in
the gestalt. But the bringing forth of the gestalt is not a simple reproduction
of the rift-design of nature, it is not a *mimesis* in the classical sense of the
word. By way of contrast, Heidegger raises the question: "How can the rift
be wrested forth except as the rift, and that means if it has not first been
brought into the open, through the creative sketch, as the strife between
measure and unmeasure?"[49] In this creative wresting there lies a productive
moment, according to Heidegger. On the one hand, the rift-design of the
gestalt belongs to nature, but on the other hand, this rift is only brought-
forth by the productive projection. "Truth will never be gathered from what
is present and ordinary. The disclosure of the open and the clearing of
beings happen, rather, only insofar as the approaching openness is projected within thrownness."[50] The truth of the gestalt *is* only *in* its bringing
forth, in its projection (*Entwurf*) of the openness, which comes forth in
the thrownness.

Heidegger also calls this projection of the truth in the gestalt "poetry." We
can understand this when we recall the Greek origin of the word: "*poiein*
is the 'bringing forth' of something in its presence, in the unconcealed."[51]
That Heidegger specifically calls his concept of the gestalt poetical should
not be taken to mean that he excludes the visual arts from such bringing
forth. However, although Heidegger does think that visual arts and architecture belong also to poetry, in a wider sense, he also accords poetry in the
narrower sense, namely, the *linguistic* work of art, a privileged position in
relation to the other arts.

This brings us to Heidegger's concept of language in the 1930s. His concept of language is in at least three respects distinguished from traditional
concepts of language.[52] First of all, the essence of language does not primarily consist in making *assertions* about beings in the world, but in naming.
Heidegger speaks about the "naming force of language and words."[53] The
primary function of names consists of their demonstrative function; names
show something.[54] "Language, by naming beings for the first time, first
brings beings to word and to appearance. This naming nominates beings *to*

their being *from out* of that being. Such saying is a projection of the clearing in which announcement is made as to what beings will come into the open as."[55] In language, in names, a meaningful world is articulated. An example of such naming is truth as "correctness," in light of which our world appears *as* fitting (*rectus*) or uncanny (*sinister*), about which we can utter cor*rect* or in*correct* statements. Another example of such naming is the name "will to power" in which light our world appears as represented (will to power) to thinking as representation (will to power).

Although this naming is performed by the poet, this poetry is not an act of a subject, but a bringing forth of the name, in whose light the disparate appears as the same and can be considered the same: "*poiein* is the 'bringing forth' of something in its presence, in the unconcealed. We have to take our German word *hervor-bringen* completely literally at this point: 'here'—from out of the heretofore concealed; and 'forth'—into the unconcealed, the open, which human has before and around itself; and 'bringing'—which means receiving something, administering, and giving."[56] With this demonstrative function of names it becomes clear, in the second place, that language is not understood as an *instrument* which is in control of human existence: "Human being does not have a language—but conversely, language 'has' human being, i.e., he 'is' only the one who he is (i.e., exposed amidst the disclosed beings) on the ground of language."[57] The example of the will to power shows that human being is involved in this meaningful world, in which the will to power structures the way we understand and interact with the world around us (will to power).

As such, third, this poetic naming is not an *expression* or mimetic reproduction of reality, because the rift-design of the gestalt belongs to nature on the one hand and is brought-forth by the productive projection. In this view, language *itself* is poetry, because language *names* a pregnant meaning of the word (unconcealment) which is surrounded by its concealed horizon of meaning; this clearing of self-concealment is shown through the name *aletheia* in previous subsections.

The particular position of linguistic poetry lies therein, that it is best able to preserve the primordial poetry of language itself according to Heidegger. Other modes of poetry, such as visual arts and architecture, only occur within the clearing of beings, which is opened by language: "Building and plastic creation, on the other hand, happen, always and only, in the open of saying and naming. It is this open which permeates and guides them. For this reason, they remain their own particular ways and manners in which truth orders itself into the work. They are an always unique poeticizing within the clearing of beings which has already happened, unnoticed, in the language."[58] Although the poetry of the gestalt and the poetry of the name seem to be convertible at first sight,[59] a hierarchical difference occurs here between the poetry of language, poetical *naming* and the poetics of the gestalt. Heidegger sees that the poetry of the gestalt is originally marked by the poetry of naming and ultimately by the poetry of language.

In *The Origin of the Work of Art*, this hierarchical difference is determined *positively*, for although the poetical naming preserves the essence of language best, Heidegger does not reject the poetical bringing forth of the gestalt here as in-essential. He only speaks about a relation of primordiality, because the creation of the gestalt is *secondary* and originally guided by the poetical saying and naming, in which the openness of unconcealing-concealing is happening.

In other texts of the same period, however, this hierarchical difference is quite *negatively* determined. In his *Contributions to Philosophy*, written around 1936–1938, Heidegger says explicitly:

> This thinking [of be-ing] should never seek refuge in a gestalt of a being and in that gestalt experience all the light of what is simple out of the gathered richness of its enjoined darkness. This thinking can also never follow the dissolution into what is without gestalt. In the abground of the gestaltground—this side of gestalt and gestalt-less (which is, of course, only in a being)—this thinking must seize the resonating throw of its thrownness and carry it into the open of the projecting-opening.[60]

Here it becomes clear that Heidegger is not solely criticizing the metaphysical concept of the gestalt because it is understood as present *eidos,* idea or form of a being or *as* idea of the subject (the gestalt of a people). In the *Contributions,* Heidegger states that *every* concept of the gestalt is metaphysical, because it starts with beings and therefore only thinks gestalt in relation to these beings. Heidegger here realizes that the gestalt is always the gestalt of a being and that this relation cannot be destructed. Therefore, the gestalt is no longer secondary but in-essential; in the gestalt, unbeknown to itself, the unconcealing-concealing of being has fallen into oblivion, is closed off and concealed.[61]

So, whereas Heidegger in *The Origin of the Work of Art* seems to introduce only an hierarchical difference between the poetical bringing forth of the gestalt and poetic naming, later on he rejects the concept of the gestalt explicitly in favor of the name. Language is not a being according to Heidegger, but rather names the clearing of self-concealment, as is shown by the example of the "name" *aletheia.* Only language is "*the original resonance of the truth of a world.*"[62]

Why did Heidegger change his mind? What convinced him that the concept of the gestalt cannot after all be destructed and so must be rejected? Our hypothesis is that this is the consequence of his later critique of his own thinking in *The Origin of the Work of Art.* We will finish this section with an elaboration of this hypothesis.

As we have seen in Section 8.3, Heidegger says in *The Origin of the Work of Art* that truth has to establish itself as unconcealing-concealing in a being, and that this establishment of truth in a being is said to be the gestalt. When Heidegger in his *Contributions* remarks that the gestalt is inherently related to beings, he has been seduced by exactly this concept of the gestalt into the idea that truth has to establish itself in beings. What is the problem of *establishment*? In his essay on art, Heidegger says that with the concept of the self-establishment of truth, we step into the domain of the question-worthiness of the ontological difference. The problem for Heidegger is this: in the metaphysical tradition, being is understood out of beings (beings as such), whereas Heidegger tries to think *being as such*. When Heidegger, at the same time, states that being has to establish itself in a being, then the question arises as to how this established being is differentiated from the metaphysically understood *beingness* of beings (i.e., ontological *in*difference).

Our discussion of Heidegger's destructed concept of the gestalt in the previous sections made clear that it cannot be understood as the beingness of beings. And yet, later Heidegger came to see that he could not withdraw his concept of the gestalt completely from this tradition, because it is inherently related to beings and thinks being out of beings. For instance, when Heidegger in his *Rectorial Address* is talking about the task before the Germans of finding their identity and when this identity can be found in a gestalt of the German people, then it is not clear how this gestalt is differentiated from an onto-typology, or from the beingness (gestalt) of beings (Germans).[63] As long as the truth of being has to establish itself in a gestalt, being as such is not only thought of in relation with beings, but also *out of* beings, and we are then incapable of differentiating it from the beingness of beings.[64] That is why Heidegger, in his *Contributions*, finally rejects the establishment of the truth in a gestalt and attempts to think the truth of being *without* beings: "Mindfulness transports the man of the future into that 'in-between' in which he belongs to being and yet, amidst beings, remains a stranger."[65] Because the concept of the gestalt is, according to Heidegger, inherently bound up with beings, the departure of establishment implies also the departure of the gestalt.

In the context of this chapter, we leave aside the question of whether the essence of truth can occur without such establishment in an entity. Instead, we raise the question whether the departure of such establishment *must* imply the departure of the gestalt. In the next chapter, we will see that Jünger's concept of the gestalt is precisely related to naming, to language.

Notes

1. Heidegger, Martin, *Beiträge zur Philosophie*, 422 (tr. 298).
2. Heidegger, Martin, *Beiträge zur Philosophie*, 422 (tr. 298).
3. In this book, we shall not focus on Heidegger's being-historical thinking and its connection with the gestalt. For Heidegger's being-historical thinking, cf. Emad, Parvis, *On the Way to Heidegger's Contributions to Philosophy* (Madison: The University of Wisconsin Press, 2007); Herrmann, Friedrich-Wilhelm von, *Wege ins Ereignis: Zu Heidegger's "Beiträge zur Philosophie"* (Frankfurt am Main: Vittorio Klostermann, 1994).
4. Michael Zimmerman points out that Heidegger's explanation of enframing *(Gestell)* as the essence of modern technology . . . owes a great deal to Jünger's

term of the gestalt as the hidden ontological principle" (Cf. Zimmermann, "Die Entwicklung von Heideggers Nietzsche-Interpretation," 110; cf. Zimmerman, *Heidegger's Confrontation with Modernity,* 80–83).

5. Heidegger, Martin, "Der Ursprung des Kunstwerkes," *Holzwege,* Gesamtausgabe, vol. 5 (Frankfurt am Main: Vittorio Klostermann, 1977) 51 (tr. 38).
6. Heidegger, Martin, "Ursprung des Kunstwerkes," 38 (tr. 28).
7. Heidegger, Martin, "Ursprung des Kunstwerkes," 39 (tr. 29).
8. Heidegger, Martin, "Ursprung des Kunstwerkes," 39 (tr. 29).
9. Heidegger, Martin, "Ursprung des Kunstwerkes," 39–40 (tr. 30).
10. Heidegger, Martin, "Ursprung des Kunstwerkes," 40 (tr. 30).
11. Heidegger, Martin, "Ursprung des Kunstwerkes," 41 (tr. 31).
12. Heidegger, Martin, *Einführung in die Metaphysik,* 4 (tr. 2–3); Because of this recoiling back, our questioning becomes entangled in its object, and according to Heidegger, this is a sign that our questioning is *really* philosophical (cf. for the role of questioning in Heidegger's philosophy: Blok, Vincent, "Heidegger and Derrida on the Nature of Questioning: Towards the Rehabilitation of Questioning in Contemporary Philosophy," *The Journal of the British Society for Phenomenology,* vol 64 2015: 307–322.
13. Heidegger, Martin, "Ursprung des Kunstwerkes," 37 (tr. 28 modified) (my italics).
14. Heidegger, Martin, "Platons Lehre von der Wahrheit," *Wegmarken,* Gesamtausgabe, vol. 9 (Frankfurt am Main: Vittorio Klostermann, 1979) 238 (tr. 182).
15. Heidegger, Martin, "Ursprung des Kunstwerkes," 41–42 (tr. 31 modified).
16. Heidegger, Martin, "Ursprung des Kunstwerkes," 41 (tr. 30–31).
17. Cf. Heidegger, Martin, "Das Ende der Philosophie und die Aufgabe des Denkens," *Zur Sache des Denkens,* Gesamtausgabe, vol. 14 (Frankfurt am Main: Vittorio Klostermann, 2007) 88.
18. Heidegger, Martin, "Ursprung des Kunstwerkes," 41–42 (tr. 31).
19. Heidegger, Martin, "Ursprung des Kunstwerkes," 47 (tr. 35).
20. We follow Heidegger's interpretation of the *Sophistes* in his lecture on this of 1924–1925 (Heidegger, Martin, *Platon: Sophistes,* Gesamtausgabe, vol. 19 [Frankfurt am Main: Vittorio Klostermann, 1992] 269–275 [tr. 184–189]).
21. Heidegger, Martin, "Ursprung des Kunstwerkes," 47 (tr. 35).
22. Heidegger, Martin, "Ursprung des Kunstwerkes," 38 (tr. 28).
23. Cf. "φύσις δὲ καθ' Ἡράκλειτον κρύπθεσθαι φιλεῖ" (Heraclitus, fragment 123).
24. *Arb,* 37–43.
25. Heidegger, Martin, *Zu Ernst Jünger,* 81.
26. Heidegger, Martin, *Zu Ernst Jünger,* 132–133.
27. "Jünger's entanglement in the metaphysical shows itself most decisively because he thinks in 'gestalten' . . . 1. The gestalt generally and the correctly understood *eidos,* the appearance in which the 'essence' is placed and stands, shows itself, not 'idea' as modern *perceptum*!—is metaphysical! 2. Man as *the* gestalt and the first gestalt-like is *modernly* metaphysical" (Heidegger, *Zu Ernst Jünger,* 93–94).
28. Heidegger, Martin, *Zu Ernst Jünger,* 141.
29. Heidegger, Martin, "Ursprung des Kunstwerkes," 48 (tr. 36).
30. Such an establishment is not restricted to art; the act which founds a state or the questioning of thinkers can also be said to be the establishment of the truth in a being.
31. Heidegger, Martin, "Ursprung des Kunstwerkes," 51 (tr. 38).
32. Heidegger, Martin "Ursprung des Kunstwerkes," 51 (tr. 38).
33. We defer any discussion of whether a word is or is not to be understood as a being (for this, cf. Section 8.4).
34. Radloff, Bernard, *Heidegger and the Question of National Socialism* (Toronto: University of Toronto Press, 2007) 3.
35. The reproach of Lacoue-Labarthe, that the philosophical thinking of Heidegger in the 1930s is still reigned by *onto-typology,* is thus incorrect (Lacoue-Labarthe,

Heidegger, Art and Politics, 85). Nevertheless, Heidegger saw later on that he could not withdraw his concept of the gestalt completely from the onto-typology, insofar as every thinking of the gestalt thinks being not only in relation with beings, but also *out of* beings (for this, cf. Section 8.4).

36. Heidegger, Martin, *Einführung in die Metaphysik*, 46 (tr. 63).
37. Heidegger, Martin, *Sein und Zeit*, 62 (tr. 89–90).
38. Cf. Heidegger, Martin, *Logik. Die Frage nach der Wahrheit*, Gesamtausgabe, vol. 21 (Frankfurt am Main: Vittorio Klostermann, 1976¹⁹⁹⁵) 56 (tr. 47).
39. Therefore, it is not true that the word 'gestalt' is convertible for the word 'form', as van Peperstraten suggests, because Heidegger tries to draw his concept of the gestalt from the *Sache* itself (Peperstraten, Frans van, *Sublieme Mimesis* [Budel: Damon 2005] 143). Form is like *eidos* and *idea* not a definition which is derived from the phenomena, the *Sache* which have to be defined. As we will see, Heidegger advances his concept of the gestalt in connection with consummation and *outline*.
40. Therefore, Heidegger says that the gestalt has to be thought of out of "Ge-stell," although this word cannot primarily be thought of as the basic concept of the modern technical era.
41. Heidegger, Martin, "Ursprung des Kunstwerkes," 71–72 (tr. 54).
42. Heidegger, Martin, "Ursprung des Kunstwerkes," 71 (tr. 53).
43. Heidegger, Martin, *Einführung in die Metaphysik*, 46 (tr. 63 modified).
44. Heidegger, Martin, *Nietzsche: Der Wille zur Macht als Kunst*, Gesamtausgabe, vol. 43 (Frankfurt am Main: Vittorio Klostermann, 1961¹⁹⁸⁵) 94.
45. "In short, the unconcealing of beings is a matter of going under, enownment and allotment, and those who unconceal beings are those who go under, are enowned by be-ing, and who are allotted to be-ing" (Emad, *On the Way to Heidegger's Contributions to Philosophy*, 50).
46. Heidegger, Martin, "Ursprung des Kunstwerkes," 62 (tr. 47).
47. Heidegger, Martin, "Ursprung des Kunstwerkes," 55 (tr. 41; The further analysis of this *Bewahren* and the question how we have to distinguish this *Bewahren* of the truth from an *adaequatio* between being and thinking, is beyond the scope of this chapter.
48. Heidegger, Martin, "Ursprung des Kunstwerkes," 58 (tr. 43).
49. Heidegger, Martin, "Ursprung des Kunstwerkes," 58 (tr. 43).
50. Heidegger, Martin, "Ursprung des Kunstwerkes," 59 (tr. 44).
51. Heidegger, Martin, *1. Nietzsches Metaphysik 2. Einleitung in die Philosophie. Denken und Dichten*, Gesamtausgabe, vol. 50 (Frankfurt am Main: Vittorio Klostermann, 1990), 112 (tr. 21).
52. For a critical assessment of the development of Heidegger's philosophy of language as naming, cf. Thomä, Dieter, "The Name on the Edge of Language: A Complication in Heidegger's Theory of Language and Its Consequences." ed. R. Polt and G. Fried, *A Companion to Heidegger's Introduction to Metaphysics* (New Haven: Yale University Press 2001), 103–122.
53. Heidegger, Martin, *Einführung in die Metaphysik*, 16 (tr. 15).
54. "The essence of language consists much more of that man first ventures out into being—the original unveiling and revelation of being happens in it; language is not first the subsequent expression of this unveiling of things, rather it is the unveiling itself" (Heidegger, *Reden und andere Zeuchnissen eines Lebensweges*, 329–330). The Greeks already knew that names primarily show something *(deloen)*.
55. Heidegger, Martin, "Ursprung des Kunstwerkes," 61 (tr. 46).
56. Heidegger, Martin, *Nietzsches Metaphysik*, 112 (tr. 21).
57. Heidegger, Martin, *Reden und andere Zeuchnissen eines Lebensweges*, 330–331.
58. Heidegger, Martin, "Ursprung des Kunstwerkes," 62 (tr. 46–47).
59. About the poetry of the gestalt, Heidegger says: "What poetry, as clearing projection, unfolds of unconcealment and projects into the rift within the gestalt is

the open; poetry allows this open to happen in such a way, indeed, that now, for the first time, in the midst of beings, it brings them to shine and sound" (Heidegger, "Ursprung des Kunstwerkes," 60 [tr. 45] sometimes tr. = [. . .] and sometimes (. . .)). The poetry projects a gestalt in which the openness (truth) can show itself (cf. Heidegger, "Ursprung des Kunstwerkes," 63 (tr. 47). About poetry as naming, Heidegger says: "This projective announcement immediately becomes a renunciation of all dim confusion within which beings veil and withdraw themselves." (Heidegger, "Ursprung des Kunstwerkes," 61 [tr. 46]). Poetry projects the name in which the openness (truth) can show itself.

60. Heidegger, Martin, *Contributions to Philosophy*, 422 (tr. 298 modified).

61. Therefore, I do not agree with Radloff's "fundamental claim [. . .] that *being 'takes gestalt' in beings*, and in the comportment of Da-sein, and that this event overcomes the separation of being and beings to found the historicity of Da-sein and the being of entities" (Radloff, *Heidegger and the Question of National Socialism*, 317). Radloff suggests that Heidegger in the *Contributions* still thinks that the truth "takes gestalt in beings" (Radloff, *Heidegger and the Question of National Socialism*, 327) and he refers to page 389 of the *Contributions*. Here, Heidegger says indeed that truth needs "sheltering the truth" in a being, but he explicitly is not talking about the gestalt in a positive way anymore. On the contrary, he says on the next page: "For sheltering of truth in a being—does that not remind one all too clearly of the shaping of 'idea,' of *eidos* into *hule*? . . . Truth holds sway always already and only as Da-sein and thereby as the strifing of the strife" (Heidegger, *Beiträge zur Philosophie*, 390 [tr. 272]).

62. Heidegger, Martin, *Nietzsches metaphysische Grundstellung im abendländischen Denken*, Gesamtausgabe, vol. 44 (Frankfurt am Main: Vittorio Klostermann, 1986) 110. In this chapter, we cannot elaborate on Heidegger's understanding of the essence of language any further, and restrict ourselves to the given indications in the artwork essay.

63. Cf. Lacoue-Labarthe, Philippe, Heidegger, *Art and Politics*, 85.

64. Although Heidegger in *The Age of the World Picture* from 1938 still speaks about *establishment*, he no longer uses this word on his own account. In this essay, establishment concerns the way subject and object are built into each other. "In the planetary imperialism of technologically organized man the subjectivism of man reaches its highest point from which it will descend to the flatness of organized uniformity and there establish itself. This uniformity becomes the surest instrument of the total, i.e., technological, dominion over the earth. The modern freedom of subjectivity is completely absorbed into the corresponding objectivity" (Heidegger, "Die Zeit des Weltbildes," 111 [tr. 84]). This establishment bears witness of the *presence* of subject and object for each other, and is therefore unsuitable to think the truth of being.

65. Heidegger, Martin, "Ursprung des Kunstwerkes," 96 (tr. 72 modified). In the *Contributions*, Heidegger still speaks about the "sheltering the truth of be-ing that is in beings" (Heidegger, *Beiträge zur Philosophie*, 27 [tr. 20]), but here, he no longer thinks *sheltering* in connection with *establishment* and *Gestalt*. As long as we think of sheltering as *self-establishing* in a *gestalt*, we understand being not only in relation with beings, but also *out of* beings: "Inceptually Da-*sein* stands in the grounding of enowning, engrounds the truth of *being*, and does not go from *a being* over to its being. Rather, the engrounding of enowning occurs as sheltering of truth in and as a being; and thus, if a comparison were at all possible—and it is not—the relationship is the other way around" (Heidegger, *Beiträge zur Philosophie*, 322 [tr. 226]).

9 Controversies over Language
The One-Sidedness of Heidegger's Examination of Ernst Jünger

In the last chapter of this part, we will identify a one-sidedness in Heidegger's examination of Jünger. As we have seen in the previous sections, Jünger's concept of the gestalt is modernly metaphysical according to Heidegger. In this section, we ask whether Jünger's actual concern is based in a "transformation of saying" and "an altered relationship to the essence of speech." Indeed, Heidegger asks in *On the Question of Being* whether Jünger's concept of language is not conceptualized in such a way that it cannot be identified with the language of the sciences. However, Heidegger does not develop the possibility anywhere. He emphasizes the fact that Jünger's descriptions do not distance themselves anywhere from Nietzsche's basic metaphysical position, as we have seen in the previous chapter. Thus, for Heidegger, it is established that Jünger understands language as well as the totally mobilized world from Nietzsche's metaphysics of the will to power: his 'way of speaking' also has work-character and the 'essence of language' is found in its instrumental character.[1]

But Jünger's experience of the gestalt of the worker extends beyond its correspondence in terms of the idea of the subject, as we have seen in Chapter 4. The one-sidedness of Heidegger's examination of Jünger becomes clear when one considers that Jünger's manner of speaking is *poetic*; he *writes poetry about* the gestalt. Heidegger, however, should not be accused of a deficient interpretation of Jünger, nor can one blame a hidden influence of Jünger on his thought. On the contrary, Heidegger's thought about the essence of art provides an indication of the specific nature of Jünger's poetics.

In Section 9.1 we will discuss the poetic nature of Jünger's speech. In Section 9.2 the specific kind of this poetics will be more closely determined with the help of some of Heidegger's thoughts about the essence of art.

9.1 The Poetic Nature of Jüngerian Speech

A first reference to the "transformation of saying" in *The Worker* can be found when one bears in mind that Jünger understands the concept of the gestalt from the will to power as *art*, thus as poetics.[2] In nihilism, Jünger's poetics performs the *transition* from the total mobilization to a world in which a new type of man—the worker type—represents the gestalt of the worker. It *brings forth* the worker type as representative of the gestalt of the worker, so that the total mobilization can be overcome in a new necessary order (see Chapter 3). What is this poetic bringing forth other than an idea produced by man as subject?

The altered nature of Jünger's speech becomes clear when we consider that he does not link the gestalt of the worker with the metaphysical understanding of "being"—*ideĩn, idéa*—as Heidegger says in *On the Question of Being*. In *The Worker* the gestalt is linked namely to language: "The more we devote ourselves to movement, the more deeply we must be convinced that a dormant being hides below it, and that every increase of speed is only the translation of an immortal original language."[3] According to Jünger, "the language of work" is indicated in the total mobilization, which is anxious to translate itself into everything that can be thought, felt, wanted."[4] What is meant with this language?

The gestalt of the worker is the "summarizing unity" in which reality and its human responsiveness appear *as* work. For the gestalt of the worker, this unity must be sought in work, that is, in the stamped appearance of our technological reality as technological space and human responsiveness as the worker type (see Chapter 1). This *appearance* can be designated as *word*. Here, language is not understood as an instrument which man *has*. The word refers here to the appearance within which we *see* the disparate *as* the same, *as* work.[5] The altered relationship to the essence of language in Jünger's poetics thus exists in that language for Jünger also relates to the design of the appearance of things and human responsiveness (see Chapter 4). This reconciliation of our technological reality *as* technological space and human responsiveness *as* the worker type through the gestalt of the worker is the *design* of the word "*work*." In Chapter 4, however, we saw that the unity of the gestalt extends further than the unity of the language of signs; signs are "projections of gestalts from a hidden dimension." The gestalt is not only the language of signs within which the disparate appearances of our totally mobilized world appear *as* work, but also the hidden *horizon* of meaning of the language of signs, which is only accessible in an indirect way (see Chapter 4).

How is it demonstrated that man is not the subject of this language according to Jünger? "It has far more to do with a new language that is suddenly spoken and man answers, or he remains silent—and this decides his reality. . . . The clatter of looms from Manchester, the rattle of machine guns from Langemarck—they are signs, words and sentences of a prose that wants to be interpreted and mastered by us."[6] Man is not the subject of this language, because it "translates itself into everything that can be thought, felt, wanted." Man responds to this language or remains silent. In the indication of this hidden horizon of meaning of the language of signs of the gestalt, Jünger's altered relationship to the essence of language shows itself.

Now we are going over to Jünger's altered nature of speech. His altered nature of speech appears when we ask about the relationship between the hidden horizon of meaning of the language of signs of the gestalt and its human responsiveness.

In *The Worker*, Jünger says his reference to the gestalt should not raise the impression that the gestalt *is* in any way as we have seen (see Chapter 3). A new stamping of the gestalt does not follow directly on nihilism and it is exactly this vacuum of power that we call *nihilism*.[7]

In this state we must first of all learn to see that the world of total mobilization can be seen in a completely *different* manner, namely as an *order* stamped by the gestalt. The poetics in *The Worker* depicts the transition from the total mobilization to a world in which the "worker type" represents the gestalt and so corresponds to the "turning of Being." With the presumption of the gestalt in the First World War, the transition is already *essentially accomplished*, and *our* transition to the worker type consists therefore of a *becoming of who you are*.

But that does not mean that man is the object of the gestalt. According to Jünger the language of signs of the gestalt wants to be interpreted and mastered by us, that is that the dominion of the gestalt "is already essentially accomplished," but needs a language in order to emerge from its "anonymous" character.[8] The poetics in *The Worker* is led by a gestalt that is not and is thus transformative to the worker type, that is, the poetics recognizes itself as representative of the gestalt of the worker (see Chapter 3).

The transition to the type exists in the *naming* of the technological reality and the human responsiveness.[9] The domination of the gestalt emerges from its "anonymous" character through the name work, and the transformation of saying that arises in *The Worker* exists in this poetic naming. Jünger's poetics shows us that the transformed "way of speaking" is incommensurable with an instrumental view of language, and cannot be represented by the human subject.

9.2 The Essence of Naming

Although Heidegger also misjudges Jünger's actual concern in relation to language, his thought about the essence of language (see Section 8.4) helps more closely articulate the poetic nature of Jünger's speech.[10] We are limiting ourselves here to the three references that we received there.

We can call the naming in *The Worker* *poetic*, if we think back with Heidegger to the Greek origin of this word; poetics is not an act of the subject, rather *brings* the name *forth*, in whose light the disparate appears *as* the same and can be understood as such. An example of that is the name "total mobilization," which in the meantime is adopted into our speech and in whose light *our* world of technology and work appears and is understood. Jünger poetizes this name in *The Worker*, i.e., the disparate appearances are made into one denominator through this name and so appear *as* a unity.

A further reference to the essence of poetic naming is that it does not exist in the invention of the gestalt, rather in the bringing forth of a rift of nature that first thanks to this bringing forth *is* in the actual sense. A productive moment hides in design, for the rift of the gestalt belongs on the one hand to nature and on the other hand is first "brought-forth" by a creative idea or act. The gestalt *is* first *in* the poetic naming. Exactly this productive moment plays a role in poetics in *The Worker*. The dominion of the gestalt is already essentially realized, but needs the poetic nature of speech in order to emerge from its anonymous character. Human speaking is neither subject nor object of the gestalt, rather it *recognizes* itself in the creative design of the gestalt as its representative. In naming the world *as* technological space and its human responsiveness *as* worker type, the poetics *recognizes* itself as representative of the gestalt of the worker, that is, that the poetics is led by the gestalt like a *magnet*. The poetic naming is thus led by the gestalt like a magnet and this magnetism is the essence of poetics in *The Worker*.

Therefore, we must conclude that Heidegger's examination of Jünger is one-sided. Heidegger emphasizes that Jünger speaks of the gestalt of the worker, thus is bound to the modern understanding of man as subject: "The source that gives meaning, the power that is present in advance and thus shapes everything, is *gestalt* as the *gestalt* of a particular *kind of human*."[11] Insofar as Jünger speaks of a gestalt of a humanity, Heidegger is correct that *The Worker* "*remains housed within metaphysics.*"[12] In *The Worker*, Jünger also literally says he is the subject of the technological processes.[13]

But there where Jünger links language with the hidden horizon of meaning of the language of signs, he is *on his way* to an understanding of the essence of language that is no longer metaphysical. The other side of Jünger's poetics highlights the dual meaning of Jünger's language. On the one hand he testifies to an instrumental understanding of language when he says that his statements themselves have work-character (see Chapter 7). On the other hand, he testifies to a transformation of saying in the sense of Heidegger which no longer exists in representation, rather in poetic naming.

Notes

1. Cf. Heidegger, Martin, *Heraklit*, Gesamtausgabe, vol. 55 (Frankfurt am Main: Vittorio Klostermann, 1979, 1994) 70–71.
2. Cf. *Arb*, 64–65; Schwarz, Hans-Peter, *Der konservative Anarchist*, 45–55.
3. *Arb*, 40.
4. *Arb*, 104.
5. Cf. Heumakers and Oudemans, *De horizon van Buitenveldert*, 180.
6. *Arb*, 141.
7. The question as to whether the basic experience of Jüngerian writing in *The Worker* must be found in the experience of nihilism was not answered conclusively until now. While Heidegger says candidly in *The Question of Being, The Worker* has "provided a description of European nihilism in its phase following the first world war" (Heidegger, "Zur Seinsfrage," 389 (tr. 294), Günter Figal is of the opinion that Jünger's basic experience precisely consists of the new

orientation provided by the gestalt: "Thus the interim thinking of nihilism, the directionless being-fixed between no-longer and not-yet is completely foreign to him." (Figal, "Der metaphysische Charaktere der Moderne," 188). In Chapter 1, we developed the idea that Jünger's basic experience is that of nihilism; however, he also experiences a *gestalt-switch* during the First World War. The experience of the *worker* is thus thoroughly one of an *interim*. "How far away is the situation in which we find ourselves from any unity that can ensure a new security and rank order of life. Here there is no visible unity other than rapid change" (*Arb*, 99; cf. *Arb*, 88, 100–101). The *thing* or *Sache* of *The worker* is precisely to become transitory to a world in which the worker type represents its gestalt and corresponds in this sense to the "new turning of being" (cf. Chapter 3).

8. *Arb*, 98.
9. Cf. *Arb*, 67.
10. We are limiting ourselves in this chapter to the references of Heidegger in order to understand the poetic nature of Jünger's speech in *The Worker*, without wanting to identify their understanding of art in general and the gestalt specifically or compare them to each other.
11. Heidegger, "Zur Seinsfrage," 396 (tr. 299).
12. Heidegger, "Zur Seinsfrage," 395 (tr. 299).
13. *Arb*, 170.

Part III

The Essence of Language and the Poetics of the Anthropocene

Speluncam exploravimus . . . Votre Majesté sait comme moi que l'avenir est gros de plus d'occurrences qu'il n'en peut mettre au monde. Et il n'est point impossible d'en entendre bouger quelques-unes au fond de la matrice du temps. Mais l'événement seul décide laquelle de ces larves est viable et arrive à terme. Je n'ai jamais vendu au marché des catastrophes et des bonheurs accouchés d'avance.

(Yourcenar, *L'Oeuvre au Noir*)

Introduction

In the previous chapter, we obtained an indication of Jünger's concept of the "essence of language" and the "transformation of saying" in his early work, i.e., the poetic naming of the gestalt of the worker. Jünger's language is indeed ambiguous in *The Worker,* but his notion of the hidden horizon of the language of signs clearly shows that he is on the way to a non-metaphysical concept of the essence of language. Is this ambiguity of the essence of language removed in his later work after *Across the Line* from 1950 and Heidegger's *Concerning "The Line"* from 1955?

In his *Notes on "The Worker"* from 1964, Jünger says that *Type, Name, Gestalt* from 1963 once again reflects on the gestalt of the worker. In *Type, Name, Gestalt,* the term Gestalt is explained anew and in a systematic manner. Here, the gestalt is also bound with language. However, in this later book, language does not have the ambiguous status it has in *The Worker,* rather it is bound with poetics and naming. In this chapter, *Type, Name, Gestalt* will be consulted in order to better understand Jünger's later understanding of the nature of language. On this basis, Jünger's transformation of saying toward a non-metaphysical language can first be determined.

But before we can inquire about Jünger's terms "gestalt" and "name," the question must be answered as to whether his later work can be understood as part of a continuum that includes his earlier concept of the gestalt. His observation in *Notes on "The Worker"* from 1964, that "*Type, Name,*

Gestalt reaches back once more to the seed of the topic," is not a sufficient justification.[1] In Chapter 10 we will therefore analyze the poetry of the gestalt of the worker in his later work. After exploring Jünger's concept of the essence of language in *Type, Name, Gestalt* in Chapter 11, we will concentrate on Jünger's transformation of saying in *At the Time Wall* in Chapter 12.

Note

1. *MM*, 333.

10 The Poetry of the Gestalt of the Worker in Jünger's Later Work

An initial reading of *Type, Name, Gestalt* reveals that Jünger maintains here the same thoughts as in *The Worker*. Jünger also notices here a decline of the type in the century of the worker,[1] "that both assume the hastening and dynamization of life, and is its result as well."[2] We have already seen this decline of the type or nihil of typicality for the sake of dynamization—he also calls the nihil of typicality a vacancy or a blank[3]—in *The Worker;*[4] it concerns the destruction of the categories of the *Animal Rationale*. And Jünger also speaks here of a "workshop landscape" in which neither the establishment of new types nor the restoration of older types makes sense.[5]

At the same time, he sees indications of a new epoch of the worker in the workshop landscape. In the prevalence of materialism in the workshop land-scape, Jünger sees the upswing of the new earth power of the worker.[6] On the one hand, this materialism destroys the categories of the *Animal Ratio-nale* and on the other hand, it "forms the ground floor for the workshop in which the scaffolding for the workers is forged."[7] The earth is here under-stood as an inexhaustible fertile field of possibilities for a new metaphysical position of the worker as representative of the gestalt of the worker and in this respect, the earth is homeland of the worker.[8] "The world of the worker will also be the homeland of man."[9] As in *The Worker,* the worker is son of the earth and enemy of the ideas of the *Animal Rationale,* i.e., a new titan who destroys the categories of the *Animal Rationale* in favor of the gestalt of the worker: "The worker fights and dies in apparatuses, not only without 'higher ideas,' but also in his conscious rejection. His ethos flows into the clean service of the apparatus. He does not have to think; he does not have an overview of the plan."[10] The worker trusts that the earth will respond and give rise to the gestalt. Also in *At the Time Wall* from 1959, he calls this type of man the worker: "It is about . . . the appearance of a new type . . . The dominant world and attitude towards life correspond to him, the growing optimism of the worker, his theoretically as well as poorly supported trust of its transitional power, which nonetheless is fundamentally justified and has prognostic worth."[11]

But contrary to *The Worker,* Jünger is not univocally positive about this phase of nihilism and its destruction of the categories of the *Animal*

Rationale in his later work. He experiences this decline as frightening and threatening as well. In the workshop landscape, technological comfort and relief by the increased automaticity and technical nature of human life goes hand in hand with a decrease of human freedom and control over these technologies according to Jünger. This poses no problem as long as it leads to convenience and comfort, but as soon as the destructive or catastrophic powers of technology show themselves, the lack of freedom becomes apparent and results in times of fear and apocalyptic panic according to Jünger.[12] What precisely is threatening in the workshop landscape?

In *At the Time Wall*, Jünger on the one hand believes that the nihilistic phase of destruction is necessary but will not end in a total technological disaster. As in *The Worker*, he still believes that this nihilist phase will be counterbalanced: "the unease has to do far more with things that are missing than with ones that are available. Insofar it is also necessary, for it points to the fact that the cost is much larger than the gain; that we are thus creditors. It has been sacrificed a little; an abandonment has taken place, one whose presence has not yet made an appearance."[13] And just as in *The Worker*, he still believes that this counterbalance of the technological disaster is only performed by the gestalt of the worker:[14] "We see only the gestalt of the worker emerge more powerful from every fire. One can surmise that the fieriest elements are hidden in it and that it has not yet found its pure cast."[15] But on the other hand, he argues that the danger of technology is that the metaphysical hunger, i.e., our ability to conceive this gestalt, dies away.[16] Why?

In the workshop landscape, "only that which can be quantified is valid"[17] and is subject to automaticity. This quantification corresponds with a lack of metaphysical sense. This means that the workshop landscape is not only the precondition of the future rise of the gestalt of the worker, but is also dangerous because it can lead to a *perfection of technology*[18] in which the metaphysical sense for this gestalt has died:[19] "The 'last man,' as an insect type, would then populate the world; his structures and works of art would achieve perfection, as the goal of progress and evolution, at the cost of freedom; they would open forth from the technological collective like a butterfly's wings or mussel shells in great, but unfree splendour, perhaps for millennia."[20] The perfection of technology is the dark side of the workshop landscape in Jünger's later work, because it lets the metaphysical hunger for the gestalt erode.

In the end, however, Jünger is convinced that this metaphysical longing will never die: "Always, and up until the last breath, he will be pacified by the internal feeling of another, infinite and larger life, by a flood of light that saves him, even if he has never seen the sun, never heard its name."[21] And as in his early works, he legitimizes this conviction by referring to the first law of thermodynamics, i.e., the law of the conservation of energy.[22] For Jünger, the experience of a decline—nihilism—corresponds with the intuition of a new rise of the gestalt. "Something similar applies to the decline of metaphysical power. A loss within the historical landscape remains relatively within the larger context—the universe is a house that loses nothing."[23] Not only does every light have its dark side, but every shadow also has a light side.

For Jünger, the perfection of technology will be prevented by the "spirit as the cosmic power"[24] of poets,[25] who are responsible for mastering and taming the abstract world of technology. Although art and poetry adopt functional, technological and mechanical features in the workshop landscape, and become the material of automatic replication in this way, the poet must stand in opposition and not engage in the workshop landscape.[26] How are we to understand this resistance to the perfection of technology by the poet?

In *The Forest Passage* from 1951, this poet is called a forest rebel. The forest passage of the forest rebel involves first of all a movement *off* the blazed trails of the categories of the *Animal Rationale* and into the forest, i.e., the farewell to such categories. This will lead secondly *beyond* the limits of the nihilist criticism of these categories. Although the nihilist critique is seen as a necessary phase, its role diminishes as soon as the categories of the *Animal Rationale* are destructed and *nihil* is left:

> If the upheaval succeeds, a short but significant interim follows it, in which everything is possible. The primary cause shows itself as chaos. The anarchist copes with this encounter as a son of the earth and as a worshipper of the earth, but not the nihilist, whose character adheres to the institution that he, like Sampson, appears to destroy, but actually is buried underneath its rubble.[27]

The nihilist critique results in a wasteland without any *idea* or category left, i.e., a *tabula rasa*. But because this *tabula rasa* is perfectly compatible with the perfection of technology, the forest passage of the forest rebel moves second of all beyond the limits of the nihilist critique and the perfection of technology. His resistance to the threat of the perfection of technology consists precisely in his movement off the blazed trails and into the forest.

This resistance doesn't mean that the forest rebel is an anarchist who is against the machine world. First of all, the abandonment of technology would lead to even more terror and fear as the perfection of technology itself, according to Jünger. Secondly, it doesn't mean either that the forest rebel opts for an alternative way of human existence. That would be a romantic gesture. Every alternative way of existence already contributes to the perfection of technology, namely as its mirror image.

In order to show this, Junger gives the example of voting. Whether one votes for or against something, even if one puts a cross on the ballot paper, one's vote is processed in the statistics. In this respect, there is no place *outside* technology. But, although we do not have a free relationship to the technological world we live in, we have a free relation to the *categories* in which the perfection of technology is understood, according to Jünger.[28] In order to understand this free relation, we return for a moment to the example of voting. The one who votes no or puts a cross on the ballot paper is not free, rather the one who rejects the categories in which the majority has the say and the minority is without meaning.[29] The resistance to the perfection of technology by the forest passage consists in the rejection of the *categories* of the *Animal Rationale* and of the categories of automaticity and calculation, in which the workshop landscape is understood.

This makes clear why passing through the forest is called a death march, namely the destruction of the prevailing categories in which human existence is understood. At the same time, the forest passage enables us to assess whether there are refractory elements that resist this destruction in the nihilist phase. This refractory element is found in individual freedom.[30] This individual freedom in the end enables human existence to resist the perfection of technology and its categories of automaticity and calculation: "Artistic man raises objections from his inborn freedom against the pure application of the logical calculus."[31]

What is the nature of this freedom according to Jünger? The experience that there is no place outside of technology makes clear that this concept of freedom can no longer be understood in terms of the *Animal Rationale:*

> It is at this point that the question arises, not merely theoretically but in every human existence today, whether another path remains viable. After all, there are mountain passes and mule tracks that one discovers only after a long ascent. A new concept of power has emerged, a potent and direct concentration. Holding out against this force requires a new concept of freedom, one that can have nothing to do with the washed-out ideas associated with this word today.[32]

But if we want to resist the perfection of technology, we are in need of a new concept of freedom beyond the free will of the *Animal Rationale* and the uncritical embracing of the perfection of technology. This "third way" has to be found in a new concept of human freedom according to Jünger.[33]

"The locus of freedom is to be found elsewhere than in mere opposition, as nowhere that any flight can lead to. We have called it the forest."[34] For Jünger, "forest" means a fertile field of possibilities or a "treasure chest of Being." It is understood here as fertile soil that continually brings forth new "harvests."[35] We encounter here Jünger's concept of the earth as fertile field of possibilities, from which the worker type as representative of the gestalt of the worker arises (see Chapter 3). The one who turns off the blazed trails of prevailing categories of the *Animal Rationale* (*Libertè*) on the one hand and the technological world we live in on the other (automaticity, calculation) into the forest is called free. This freedom defies in the end all calculation and automatization and is found in the individual. "In the triumph of the individual a power liberates itself that is immeasurable, freedom in the deepest sense, that mocks every cipher."[36] This freedom is no longer found in the individual *as* individual but in the singularity of the individual as *connected* with the earth as a fertile field of possibilities; the earth is an intellectual contingent that precedes intellectual freedom.[37] The earth is a fertile field of possibilities and its variability and fertility resists technological control. "The home of freedom is the infinite."[38]

With this, it becomes clear that the forest passage is not only a death march but provides access to the overflow of Being, in which the forest rebel finds his freedom to resist the perfection of technology:

> Freedom, however, does not live in emptiness; it resides much more in the disordered and unseparated, in those areas that are organizable, but aren't counted among organization. We want to call it 'the wilderness'; it is the space from which man hopes to be allowed to not only lead the battle, but also triumph. That is then clearly no longer a romantic wilderness. It is the primal source of his existence, the thicket from which he will break forth as a lion.[39]

It is the worker type, as son of the earth, that will invoke the earth as a fertile field of possibilities—the unseparated—for the new rise of the gestalt and in this sense is called free.

In the workshop landscape, with its preference for automatization and calculation, which is associated with high levels of un-freedom, the forest rebel fights for this new concept of freedom. This new concept of freedom enables the individual to resist the perfection of technology: "We may imagine an elite opening this battle for a new freedom, a battle that will demand great sacrifices and which should leave no room for any interpretations that are unworthy of it."[40] Individual freedom is understood here as the primordial substance of human existence, that "ensures fertility, again and again."[41] It is this experience of the primal creative force of man that will initiate the forest passage: "A person scraping by, if not in an actual wasteland then in a wasted zone such as an industrial city, to whom a mere glimmer, a brief whiff of the immense power of being is imparted—such a person begins to sense that something is missing in his life. This is the prerequisite for him to start searching."[42]

With this, it also becomes clear that the forest is not primarily a geographical location:

> In reality, it is concealed in every individual, entrusted to him in code, so that he might understand himself, in his deepest, supra-individual power. This is the goal of every teaching that is worthy of the name. Let matter condense into veritable walls that seem to block all prospects: yet the abundance is closest at hand, for it lives within man as a gift, as a time-transcending patrimony. It is up to him how he will grasp the staff: to merely support him on his life path, or to serve him as a scepter.[43]

The freedom of the individual is to resist the threat of the perfection of technology and to find a way beyond the nihilist reduction and the perfection of technology,[44] based on this individual freedom.

As soon as the individual experiences the forest as a fertile field of possibilities, the perfection of technology is broken:

> The illusion of encirclement will also disappear therewith, and another solution will always become visible beyond the automatic one. Two paths will then be possible—or, in other words, free choice will have been restored. Even assuming the worst possible scenario of total ruin, a difference would remain like that between night and day. The one path climbs to higher realms, to self-sacrifice, or to the fate of those who fall with weapon in hand; the other sinks into the abysses of slave pens and slaughterhouses, where primitive beings are wed in a murderous union with technology. There are no longer destinies there—there are only numbers. To have a destiny, or to be classified as a number—this decision is forced upon all of us today, and each of us must face it *alone*.[45]

According to Jünger, the singularity of human existence always makes it possible to decide against the perfection of technology. The forest rebel longs for a higher form of life beyond the "empty doctrines" of nihilism[46] and resists "the automatism and *not* to draw its ethical conclusion, which is fatalism."[47] In this respect, we can say that the automatization and calculation of the perfection of technology is opposed to individual freedom according to Jünger. In his turn off the blazed trails, i.e., in the movement across the line, the forest turns out to be a fertile ground for a movement across the line,[48] which consists in the poetic naming of the hidden dimension of the gestalt of the worker.

In general, we can conclude therefore that Jünger's later essays are in line with his early work on the gestalt of the worker. A first main difference between his early and later work on the gestalt of the worker is that nihilism opens two ways in his later work, namely the perfection of technology and the poetry of the gestalt of the worker. The freedom of human existence consists precisely in this ability to decide for one of these two ways, i.e., the poetic leap away from the perfection of technology *across the line,* which consists in the poetic *naming* of the gestalt (cf. Chapter 11).

This brings us to a second main difference between Jünger's early and later work. In *The Worker,* the word "type" primarily concerns a new race of man—the worker type—which finds its determination in the representation of the gestalt of the worker. The worker type relates to the unity of the human being in the epoch of the worker. In his later work—in *Type, Name, Gestalt* from 1963 for instance—type has another meaning. The word "type" is not only related to the unity of the human race, but also to the unity of the relationships that can be delimited by names; the unity of the different lilies under the name "lily," the unity of the different types of cats under the name "cat" or "predator" for example. Because type as well as gestalt are brought together in relationship with poetic naming in *Type, Name, Gestalt,* we ask in the next section first about the poetic naming of the type, in order to conceive of Jünger's concept of the essence of language and the transformation of saying in his later work, i.e., the poetic naming of the gestalt of the worker.

Notes

1. *TNG*, 113.
2. *TNG*, 111–112.
3. *TNG*, 85.
4. *TNG*, 87, 112–113; *Arb*, 12; *ÜdL*, 256–261.
5. *TNG*, 116; cf. 122.
6. Jünger, Ernst, *An der Zeitmauer. Sämtliche Werke*, vol. 8 (Stuttgart: Klett-Cotta 1981), 632.
7. *ZM*, 633.
8. We call the position of the worker *metaphysical*, because human existence is understood here in its relation with the gestalt as a new turning of being. At the same time, it will become clear that this gestalt can no longer be understood as metaphysical in the sense of Heidegger.
9. *MM*, 387; cf. 332.
10. *MM*, 328.
11. *ZM*, 606.
12. Jünger, Ernst, *Der Waldgang. Sämtliche Werke*, vol. 7 (Stuttgart: Klett-Cotta, 1980), 308–309.
13. *ZM*, 543.
14. *ZM*, 632.
15. *ZM*, 526.
16. *ZM*, 540.
17. *MM*, 339.
18. With *the perfection of technology*, Jünger explicitly refers to the title of a book of his brother (*MM*, 361; *ZM*, 613). Jünger, F., *Die Perfektion der Technik* (Frankfurt am Main: Vittorio Klostermann, 1946). For a good introduction, see the work of Friedrich Georg Jünger, Geyer, A., *Friedrich Georg Jünger. Werk und Leben* (Wien und Leipzig: Karolinger Verlag, 2007).
19. cf. *MM*, 360.
20. *ZM*, 540; cf. 610.
21. *ZM*, 440.
22. cf. *ZM*, 547; 608.
23. *MM*, 322–323; cf. 334; 343.
24. *ZM*, 644.
25. *MM*, 325; *ZM*, 613.
26. *MM*, 325.
27. *ZM*, 637.
28. Note that Heidegger's ambition in *The Question Concerning Technology* is precisely a *free* relationship, not with technology but with the *essence* of technology (cf. Heidegger, Martin, *Vorträge und Aufsätze*, Gesamtausgabe, Band 7 (Frankfurt am Main: Vittorio Klostermann, 2000), 5–36 (tr. 3–35).
29. "This all changes the moment we abandon the statistics and turn to evaluative considerations. In this regard the solitary vote sets itself so far apart from all others that it even determines their market value. . . . Viewing the matter from this angle, it appears that the power of an individual in the midst of the undifferentiated masses is not inconsiderable" (*WG*, 297–298). An indication of the potential power of the individual is found by Jünger in the enormous police and intelligence force which is needed to control this minority and to which the individual is extradited.

30. cf. WG, 336–337.
31. ZM, 613.
32. WG, 304.
33. ZM, 528.
34. WG, 312–313.
35. WG, 366.
36. ZM, 529.
37. ZM, 564.
38. ZM, 577.
39. *ÜdL*, 273; cf. "The home of freedom is the limitless; it is a cosmic absolute that appears as something specific within the limited. That means that every state and every person deserves the freedom which comes to him and which he has earned. He who pushes forward into a new world not only has to explore the space, but also has the freedom to do so" (ZM, 577–578).
40. WG, 304–305; cf. "The forest passage leads to difficult decisions. The task of the forest rebel is to stake out vis-à-vis the Leviathan the measures of freedom that are to obtain in future ages. He will not get by this opponent with mere ideas" (WG, 344).
41. WG, 336; cf. 337.
42. WG, 340.
43. WG, 327.
44. "Caught in such straits, where is he to find a third element that will not simply go under in the movement? This can only be in his quality of being an individual, in his human Being, which remains unshaken" (WG, 325–326).
45. WG, 312.
46. WG, 335.
47. WG, 306.
48. *ÜdL*, 247–251.

11 Type, Name, Gestalt

11.1 Types and Names

In Jünger's systematic examination of the term "type" in *Type, Name, Gestalt*, it becomes directly clear that everything begins with the sensory perception. Perception does not however begin with the observation of different objects in reality, rather with the "limitless fertility of appearances" of nature. The original appearances still have no limits, separations and determinations, rather is described here as the unseparated. This unseparated of nature is the *ground* for separation, determination or limitation of objects in reality, but cannot itself be limited. The fertility does not let itself be recognized therefrom—in addition the unseparated must be able to be limited and determined—rather it can only be perceived. Perceiving the fertility of appearances is the point of departure of Jünger's poetics.[1]

The unseparatedness of nature brings forth separations and limitations (types) and thus does Jünger speak also of the "formative" and "type-setting power of the universe": "the type-setting power directly affects perception. It first generates surprise and then a nameless recognition: intuition. 'Intueor' is a verb that the ancients knew only in the passive for good reason. Naming follows after it: things bear no names, rather names are given to them. The world of names differs from that of images: it is a reflection."[2] Separations or limits (types) thus emerge from the inexhaustible wealth of appearances (the unseparated), which according to Jünger astonish us and are then intuitively understood as types.

This astonishing of the type harks back to the metaphysical tradition. In the metaphysical tradition, the origin of philosophical contemplation is found in an *aporia* in relation to the identity of things, whereby the philosophical question of the *Being* (*idea*, category) of things develops (cf. Chapter 4). According to Jünger, this Being (type) is understood intuitively. In looking at lions, tigers and house cats for example, we encounter relationships that enable the different types of cats—lions, panthers, house cats—to appear as unity, namely as "cat" or as "predator."[3]

The naming of the type by man follows the intuitive understanding of the type. The name is reflected back "to the intuitively understood type, as an answer of the inner disposition of man towards an inner image."[4] The intuitive understanding of the type must be "completed" by the type-setting naming of man.[5] The name is a reflection of the representation of the type, and through this naming the previously anonymously understood type is *repeated and confirmed.* "The choosing and naming of types are subordinate to free will; if both are successful, the chosen word confirms the type-setting power of the unseparated."[6]

Jünger compares the repetition and confirmation of the type through naming with the development of an image:

> The word "develop" can also be taken in the sense that photographers apply it: the image of an object is developed after light has been cast onto film. Without development, the picture would rest in darkness, unseizable, without contour and nameless. It would be the same as the innumerable pictures that, without our ever having paid them attention, have touched our retinas. Naming means: developing from the nameless, means choosing.[7]

Out of the multiplicity of the types that show themselves, a type will be contoured, described, branded or "fixed" in another way through human naming. Therefore, the type *is* first in the actual sense of the word due to the *naming* of this type.[8] An example is the name "cat," in whose light different cats appear *as* cats. The name "cat" becomes with that a model by which we measure for our assessment of other cats. The name defines not only real but also possible and self-invented cats. Therefore, Jünger says: "The perceived is disguised by it with a cloak; it is enfeoffed. It is not given reality through that, but function."[9] With that it becomes clear that language here is not primarily conceptualized as statement or proposition, rather as name. The intellectual power of man exists in the type-setting or naming of the type.

The difference between type and name exists according to Jünger in that type, in contrast to name, does not lie in the "domain" of man. "Due to this power he may not be able to decide about the reality of the things he encounters, but he can determine the order, scope and duration that he wishes to grant the perceived as taken 'for real.'"[10] The freedom of man exists in the choice, articulation and fixing of each type that are taken for meaningful and true. Does Jünger not testify with that to a subjective concept of language in which man is the namegiver and the name only an instrument in the hand of man?

There is nevertheless good reason to nuance the role of man in naming. Jünger says first, that we are not allowed to apply our measurements to nature, rather we must follow the laws of the universe.[11] Second, Jünger says that names are not invented *by us,* rather erupt *from the nameless.* Types that are understood intuitively emerge from the unseparated and are then established through naming:

> But the earth must always contribute . . . He [man] has to contribute. Without the word with which he exercises his type-setting force,

only a new unfolding of the earth would follow as has already occurred multiple times—wonderful in every way but without isolated, higher consciousness, without art and free thinking, without worship, either. That is all testified to through image and name.[12]

This name is not a subjective invention of man, rather in it plays,

> an inexhaustible back and forth [. . .] between that which is shown to man and that which he grasps—between the limitless fertility in which the world introduces its puzzle and the manner in which man answers. The type-setting power of the universe corresponds to a perceiving power and vigilance of man: he first answers that which is shown to him in images with astonishment and then with the word, the original image of the work of art.[13]

This reciprocity between the named (the intuitively understood but still nameless type) and the name shows that the name is no subjective invention, rather a creative act that is responsive to the type. "Answering does not mean anything other than: giving the word back."[14] Creative man sees the things "in their fresh state"[15]—the intuitive understanding of the type—creates the name directly from the nameless and exerts his type-setting force—naming—on the unseparated.

On the one hand, every name of the type stands in the end related to the unseparated as a type-creating power:

> Where we penetrate into nature, it happens with the aid of names. We are like the miner, who moves in the shaft. What is for him the mining light is for us names—but exactly as the shaft leads deeper and further, or in any case could lead in every direction than to a place on which the light falls, so is the nameless eternally greater than everything that we can lift out of it.[16]

The names are traces and symbols "on the way to the absolute, which is inaccessible."[17] On the other hand, every name of the type is in the end related to the intuitively understood type. The types as well as the names used to name them change. Every attempt to fix the type is therefore only an approximation of the type. The freedom of man exists in the naming of the given type, but this name always remains in the end related to the type: "Every name sooner or later departs from us. But that which preceded the naming remains with us, and we with it."[18] With that it becomes clear that the intuition of the type is given priority. Do we not have to conclude then, that Jünger, contrary to his early work, embraces a metaphysical concept of language in his later work?

Jünger's differentiation between the intuitive concept of the type and the free act of naming harks back to the metaphysical tradition. According to the metaphysical concept of language, the name is an *expression* (reflection, representation) of an inner image (*idea, mental image,* type) that is given. In addition, the inner image lies for Jünger not within the domain of man, rather it is given, while the name as expression of this inner image lies within the domain of man: "The image rests deeper than the name. When we arrive in a foreign land, we must let another word imprint us; but we do not need to learn anew what a lily is."[19] Jünger's differentiation between the inner image of a "pipe," for example, and the different expressions of this type in different languages—"Pfeife," "Pipe" and "Pijp"—is embedded within the metaphysical tradition. The name is mainly an expression that is ultimately determined conventionally.[20] With that it appears to be that Jünger's concept of language with regards to the type is indeed not subjective, but remains embedded in the metaphysical tradition. Do we not encounter here a third distinction between Jünger's early and later work? While he takes leave of the law of the homecoming of metaphysics, in which the permeability of being and thought is re-established through the naming of the type and gestalt, as we have seen in Chapter 9, he seems to embrace this metaphysical concept of language in *Type, Name, Gestalt.*

Man is not only master of names. The name is also a "transient medium"[21] or called an "aid in the moving"[22] that makes "the things named so . . . subservient."[23] With that, Jünger also appears to testify to an instrumental metaphysical concept of language regarding the type, mainly as instrumental representation of the type. How can we then still assert that Jünger's concerns are situated in another concept of the essence of language and the transformation of saying?

11.2 Nihilism and the Experience of the Unseparated

We must, however, remember that Jünger's basic experience is that of nihilism. In *Across the Line,* Jünger argues that we already crossed the line. But this crossing doesn't prove a new metaphysical position: "The crossing of the line, the passage of the zero point, divides the play; it indicates the middle, but not the end. The certainty is still far in the distance. One can hope for that certainty."[24] According to Jünger, we already left the metaphysical position of the *Animal Rationale* and crossed the line, but we didn't arrive at a new position across the line yet; we are still living in the *interim* of the workplace landscape. He brings to our attention the decline of the type and dynamization of life; that means, *there is no type* in our era of nihilism, much less the possibility of type-setting or naming of the type. The decline of the type correlates with a "reduction of the type-setting ability of man."[25] In the workshop landscape there is no type, which means that Jünger speaks of an instrumental metaphysical concept of language regarding the type, but does not take this concept on in *Type, Name, Gestalt.*

Jünger refers in contrast to something else, which is only possible due to the facticity of the decline of the type. While man first responded to the intuitively understood type through naming, the decline of the type in our era first gives access to the type-creating power in the unseparated, which means to the unseparated itself as the origin of types. While Jünger calls this "nameless life" and the "elementary" in his early work, he calls it the unseparated or the forest in his later work as we have seen. The forest rebel's movement across the line or his forest passage points to a "change in attention of being"[26] in our lifetime, namely a shift from the type as spiritual power to the "last approximation of the unseparated."[27] In this approximation, all separations (types) are destroyed—Jünger compares this destruction with the whiting-out of an image by a painter—and man approximates the unseparated, in the end fusing with it.[28] The forest passage makes clear that the passage across the line doesn't result in a new metaphysical position, and the im-possibility to achieve this new metaphysical position provides an indirect access to the hidden dimension of types and names, the unseparated. It can be seen as approximation of the unseparated, in which the actualization of the possible—a new turning of being—can be prepared.[29] Because of this positive experience of the fertility of the unseparated, the dissatisfaction with nihilism or perfection of technology increases and calls for a third way beyond the nihilist critique of the *Animal Rationale* and the embracing of technology, which consists in the preparation of this new turning of being. This third way requires our fusion with this unseparated.

What is the meaning of this fusion? In contrast to the type, gestalts are not derived from appearance, rather, they come from the unseparated as the unmeasured. The meaning of the approximation of the unseparated is therefore, that these approximations enable the encounter with a new attention of being, namely the encounter with the gestalt of the worker, in the case that it emerges. This is why the next section will examine first the gestalt and naming of the gestalt in *Type, Name, Gestalt*, in order to fully understand his concept of language, before we come back to Jünger's transformation of saying in Chapter 12.

11.3 Gestalt and Name

In the second section of *Type, Name, Gestalt*, Jünger thematizes the naming of the gestalt. There, he says that much is anticipated with the relationship of type and name, which also counts for the relationship between gestalt and name. He makes the difference between gestalt and name clear through an example, is basically like the difference between "lily" and "plant." The name "lily" articulates a type that represents the different lilies—iris, tiger lily or white lily (cf. Section 11.1). There are different plant families that are to be differentiated from each other and can be compared with each other: "If the lily were not available to or known by us, it would not stunt our concept of the plant. However, if we did not know "the plant," our knowledge of the lily would also naturally not apply. The lily thrives within an order, the plant harbors orders. The lily forms a family, the plant a kingdom."[30] The plant is named a gestalt.

According to Jünger the difference between types and gestalts is to be understood on the one hand gradually and on the other hand qualitatively.[31] He says that the reduction of separations leads to the gestalt: "It leads from object (the shown lily) to the type (the named lily) to the gestalt (plant) and finally into the unseparated. The answers become broader, and at the same time the separations are reduced."[32] For example, we understand a "worker" first as a person who works (object). But the worker can also be addressed as type or race (cf. Chapter 1). If the word were now also addressed as gestalt, then a system or kingdom would be understood. As the gestalt of the worker in *The Worker* is addressed as a new unity or standard that can guarantee a new security and rank order of life, so does Jünger speak here of systems and kingdoms that give the type a higher meaning. We have seen already in *The Worker* that the gestalt is the source of meaning and stamps a meaningful order (cf. Chapter 1).

But we can conceive of the gestalt as not only more comprehensive than the type. "The transition to them leads not through quantities, and can therefore not be reached through better instrumentation. Much more the qualities are to be grasped, which ultimately give every kind of expansion meaning. For that, one does not need a new optics, but a new eye."[33] A new eye is necessary, which means that not only the appearance of things has changed, but also human responsiveness to it. "The naming of types is connected to a being taken possession of by man. Where in contrast gestalts are named with names, we may assume that man has to be taken into possession by the gestalt."[34] While the type is the unity in which the different lilies appear as unity, namely *as* lily, man is included in the stamping of the gestalt, that is, it relates to the appearance of the world and their responsiveness as *belonging together*, as *unity*. The unity of the gestalt is therefore called system-forming or light-giving,[35] for in the light of the gestalt of the worker the world shows itself as technological space for human responsiveness *as* worker type. Exactly therein lies the difference between type and gestalt.[36]

However, if we had to establish in Section 11.1 that there are no types and gestalts in our era of nihilism, can we then articulate the gestalt as a common feature through the *reduction* of the singularity of the different types? We are to understand the reduction of separations in our lifetime of nihilism as the *destruction* of separations, "as last approximations of the un-separated." According to Jünger, gestalts emerge from the unseparated, and only due to the destruction of separations (decline of types); the area from which gestalts can emerge is unlocked, the hidden dimension of the gestalt. "The movement towards the material, even where it appears as nihilism, must lead to a layer in which the material answers."[37] This answer of the material—Jünger speaks also of a "progress of material"—is the rise of the gestalt, which emerges from the unseparated.

In the case that the gestalt actually arises from the unseparated, then this is not intuitively understood by man as the type is. The concept of the gestalt exceeds the capacity of man and requires in contrast a taking possession of man by the gestalt: "This encounter [with the gestalt] is more shaking than that with the types: As the type announces itself in the consciousness through intuition, so does the gestalt through divination."[38] In contrast to the type, man has no position opposite the gestalt, rather he is *included* in the shaking of the gestalt. That means that this shaking of the gestalt applies not only to the separations or limitations of the world, but also the identity of man himself.

With that, the meaning of the change in attention in the human spirit shows itself (cf. Section 11.1). In the workshop landscape man can only approximate the unseparated. Through that he contributes to the destruction of the separations of man and world (decline of the type); he "leaves behind his body, his I."[39] Through this destruction of the separated, man fuses with the unseparated and he experiences for the time being the silent power of this unseparated in himself.[40] According to Jünger, this is an important fusion, basically the condition for the possibility to poetically name the gestalt: "Man is capable of grasping and with that of capturing gestalts only because something related, yes, the same, lives in him."[41] Man experiences this related and same—the nameless as the unseparated in man—first due to his last approximation of the unseparated, that is, due to his fusing with it. Merged with the unseparated, man can first be called upon by the gestalt, in the case that it emerges.[42] In this "divination of the gestalt"; man is named anew,[43] he finds his identity and determination: "The appearance of the one [gestalt] is more forceful than that of the multiple; it overwhelms the cognitive spirit. Powers of perception and vision unite in the encounter, and with that cognition fuses with recognition: 'Is that you?—That's you!' "[44]

With that the question arises as to whether the gestalt can be set by man in a way similar to the type by way of naming. Jünger says about the encounter with the gestalt: "We will address it after a moment of silence with the strongest name that is available to us. Thereby our silence is applied to something different than our word. A shadow of the gestalt has grazed us lightly: the overwhelming."[45] Although man names the gestalt, it is not *set* by man through naming, in contrast to the type. "Here fails the dominance of man, fails the spirit with his type-setting force. The gestalt can be experienced, but not be set."[46] In *Maxima Minima* he writes, "that the gestalt begins spontaneously to stir in the material and emerges from it at a certain moment."[47] Although the naming of the gestalt does not lie in the domain of man, he is not to be thought of only as *receiver* or as *object* of the gestalt. According to Jünger, the gestalt first *is* in the actual sense of the word when it is captured by man.[48] This relationship between the gestalt and the name harks back to *The Worker* (cf. Chapter 1 and Chapter 9). The gestalt erupts from the unseparated, but needs the human naming in order to emerge from its a-nonymous character. "Something new appears not only in man, but it also is named by him and with that not only recognized, but also acknowledged. Therefore, a peculiar responsibility lies in every naming, in every bestowal of a name."[49]

The responsibility of man does not exist in the setting of the gestalt, but rather in *living* and *acting* in the light of this name of the gestalt: "In order to act as the gestalt . . . other things must correspond to it—the creation with a word of works, acts and thoughts, sacrifices and love, history, destiny."[50] The naming of the gestalt of the worker exists in the active *formation* of the world as technological space for man as type of the worker, that is, in the recognition of his identity as representative of the gestalt of the worker. In this representation, name and gestalt are *one*.[51]

How do name and gestalt then relate to one another? Jünger says, "In image and in word, in the gestalts and in their names, two outposts encounter each other. Behind the image stands the unseparated in its abundance, while behind the word, man in his silent power."[52] Here, Jünger speaks of outposts, because he understands the gestalt as well as the name as a separation or delimitation from the unseparated: "Every gestalt is only a possibility, an oasis in it."[53] If we encounter the gestalt, then this encounter leads to a moment of silence, followed by the naming of the gestalt. Just as the gestalt is rooted in the unseparated, so is the name a separation or branching-off of the language that is for its part rooted in silence, that is, in the unseparated of man. "Man limits and separates through his word, but the word juts from the depths, juts from the silence. There rests the inexpressible, rests a cosmic fundamental power that man possesses via language."[54] Jünger concentrates on the equality of the gestalt and the name, that is, that naming is to be understood *iso-pathically*.[55] In poetic naming, these outposts fuse and become identical.[56]

11.4 Conclusion: Jünger's New Non-Metaphysical Concept of Language

We have already seen Jünger's concept of the nature of language in *The Worker*. There it became clear that the attuning of our technological reality as technological space and the human responsiveness as the worker type through the gestalt of the worker is to be understood as the design of the name "work." The name "work" articulates a meaningful world. Jünger's altered relationship to the nature of language shows itself in this language of signs of the gestalt. This is confirmed in his later work, as we have seen in this chapter. Although the naming of the type in *Type, Name, Gestalt* has unmistakable metaphysical connotations (cf. Section 11.1), the naming of the gestalt leads to a closer determination of the Jüngerian concept of the nature of language.

Unlike in *The Worker*, language in *Type, Name, Gestalt* is not brought into connection with the gestalt in a direct, but rather an indirect manner. Jünger speaks here not of the language of signs of the gestalt, for language here is described explicitly as *human*. But both the name and the gestalt are of equal birth insofar that both have their origins in the unseparated. If the name and the gestalt encounter one another in the poetic leap away from the perfection of technology and across the line, i.e., in the poetic naming of the gestalt of the worker, a meaningful world is then articulated. The encounter of the gestalt and the name, however, not only articulates a meaningful world (light), for this remains surrounded by the hidden horizon of meaning of the unseparated (darkness).[57] In that Jünger concentrates on the unseparated as the joint origin of names and gestalts in *Type, Name, Gestalt,* it becomes on the one hand clear that Jünger no longer thinks of the gestalt metaphysically as a *present* form, rather as an articulation of a meaningful world. On the other hand it becomes clear that the name cannot be understood as an instrument in the hand of man, nor as an expression of the gestalt. Language is equally original as the gestalt; that means that language is not only light-giving, but concerns a *finite* articulation of the unseparated (light). "That which man conceives, also the innermost and largest, comes from the nameless abundance that he addresses and delimits with names. This abundance is larger than any idea; it can indeed be delimited through names, but can be grasped neither in its scope nor in its depth. The names are like probes in a massif; they draw like cups from the sea."[58] Jünger's non-metaphysical concept of the nature of language exists thus in that it articulates a meaningful world (light) that however is surrounded by the hidden horizon of meaning and remains housed therein (darkness).

Notes

1. His brother Friedrich Georg called him a visionary person, because his works are to be understood as "exercises in perceiving" (Jünger, *Die Perfektion der Technik*, 10). Günter Figal calls Jünger's approach therefore a "phenomenology oriented towards last and thus original appearances" (Figal, Günter, "Gestalt und Gestaltwandel—Ernst Jünger und Goethe," *Jünger Studien* 5 2011: 20). Although Jünger's approach can be called phenomenological, the question remains as to whether the unseparated that evades every separation and limitation can at all be shown phenomenologically. This also explains Jünger's efforts concerning the right access regarding the topic of his poetics; crystallography, stereoscopy, trigonometry etc. (cf. Figal, "Flugträume und höhere Trigonometrie," 175–188; Gorgone, "Naturphilosophie und stereoskopische Sicht bei Ernst Jünger," 21–39).
2. *TNG*, 100.
3. One can ask whether we already have to require the unity of the type in order to be able at all to compare the lion with the tiger and not man or cars, for example. But then the general characteristics of the cat-type (type) cannot also be achieved through abstraction.
4. *TNG*, 104.
5. *TNG*, 112.
6. *TNG*, 99; cf. "A name stamps a type, one that already exists before its stamping, waiting. The naming takes it and exposes it. The naming is a compliant stamping. In it repeats the creation of the nameless, intuitively understandable type that already always is anticipated" (Figal, "Gestalt und Gestaltwandel," 17).
7. *TNG*, 88–89.
8. *TNG*, 102; cf. 115, 138.
9. *TNG*, 109.
10. *TNG*, 109.

11. *TNG*, 126.
12. *TNG*, 131.
13. *TNG*, 90.
14. *TNG*, 140.
15. *TNG*, 100.
16. *TNG*, 141.
17. *TNG*, 126.
18. *TNG*, 101.
19. *TNG*, 137.
20. Cf. *TNG*, 140.
21. *TNG*, 128.
22. *TNG*, 141.
23. *TNG*, 151.
24. *ÜdL*, 261.
25. *TNG*, 112.
26. *TNG*, 113.
27. *TNG*, 119.
28. *TNG*, 119, 140.
29. *ÜdL*, 267.
30. *TNG*, 137; It is clear that Jünger's example of the plant is inspired by Goethe's concept of the "original plant" *(Urpflanze)* (cf. Figal, "Gestalt und Gestaltwandel").
31. *TNG*, 136.
32. *TNG*, 138.
33. *TNG*, 139.
34. *TNG*, 161.
35. *TNG*, 157.
36. Cf. Section 1 for this difference between type and gestalt in *The Worker*.
37. *TNG*, 125.
38. *TNG*, 152.
39. *TNG*, 164.
40. Cf. *TNG*, 170; *WG*, 327–328.
41. *TNG*, 164.
42. *TNG*, 159.
43. *TNG*, 153.
44. *TNG*, 164.
45. *TNG*, 150.
46. *TNG*, 155.
47. *MM*, 351.
48. *TNG*, 164.
49. *TNG*, 160.
50. *TNG*, 161.
51. *TNG*, 166.
52. *TNG*, 156.
53. *TNG*, 165–166.
54. *TNG*, 159.
55. cf. "Like heals like—The saying also applies to the unseparated, which hides in man as well as in the material" (*TNG*, 118).
56. "On the primal ground, the word is no longer form, no longer a key. It becomes identical with being. It becomes creative energy. *That* is the source of its immense, unmintable power" (*WG*, 373; Heumakers and Oudemans, *De horizon van Buitenveldert*, 180).
57. With that an affinity reveals itself between Jünger's concept of the gestalt and the Heideggerian gestalt in his *Origin of the Work of Art* (cf. Chapter 8).
58. *TNG*, 159.

12 Living and Acting in Light of the Absence of the Gestalt

In the previous sections, we have seen that Jünger is underway to a "non-metaphysical" concept of the essence of language in his early work, which is further articulated in his later work. We are sufficiently prepared now to answer the question, to what extent Jünger speaks the same language "in the space on this side of the line and beyond it," as Heidegger suggests. Does Jünger's language deny the overcoming of nihilism in his later work as Heidegger asserts, because his language remains housed in the metaphysical? Or are Jünger's approximations of the unseparated to be understood as a transformation of saying and therefore as an "overcoming of metaphysics," namely the articulation of the unseparated as the hidden dimension of the gestalt?

We have already seen in *The Worker* that the transformation of saying consists in poetic naming (cf. Chapter 9). Although the naming of the type in *Type, Name, Gestalt* has unmistakably metaphysical traits in the broader sense of Heidegger (cf. Chapter 11), the naming of the gestalt leads to a further determination of the altered nature of language. The shift in attention in the human spirit of which Jünger speaks refers to this transformation of saying. The transformation of saying reveals itself in the last approximations of the unseparated. On the one hand man can, fused with the unseparated, first be called upon by the gestalt, *if* it rises out of the unseparated. On the other hand, the gestalt first *is* due to its iso-pathic representation by way of the naming that rises out of the same unseparated, that is, due to our living and acting in light of the name of the gestalt. Do we have to conclude then, that Jünger's altered nature of language consists precisely in this poetic naming of the gestalt? Yes and no.

Although name and gestalt are of equal birth, this doesn't mean that they occur simultaneously. In the technological age in which technology becomes perfect, there are no types and gestalts, and this has consequences for the way we can conceptualize Jünger's transformation of saying. "Man enters into new relations, which he does not at first grasp with his consciousness, let alone through their configuration—an eye for the meaning of the scene comes only with time. And only then does sovereignty become possible."[1] This means that in the age of technology we currently live in, the transformation of saying cannot consist in the poetic naming of the gestalt. This is confirmed in *Type, Name, Gestalt,* in which the gestalt isn't named: "Although attempts to fill the blank do not fail, its contemplation does not belong to the topic of this book, which focuses more on its prerequisites."[2] The impossibility of naming the gestalt means that the transformation of saying consists in the *preparation* of a poetic leap away from the perfection of technology *across the line,*[3] in which the gestalt is named. What is prepared is the poetic naming of the gestalt by the approximation of the unseparated as the hidden dimension of the gestalt. In fact, the impossibility to name the gestalt in the technological age is *positive,* because this im-possibility makes the approximation of the unseparated possible to begin with. Because of this im-possibility to name the gestalt, our efforts are no longer focused on direct approximations of the gestalt; contrary to a metaphysical presentation or representation of this gestalt, our efforts focus now on the unseparated as the hidden dimension of the gestalt. In other words, the approximation of the unseparated is only possible *because* of the im-possibility of naming the gestalt in the technological age in which technology becomes perfect. In this respect, Jünger's transformation of saying limits itself to the "prerequisites" of the naming of the gestalt. It concerns our living and acting in light of the *absence* of the gestalt. The "metaphysical" gestalt is overcome therein, and the emergence of a non-metaphysical gestalt is prepared.

This transformation of saying consists first of all in the fight for a new form of freedom, which is embedded in the unseparated as we have seen in Chapter 10, and secondly in the provisional *experimentation* with the unseparated as an inexhaustible field of *possibilities* for a new turning of being amidst the perfection of technology.[4] The third way beyond the nihilistic critique of the *Animal Rationale* and the embracing of the perfection of technology in Jünger's later work consists precisely in this free experimentation in light of the absence of the gestalt. In the end, the goal of this poetic experimentation is, "to ward off the force" of the perfection of technology by naming the gestalt, but without a divination by this gestalt, it consists in the free experimentation with a *possible* gestalt as preparation of the occurrence of the gestalt in the case of a new turning of being.

Although human existence is in the end not capable of naming the gestalt without a call or demand by this gestalt itself, it is our elementary freedom to choose this third way: "'Here and now' is the forest rebel's motto—he is the spirit of free and independent action. As we saw, only a small fraction of the mass populace can be counted among this type, and yet these few form a small elite able to resist the automatism, on whom the pure use of force must fail. This is the old freedom in the garments of the new times."[5] In an environment in which the technological age becomes perfect, it is the ultimate responsibility of the individual to decide for this third way beyond the nihilist criticism and the perfection of technology.[6]

In this chapter, we pose questions about Jünger's transformation of saying *within* the perfection of technology. How exactly can we encounter the unseparated amidst the perfection of technology and what is the role of human existence *within* the age in which technology becomes perfect? This is also the main question of Jünger's essay *Across the Line* from 1950: "The individual is pulled into the spell of nihilistic tension and cut down. It is therefore worth examining which behavior can be recommended to him in this battle."[7] We assume that Jünger's third way can teach us how his transformation of saying in the age of technology has to be understood. To this end, we explore Jünger's second main work *At the Time Wall* from 1959 in this last section of this chapter.

12.1 Jünger's Transformation of Saying in *At the Time Wall:* A Methodological Reading

Right at the start of *At the Time Wall,* Jünger introduces his method. With the example of the occurrence of the massive attention for horoscopes that emerged during that period, he introduces a distinction between new phenomena—the massive attention paid to horoscopes itself for instance— and another type of attention which is aroused by this phenomenon; the occurrence of the massive attention paid to horoscopes as a *sign of time,* i.e., as an indication of a different style of thinking about time in astrology when we compare it with traditional clocktime. In the first situation, we can ask for all kinds of causes for this new phenomenon, like psychological, social, cultural causes, etc., of the occurrence of the massive attention paid to horoscopes. Jünger is not interested in this question, but on the contrary in the sign of time which is at stake in the occurrence of new phenomena; the occurrence of the massive attention paid to horoscopes arouses the question how this emerging style of thinking is *connected* with the seemingly contradictory style of thinking which is at stake in clocktime. This distinction provides a first clue regarding Jünger's turning of saying. He is not interested in the meaning of time that is at stake in astrology itself, but in the *connection* between or *unity* of the different meanings of time.

Regarding the unity between astrological time and clocktime, Jünger argues:

> Scientific and astrological thought can as a matter of fact become very similar, just as a horoscope and a clock are similar. But that always remains an analogy with regard to a third, something reigning. A whale and a fish are also similar to each other, and indeed "deceptively" similar; the relationships, however, do not lie in them, rather in a third—let us call it the sea or the spirit of Neptune and its influence. The fact, though, that the issue centers on two models must remain held in consideration.[8]

This remark about the unity and difference between the two meanings of time in light of a "third" instance provides a second clue regarding Jünger's transformation of saying. The question about the unity of astrological time and clocktime should on the one hand acknowledge the fundamental *difference* between both meanings of time. In other words, it doesn't concern a metaphysical unity in which the differences are reduced to the same. At the same time, it turns out that Jünger is not even interested in this connection between the two meanings of time, but in the "third" instance in light of which the different meanings of time appear *as* the same. Jünger's example is comparable with the examples we already encountered in *Type, Name, Gestalt*. Lilies and roses are different but appear as connected in light of a third, namely "plant." In *At the Time Wall*, Jünger is interested in this third instance as well, namely the third instance in light of which clocktime and astrological time appear as connected, as unity.

In order to clarify his method to thematize this "third" instance in *At the Time Wall*, Jünger explicitly refers to his early work in *The Sicilian Letter to the Man in the Moon* that we discussed already in Chapter 4. In the *Sicilian Letter*, it becomes clear that Jünger is not primarily interested in the meaning of the moon *as* man in the moon nor in the moon *as* astronomical object, but in the unity of both meanings of the moon. Already in his early work, this interest in unity is not motivated by the wish to fuse these different meanings in favor of a new unity of the gestalt. In the *Sicilian Letter*, it turned out that the hidden dimension of the gestalt shows itself only indirectly in the stereoscopic view of *different* meanings of the moon.

If Jünger in *At the Time Wall* refers to his method in the *Sicilian Letter*, we can expect, first, that not astrological time versus clocktime is at stake in this book and, second, that the third instance has to be found in the hidden dimension of the gestalt. Jünger's transformation of saying in the technological age in which technology becomes perfect concerns the concept of the hidden dimension of the gestalt at the crossroads of astrological time and clocktime, i.e., *at the time wall*: "Both qualities can be united synoptically if the power of the spirit is capable of doing it. Then the leap, the leap backwards to the origin, is achieved, and a new dimension emerges stereoscopically from the perspectival covering of opposites, a new dimension that not only unites them spatially, but also heightens them qualitatively."[9] The stereoscopic view on the different meanings of time indirectly provides access to the hidden dimension of the gestalt as the third instance in the light of which these different meanings of time appear *as* the same. This preliminary exploration of Jünger's methodological remarks right at the start of *At the Time Wall* is important to keep in mind when reading the book.

At first sight namely, Jünger seems to concentrate on horoscopes and astrological time *as such* in *At the Time Wall*. According to Jünger, the meaning of astrological time is found in the combination of the "unshakeable passage of the world clock" and fleeting destiny,[10] i.e., "the moment and place of birth."[11] On the one hand, Jünger seems to describe astrological time as an *alternative* for clocktime. Clocktime is the prevalent conceptualization of time in the technological world of calculation and automatization we currently live in. According to Jünger, people who feel threatened by the perfection of technology are in need of a "supervening" so that life possesses meaning and sense.[12] The proponents of astrology are discontent with the perfection of technology and want to withdraw from clocktime and its categories of calculation and automatization: "The astrological principles stand in crass contrast to everything that we conduct and further extend as planning, norming, automation, traffic, comfort, insurance."[13]

Sometimes, Jünger even gives the impression that astrology provides access to the gestalt. He says:

> We approximate the astrological language of signs there where the characters acquire a power that break the personal character as well as the historical uniqueness. There, something appears to return, something long-familiar becomes temporally visible and grasped from the clouds by the people through reasons, rather as a gestalt that unveils itself.[14]

In this respect, the massive attention paid to horoscopes is considered here as a *revolutionary omen*. Astrological time is not only *contrary* to clocktime, but more important, gives an indication that in the end, human existence is not embedded in the perfection of technology but in cosmic existence: "If the significance of astrology only consisted in pointing man to the meaning of the great cycles and the attention of them, that would already be invaluable."[15] For Jünger, the occurrence of the massive attention paid to astrological time points at a counterbalance against the perfection of technology.

If we remember the methodological remarks at the beginning of *At the Time Wall*, however, we realize that the real meaning of the occurrence of the massive attention paid to horoscopes is not found in its being such a counterforce. Jünger is *not* interested in the concept of astrological time as such and is *not* looking for alternatives for clocktime in the technological world, which is consistent with our findings in the previous chapters. The ambition to slow down the perfection of technology is unavailing and although Jünger seems to be positive about the other style of thinking and the other style of spirit which is at stake in astrology, it doesn't make sense for him to decide between both meanings of time. Jünger's analysis of astrological time only serves the interest to *contrast* it with clocktime in order to have indirect access to the hidden dimension of the gestalt *via* these different meanings of time. In *At the Time Wall*, this is stated in the following way: "One should not venture to make a judgment about the reality of astrology. The debate about what is real in it becomes more revealing if one does not take part in it—if it is led onto a field on which two kinds of examining of the world abruptly collide like no other. That gives us an idea of the perfection of the debate's object, of the invisible world."[16] As in the *Sicilian Letter,* Jünger is primarily interested in the unity of astrological time and clocktime in his later work. The question whether the occurrence of the massive attention for horoscopes is a freak of fashion or a symptom of a real change in our concept of time cannot be answered according to Jünger, and instead, we should acknowledge the *co-existence* of both meanings of time as "neighboring sovereigns" with their own style, laws and consequences for human existence. As in the *Sicilian Letter,* he is primarily interested in the hidden dimension of the gestalt—which is called a "dormant depth" here[17]—that shows itself in the stereoscopic unity of the different meanings of time.

This primacy of the unity of the different meanings of time becomes clear if we turn to Jünger's discussion with Spengler in *At the Time Wall.* For Jünger, the different meanings of time represent different ages, epochs or time zones. There is an epoch in which clocktime with its calculations and automatizations is predominant—the age of technology we currently live in—and in this respect, the occurrence of the massive attention paid to horoscopes can be seen as a sign of time, i.e., as an indication of the decline of clocktime which is dominant in the technological age and the emergence of a new epoch in which human existence is connected again with the cyclical movements of the cosmos. Others have tried to analyze the decline and emergence of epochs in history, and Spengler is one of them.

Spengler's achievement in *The Decline of the West* from 1918 was analyzing the morphological relations and affinities within eight different cultures. His method can be compared with the intuitive understanding of the type we encountered in the previous section. Spengler discerns eight high cultures in history—the Babylonian, Egyptian, Chinese, Indian, Mexican, Classical, Arabian and Western culture—which evolve as organisms. Although Jünger appreciates Spengler's morphological efforts in *At the Time Wall,* he points at the fact that for Spengler these cultures have no relation to each other. They concern eight cultures that successively emerge and fade away. Contrary to Spengler, Jünger asks:

> But now this belongs to the peculiarity of the human spirit that the ordering and apposition of the similar occupies him greatly, but does not satisfy him, as long as the question about the source of the comparison and the question of the common composition of acts and occurences of the great performance remains open. Pure comparison creates relations, not standards. The question remains as to the inner unity of the multi-faceted appearance and procedures beyond these similarities.[18]

According to Jünger, the ability to recognize a morphological unity or type like a high culture in history is one thing, but it is another thing to recognize the connection between or unity of these different cultures. In other words, it is one thing to grasp a new meaning of time in the occurrence of the massive attention for horoscopes, but it is another thing to ask for the unity between astrological time and clocktime in the technological age we currently live in. In order to capture this unity, the morphological genius is not sufficient but in need of an additional synoptical genius according to Jünger. This synoptical genius is found in the stereoscopic method in which the two meanings of time appear as unity in light of the hidden dimension of the gestalt. In *At the Time Wall*, this gestalt is called the archimedial point in light of which astrological time and clocktime appear as unity.

As in his early work, this archimedial point cannot be understood as a metaphysical idea, i.e., cannot consist in a metaphysical conceptualization of the gestalt. This becomes clear if we turn to Jünger's discussion of Herodotus, the founding father of history, in *At the Time Wall*:

> Something else was before him, was mythical night. But this night was not dark, rather more of a dream, and knew another connection of man and experiences as the historical consciousness and his separate power. It brings the dawn in Herodotus' work. It stands on the ridge of a mountain that separates day and night: not only two times, but also two kinds of time, two kinds of light.[19]

Herodotus can be seen as the beginning of the epoch of historical time, in which clocktime is dominating the historical consciousness of the *Animal Rationale*. The situation of Herodotus is that he stands at the crossroads of mythical time and historical time, but already crossed the line. He already entered historical time at the other side of the time wall and looks back to mythical time. As Herodotus stands on a ridge with the darkness of mythical time behind him and the brightness of the historical consciousness of the *Animal Rationale* in front of him, we stand on a similar ridge according to Jünger. The technological world we currently live in no longer allows the *Animal Rationale* to be inserted in the context of the historical consciousness, which means that we left the epoch of the *Animal Rationale*. There is, however, also a great difference between Herodotus's situation and our situation:

> Herodotus looked back from the dawn of history to the mythical night. The new light cast a strong glow that itself fell onto the gods. There is a historical Christ, but not a historical Jupiter. We in contrast stand in the midnight of history; the clock has struck 12 and we look out into a darkness in which future things loom. This view is led from darkness by heavy ideas. It is the hour of death, but also the hour of birth.[20]

The difference between our situation and the one of Herodotus is that he obtained a new metaphysical position at the other side of the time wall—the historical consciousness of the *Animal Rationale*—and looks back to the mythical time which is now foreign and inaccessible for him. We, on the contrary, already left the historical consciousness of the *Animal Rationale* behind but still slander on *this* side of the time wall: "Herodotus' situation repeats itself with reversed signs. Herodotus looks out from the historical space that he had just entered, back to the mythical. He does it shyly. The same shyness is necessary here today where it looms beyond the time wall.

Danger slumbers in every naming."[21] The other side of the time wall is still concealed in darkness, i.e., the gestalt is hidden from us. On the one hand, this makes clear that the archimedial point of the gestalt is not found in a metaphysical idea, but concerns the hidden dimension of the gestalt. On the other hand, we have seen that the im-possibility of naming the gestalt at the time wall is positive, because this im-possibility to name the gestalt at the other side of the time wall enables us to focus on the unseparated as the hidden dimension of the gestalt. It is this hidden dimension of the gestalt that is called the archimedial point, and because this dimension is at the same time called archimedial *and* hidden, we can no longer conceive it in terms of the metaphysical tradition.

In *At the Time Wall*, this hidden dimension of the gestalt is conceived in terms of the earth's history. Like the unseparated, the earth's history is a fertile field of possibilities from which the epoch of mythical time and the epoch of historical time emerged, and from which the time of the worker will occur one day according to Jünger. The importance of the methodological remarks at the beginning of *At the Time Wall* can become clear now, because the stereoscopic method concerns the unity of different articulations of time in the earth history: astrological time and clocktime. We don't need the stereoscopic method, however, to articulate time as astrological time versus time as clocktime, but these *different* meanings of time provide indirect access to this earth's history in which clocktime and astrological time emerge and fade away. This earth history is the horizon of meaning of the different meanings of time, in which light time as astrological time and time as clocktime appear as unity, i.e., as order.

With this, it becomes clear that Jünger's transformation of saying within the technological age does not consist in the poetic naming of the gestalt, but in the stereoscopic method to have access to the unseparated or earth history as hidden dimension of the gestalt.

> Perceiving gestalts requires a more thorough scaffolding than the one prime optics, for to see and describe or even paint the gestalt is always only its signature, not its essence. If the eye has recorded the signs in their forceful inexhaustibility, then it must rather close the eyelid to receive an idea from the unity, which can always only remain an approximation: a cloaked and dormant counterpoint of the restless revolving world. . . . To name it is the actual risk of our time.[22]

Although the naming of the gestalt is the actual risk of our time, it presupposes a divination by this gestalt. Naming the gestalt too soon is also dangerous, for such a naming would obscure and mask its dimensional characteristics for the sake of an articulated meaning. In the technological age we currently live in, in which technology becomes perfect, the hidden dimension of the gestalt is only indirectly accessible. This hidden dimension of the gestalt only allows itself to be seen in indirect ways and only approximately if we simultaneously look—stereoscopically—at the different meanings of time. In *At the Time Wall,* we are at the crossroads of time as astrological time and time as clocktime, and wander back and forth between the different articulated meanings of time. Continually on the way at the time wall, human experience experiences in passing and indirectly the hidden horizon of meaning, the history of the earth as hidden dimension of the gestalt. That means that the gestalt comes *nearer* as the inaccessible and hidden only *in* this twofold.

12.2 The Necessity of Poetic Experiments in the Absence of the Gestalt

With the importance of the stereoscopic method for Jünger's transformation of saying, it also becomes clear why Jünger stresses the importance of artistic experiments with the unseparated or earth history in his later work. In the technological age in which technology becomes perfect, clocktime with its calculations and automatizations becomes the absolute and only valid meaning of time. For Jünger, the omnipresence of clocktime is problematic. If our indirect access to the unseparated or earth history requires a stereoscopic view on *different* meanings of time, the monomanic reign of clocktime prevents access to this hidden dimension. In order to have access to the hidden dimension of the gestalt in the technological age in which technology becomes perfect, the transformation of saying does therefore not only involve the stereoscopic method, but the poetic experimentation with possible *new* meanings of time next to clocktime as well. In *At the Time Wall,* this new possible meaning is found in astrological time on the one hand and the time of the worker on the other. The role of poetry in the technological age we live in is not to name the gestalt—this requires a divination by the gestalt as we have seen—but to experiment with new possible meanings of time, i.e., poetic experiments with the time of the worker in the *absence* of the gestalt.

These two aspects of the transformation of saying in the age of technology—stereoscopic method and poetic experimentation—are mutually dependent. On the one hand, the stereoscopic access to the earth history as fertile field for a new turning of being is preceded by the poetic experimentation with a new possible meaning of time next to clocktime. On the other, this poetic experimentation is preceded by the stereoscopic method that provides access to the earth history as fertile field of possibilities for a new meaning of time.

> It lies in its nature that the magical powers adhere more invisibly, but also more doggedly than the mythical and historical . . . one asserts that the earth kept here reserves of its old species-forming power. Therefore, one can surmise that magical powers not only can achieve unforseeable amounts of space, when catastrophes threaten man not only as a world-historical entity, but also earth historical entity, i.e., as species.[23]

The poetic experiment draws freely from this fertile field of possibilities provided by the earth history—which is called an "infinite universe" or "world flushed with abundance"[24] here—and like mythical and historical time emerged from this earth history, a new epoch of the worker will arise on the other side of the time wall. The task of the poet *at the time wall* is to leave historical time behind, have indirect access to the unseparated or earth history, and to experiment freely with the possibility of a new epoch of the worker. "The earth wants to be recognized in its full scope, with seed and shell, in its animation. In addition, it seeks spirits that are its keys."[25] At the time wall, i.e., in the phase where the divination by the gestalt is still awaited, we don't have new names to name the gestalt, but can experiment with the possibility of the time of the worker in the *absence* of the gestalt.

This poetic experimentation at the time wall, first with time astrological time and later on with the time of the worker, is precisely what is at stake in the second part of *At the Time Wall*.[26] The poetic experimentation with the time of the worker qualifies first of all the self-evidence of clocktime in the technological world we live in and undermines secondly the absolutation of clocktime and its calculations and automatizations, i.e., the perfection of technology. Another meaning of time is possible and in fact, clocktime concerns only one epoch in the earth's history. But more important than the acknowledgment of the finitude of clocktime by the poetic experimentation with astrological time or the time of the worker is the *distance* between both meanings of time. Because we explore *different* meanings of time, we are no longer interested in the meaning of astrological time or clocktime itself, but in the *horizon* of meaning of both clocktime and astrological time: earth history. Earth history is a fertile field for the possible occurrence of a new epoch like mythical time, the epoch of the worker. Do we have any reason to introduce a new epoch of the worker beyond the perfection of technology?

An indication for the possibility of a new epoch of the worker is found in the concept of the anthropocene in *At the Time Wall*. Jünger compares time with geological layers and the destruction of the layer of mythical time and historical time provides access to the earth in its geological history. This earth history is not confined to human history. It is possible that the end of historical time not only ends this epoch, like the epoch of mythology has ended before, but also larger time frames, for instance the epoch of human existence as such. History is considered not in human, but in sidereal categories here, which means that earth history primarily concerns the history of the planet. Jünger explores the possibility of the occurrence of a new geological layer, the anthropocene as the timeframe in which humanity has the biggest impact on the ecosystem of planet earth: "The extent of human activity was however up to this point such that its geological examination appeared as a trick. That is changing. If bare patches of land appear in an immeasurable forest region like that of the Amazon, on which stand some huts, it is meaningless for the larger balance. One individual kind of insect can intervene more deeply. If this mark however expands itself in such a manner that makes the forest disappear, then the axe, tools, determined the image of the area."[27]

In the emergence of the anthropocene as a new geological layer, Jünger sees an indication that we left historical time and entered a new transhistorical epoch of the worker as layer-forming species: "This transition now, from which point one finds man not only in a layer, but also as a layer-forming being, is one of the symptoms of his exit from the field of history; it lies at the time wall."[28] This layer-forming capacity is primarily something of mother earth itself, but in our current age, humanity contributes to a layer-forming capacity of the earth.[29]

An indication of the layer-forming capacity in the anthropocene is found in the fact that humans intervene in their own evolution nowadays. Our time, which is characterized by huge experiments with human nature itself, can no longer be understood in terms of the categories of historical consciousness of the *Animal Rationale*. For Jünger it concerns something completely new— the emergence of a new era—of which we can see now only the tip of the iceberg. And because we can only see the tip of the iceberg—the entrance of the anthropocene—and not the vast amount of ice which remains under sea level—the gestalt of the worker—Jünger experiments with the time of the worker as layer-forming species in order to fathom from there the emergence of the gestalt of the worker.[30]

And here, Jünger's method of trigonometry can help to understand his transformation of saying. As we have already introduced in Chapter 4, Jünger explains trigonometry as the method to calculate the third hidden angle of a triangle based on two known angles, and transposes this method to the sphere of the gestalt: based on two fixed meanings of time—historical time and astrological time, historical time and the time of the worker—we can fathom the hidden dimension of the gestalt. So while the stereoscopic method consists in the poetic experimentation with a possible meaning of time beyond the perfection of technology—the time of the worker next to clocktime—in order to have indirect access to the hidden dimension of the gestalt, the trigonometric method enables us to see this new possible meaning of time—the time of the worker—as the representation of the gestalt of the worker. "Whoever adheres to the gestalt of the worker as to the great representative, and applies to it the change of the world as a principle of transformation, which is itself not subject to this transformation, will find a standard that does not deceive. He will perceive that there is a power that passes through the catastrophes as through a curtain of fire."[31]

What indications can be found at the time wall that the layer-forming capacity of the worker represents the gestalt of the worker? One of these indications is the leveling of differences in the age of technology, like traditional oppositions between work and leisure, day and night, city and countryside; oppositions and differences between races and peoples are leveled, forms are simplified and standardized, boundaries and borders fuse and the technological age is characterized by increased automatism. The trigonometric method enables Jünger to see this leveling of boundaries and fusion of borders as a development that will lead to a concept of planet earth as world state of the worker as a representative of the gestalt of the worker. In this respect, the technological age in which technology becomes perfect can be seen as part of a still hidden master plan. Because no one can avoid and escape the leveling of differences and the use of technological devices in the technological age, i.e., both the proponents and opponents of technology, Jünger starts to see an emerging unity in the workshop landscape; the epoch of the worker as representative of the gestalt of the worker.[32]

An indication of this new type of man, who is the operator of technological devices in a world which is covered by electricity, steam-, explosion- and radiation technology, is that this "total" work-character cannot be understood without reference to a new passion and comprehensive lifestyle[33] of the worker type, in which he represents the gestalt of the worker.[34] As son of the earth and operator for whom the technological capabilities are a higher instinct,[35] Jünger sees the worker type as a layer-forming species, namely as producer of a geological layer of artifacts that are integrated in a global network of electrification and radiation.[36] In *At the Time Wall,* Jünger even goes further:

> Regarding man as a spiritual being, one may deduce an epochal style that spiritualizes, somewhat in the sense, that the material also becomes 'more intelligent.' . . . That is conceivable: 1. In that man as a spiritual being represents purely the potency hidden in the materiality, connects and weaves into the global style, according to the way of an artist or craftsman, 2. In that the spiritualization as earth power grasps man and pulls him in, radiating through him and his works like through peaks. In this case, matter would take possession in its deepest form, as source, of man as its workman, to place it as the service of the spiritualization of the world.[37]

This planetary network of electricity resembles our nervous system and shows the mechanization and spiritualization of planet earth in the anthropocene.

> It is based on the notion that the empirical worker . . . represents more or less the gestalt of the worker and only from there retains sovereignty. First when this limitation is acknowledged, can security increase. It is finally based on the notion that our goals are much more widely set than we hope for today, and that we are still at the start.[38]

For Jünger, the worker type shares responsibility for the rise of the gestalt because he contributes to the formation of this geological layer of interconnected artifacts in the anthropocene.

The previous discussion of Jünger's method of the stereoscopic and trigonometric method should remind us that his explorations of the worker type as representative of the gestalt of the worker are not *descriptive.* "Where the worker pushes through to dominance, things become simpler. It should be remembered that no empirical-historical dimension is understood under this word, rather a metaphysical gestalt. It shapes the new world and its forms in an assignment, that in the first instance can only be traced in the crossings over, in the workshop landscape, the plans of the site shed."[39] On the one hand, the worker type is not an empirical category but represents the gestalt of the worker. This representation presupposes a divination by the gestalt as we have seen, and this divination didn't happen yet at the time wall. On the other hand, precisely the absence of the gestalt raised the question how this worker type as representative of the gestalt of the worker can be explored in the technological age in which technology becomes perfect. "Behind the unusual appearances that move us in this time and partially with hope, partially with fear, commonality hides."[40] This *Geheimnis* of the gestalt makes clear that the new epoch of the worker is not a matter of observation but of *poetry*. "Rather, they are experiments with the supreme goal of uniting freedom and the world in a new harmony. Where this succeeds in an artwork, the pent-up fear will disappear like fog with the first rays of the morning sun."[41] Jünger's transformation of saying in the workshop landscape consists 1) in the poetic experimentation with a new meaning of time next to clocktime. These different meanings of time 2) enable his stereoscopic method to have indirectly access to the earth history as fertile field of possibilities for a new possible meaning of time, which is 3) fathomed by the trigonometric method and enables him to see the time of the worker as a representative of the gestalt of the worker in the absence of the gestalt.

Although the transformation of saying in the technological world we live in cannot consist in naming the gestalt, it is a prerequisite for our future naming of the gestalt. On the one hand, the poetic experimentation with the time of the worker next to time as clocktime is the only way to have indirect access to the earth history as the hidden dimension of the gestalt in the technological age in which technology becomes perfect. On the other hand, the poet can only be affected by a possible divination or demand of the gestalt thanks to this indirect access to the earth history as a fertile field of possibilities for a new turning of being. The hidden dimension of the gestalt can only be seen indirectly and only approximately if we simultaneously—stereoscopically—look at the different meanings of time and fathom the gestalt via the trigonometric method. It is this transformation of saying that is able to conceptualize the gestalt at the time wall.

Notes

1. *WG*, 301.
2. *TNG*, 173.
3. *MM*, 349; cf. 343.
4. *ÜdL*, 253.
5. *WG*, 344; cf. *ZM*, 528.
6. "The decision then falls to the individual, as an either-or, since a third position, neutrality, is excluded. From this point forward, a particular form of infamy lies

in non-participation, but also in making judgments from a non-participating position" (*WG*, 361).

7. *ÜdL*, 244.
8. *ZM*, 403.
9. *ZM*, 402.
10. *ZM*, 409.
11. *ZM*, 410; cf. "Human Being is with that related to a movement that is independent of will and other dimensions, such as race and inheritance, and that connects only through location and time of the entrance into the world. Not this world and its possessions—the stars determine the actual house. A new cog begins its prescribed path in the middle of the tremendous revolution" (*ZM*, 410).
12. "The more the revenue and relocation increases, the more life becomes urban, technological-abstract, the more strongly this concern must emerge. That will especially be the case, if it comes to crises or catastrophes, in the face of which technological optimism is threatened or falls apart. Then man feels in need of an interpretation, a reference to the powers that lie outside of the circulation. In order to achieve that it needs the joining concept. That is the reason for the astounding power of attraction of astrology in our time, not for it alone." (*ZM*, 415).
13. *ZM*, 426.
14. *ZM*, 437; cf. 448.
15. *ZM*, 445.
16. *ZM*, 416.
17. *ZM*, 421.
18. *ZM*, 455.
19. *ZM*, 466.
20. *ZM*, 471–472.
21. *ZM*, 468.
22. *MM*, 333–334.
23. *ZM*, 496.
24. *ZM*, 507, 577.
25. *ZM*, 575.
26. *ZM*, 593–595, 520–521.
27. *ZM*, 558; Recently, geologists announced that the earth entered this new epoch of the anthropocene at July 16, 1945, the day that the first atomic bomb detonated in New Mexico.
28. *ZM*, 576.
29. "What is in contrast novel is that his conscious being works on the forming of layers. With that enters freedom, but also the responsibility into the development" (*ZM*, 590).
30. "The great advance occurs in the invisible, in the unconscious, in the blind mass" (*ZM*, 618).
31. *MM*, 332.
32. *MM*, 381.
33. *MM*, 362.
34. *ZM*, 537, 569, 574.
35. *MM*, 385.
36. *ZM*, 574; *MM*, 348.
37. *ZM*, 560.
38. *ZM*, 574.
39. *ZM*, 632.
40. *ZM*, 639.
41. *WG*, 308.

References

Works by Jünger

AH1 Jünger, Ernst. *Das Abenteuerliche Herz (Erste Fassung). Aufzeichnungen bei Tag und Nacht. Sämtliche Werke*, Band 9 (Stuttgart: Klett-Cotta 1979), pp. 31–176.

AH2 Jünger, Ernst. *Das Abenteuerliche Herz (Zweite Fassung). Sämtliche Werke*, Band 9 (Stuttgart: Klett-Cotta 1979), pp. 177–330.

Arb Jünger, Ernst. *Der Arbeiter. Herrschaft und Gestalt. Sämtliche Werke*, Band 8 (Stuttgart: Klett-Cotta 1981), pp. 11–320.

FB Jünger, Ernst. "Feuer und Bewegung". *Sämtliche Werke*, Band 7 (Stuttgart: Klett-Cotta 1980), pp. 105–118.

FBl Jünger, Ernst. *Feuer und Blut. Ein kleiner Ausschnitt aus einer großen Schlacht, Sämtliche Werke*, Band 1 (Stuttgart: Klett-Cotta 1978), pp. 439–538.

KE Jünger, Ernst. *Der Kampf als inneres Erlebnis. Sämtliche Werke*, Band 7 (Stuttgart: Klett-Cotta 1980), pp. 11–104.

Sta Jünger, Ernst. *Im Stahlgewittern. Sämtliche Werke*, Band 1 (Stuttgart: Klett-Cotta 1978), pp. 9–300.

MM Jünger, Ernst. *Maxima – Minima. Adnoten zum "Arbeiter". Sämtliche Werke*, Band 8 (Stuttgart: Klett-Cotta 1981), pp. 321–398.

PP Jünger, Ernst. *Politische Publizistik 1919 bis 1933* (Stuttgart: Klett-Cotta 2001).

SB Jünger, Ernst. *Das Sanduhrbuch, Sämtliche Werke*, Band 12 (Stuttgart: Klett-Cotta 1979), pp. 101–250.

SBr Jünger, Ernst. "Sizilischer Brief an den Manni m Mond". *Sämtliche Werke*, Band 9 (Stuttgart: Klett-Cotta 1981), pp. 9–27.

Str1 Jünger, Ernst. *Strahlungen 1. Sämtliche Werke*, Band 2 (Stuttgart: Klett-Cotta 1981).

Stu Jünger, Ernst. *Sturm. Sämtliche Werke*, Band 15 (Stuttgart: Klett-Cotta 1978), pp. 9–74.

TM Jünger, Ernst. "Die Totale Mobilmachung". *Sämtliche Werke*, Band 7 (Stuttgart: Klett-Cotta 1980), pp. 119–142.

TNG Jünger, Ernst. *Typus, Name, Gestalt. Sämtliche Werke*, Band 13 (Stuttgart: Klett-Cotta 1981), pp. 85–176.

UdL Jünger, Ernst. "Über die Linie. Martin Heidegger zum 60. Geburtstag". *Sämtliche Werke*, Band 7 (Stuttgart: Klett-Cotta 1980), pp. 237–280.

UdS   Jünger, Ernst. "Über den Schmerz". *Sämtliche Werke*, Band 7 (Stuttgart: Klett-Cotta 1980), pp. 143–194.

W125   Jünger, Ernst. *Das Wäldchen 125. Eine Chronik aus den Grabenkämpfen 1918, Sämtliche Werke*, Band 1 (Stuttgart: Klett-Cotta 1978), pp. 301–438.

WG   Jünger, Ernst. *Der Waldgang. Sämtliche Werke*, Band 7 (Stuttgart: Klett-Cotta 1980), pp. 281–374; *The Forest Passage.* trans. T. Friese (Candor: Telos Press Publishing 2013).

ZM   Jünger, Ernst. *An der Zeitmauer. Sämtliche Werke*, Band 8 (Stuttgart: Klett-Cotta 1981), pp. 399–645.

Works by Others

Bein, S. "Der Arbeiter. Typus—Name—Gestalt". In: Arnold, H.L. (ed.), *Wandlung und Wiederkehr. Festschrift zum 70. Geburtstag Ernst Jüngers* (Aachen: Verlag Dr. Rudolf Georgi 1965), pp. 107–116.

Blok, Vincent. "Communication or Confrontation: Heidegger and Philosophical Method", *Empedocles* 1 (2009), pp. 43–57.

Blok, Vincent. "Naming Being—or the Philosophical Content of Heidegger's National Socialism", *Heidegger Studies* 28 (2012), pp. 101–122.

Blok, Vincent. "'Massive Voluntarism' or Heidegger's Confrontation with the Will", *Studia Pheanomenologica* 13 (2013), pp. 449–465.

Blok, Vincent. "Towards the Rehabilitation of the Will in Contemporary Philosophy: Heidegger's Phenomenology of the Will Revisited", *Journal of the British Society for Phenomenology* 44(3) (2013), pp. 286–301.

Blok, Vincent. "Being-in-the-World as Being-in-Nature: An Ecological Perspective on *Being and Time*", *Studia Pheanomenologica* 14 (2014), pp. 215–236.

Blok, Vincent. "Heidegger and Derrida on the Nature of Questioning: Towards the Rehabilitation of Questioning in Contemporary Philosophy", *The Journal of the British Society for Phenomenology* 64 (2015), pp. 307–322 (10.1080/00071773. 2015.1052659).

Bohrer, K.H. *Die Ästhetik des Schreckens. Die pessimistische Romantik und Ernst Jüngers Frühwerk* (Frankfurt am Main/Berlin/Wien: Ullstein 1983).

Davis, B. *Heidegger and the Will: On the Way to Gelassenheit* (Evanston, IL: Northwestern University Press 2007).

Dilthey, W. *Einleitung in die Geisteswissenschaften. Gesammelte Schriften*, Band 1 (Göttingen/Zürich: Teubner/Vandenhoeck & Ruprecht 1962).

Dilthey, W. *Ideen über eine beschreibende und zergliedernde Psychologie. Gesammelte Schriften*, Band 5 (Göttingen/Zürich: B.G. Teubner/Vandenhoeck & Ruprecht 1964).

Dreyfus, H. *Being-in-the-World: A Commentary on Heidegger's Being and Time, Division I.* (Cambridge: MIT Press 1991).

Droste, V. *Ernst Jünger: 'Der Arbeiter'. Studien zu seiner Metaphysik* (Mainz: Dissertation 1980).

Emad, Parvis. *On the Way to Heidegger's Contributions to Philosophy* (Madison: The University of Wisconsin Press 2007).

Figal, Günter. "Der metaphysische Charaktere der Moderne. Ernst Jüngers Schrift *Über die Linie* (1950) und Martin Heideggers Kritik *Über „die Linie"* (1955)". In: Müller, H-H., Segeberg, H. (eds.), *Ernst Jünger im 20. Jahrhundert* (München: Wilhelm Fink Verlag 1995), pp. 181–197.

Figal, Günter. "Nochmals über die Linie". In: Figal, Günter, Heimo, Schwilk (eds.), *Magie der Heiterkeit. Ernst Jünger zum Hundertsten* (Stuttgart: Klett-Cotta 1995), pp. 25–40.

Figal, Günther. "Erörterung des Nihilismus. Ernst Jünger und Martin Heidegger", *Etudes Germanistiques* (1996), pp. 717–725.

Figal, Günter. "Flugträume und höhere Trigonometrie", *Les Carnets Ernst Jünger*, 4 (1999), pp. 175–188.

Figal, Günter. "Gestalt und Gestaltwandel—Ernst Jünger und Goethe", *Jünger Studien*, 5 (2011), pp. 8–21.

Gehtmann, C.F. "Heideggers Konzeption des Handelns in Sein und Zeit". In: Gehtmann-Siefert, A., Pöggeler, O. (eds.), *Heidegger und die praktische Philosophie* (Frankfurt am Main: Suhrkamp 1989), pp. 140–176.

Geyer, A. *Friedrich Georg Jünger. Werk und Leben* (Wien und Leipzig: Karolinger Verlag 2007).

Gorgone, Sandro. "Naturphilosophie und stereoskopische Sicht bei Ernst Jünger", *Jünger-Studien* 5 (2011), pp. 21–39.

Gorgone, Sandro. "Machenschaft und totale Mobilmachung: Heideggers Besinnung als Phänomenologie der Moderne", *Heidegger Studies* 22 (2006), pp. 49–69.

Haar, M. "Critical Remarks on the Heideggerian Reading of Nietzsche". In: Macann, C. (ed.), *Martin Heidegger: Critical Assessments* (London: Routledge 1992), pp. 290–302.

Hasselbach, K. "Das weite Feld jenseits von rechts und links: Zum konservativ-revolutionären Geist von Ernst Jüngers *Der Arbeiter. Herrschaft und Gestalt*". In: *Literaturwissenschaftliches Jahrbuch* 36 (1995), pp. 229–242.

Heidegger, Martin. *Grundbegriffe der Phänomenologie*, Gesamtausgabe Band 24 (Frankfurt am Main: Vittorio Klostermann 1975); *Basic Problems of Phenomenology*, trans. A. Hofstadter (Bloomington & Indianapolis: Indiana University Press 2009).

Heidegger, Martin. *Nietzsche: Der Wille zur Macht als Kunst*, Gesamtausgabe Band 43 (Frankfurt am Main: Vittorio Klostermann 1961,1985); *Nietzsche, Volumes One and Two*, trans. D.F. Krell (San Francisco: Harper 1991).

Heidegger, Martin. "Einleitung zu 'Was ist Metaphysik'". In: *Wegmarken*, Gesamtausgabe Band 9 (Frankfurt am Main: Vittorio KLostermann 1976), pp. 365–384; "What Is Metaphysics", *Pathmarks*, trans. W. McNeill (Cambridge: Cambridge University Press 1998), pp. 82–96.

Heidegger, Martin. "Von Wesen der Wahrheit". In: *Wegmarken*, Gesamtausgabe Band 9 (Frankfurt am Main: Vittorio KLostermann 1976), pp. 177–202; "On the Essence of Truth", *Pathmarks*, trans. W. McNeill (Cambridge: Cambridge University Press 1998), pp. 136–154.

Heidegger, Martin. *Logik. Die Frage nach der Wahrheit*, Gesamtausgabe Band 21 (Frankfurt am Main: Vittorio Klostermann 1976[1995]); *Logic: The Question of Truth*, trans. T. Sheehan (Bloomington & Indianapolis: Indiana University Press 2010).

Heidegger, Martin. "Platons Lehre von der Wahrheit". In: *Wegmarken*, Gesamtausgabe Band 9 (Frankfurt am Main: Vittorio Klostermann 1979); "Plato's Doctrine of Truth" *Pathmarks*, trans. W. McNeill (Cambridge: Cambridge University Press 1998), pp. 155–182.

Heidegger, Martin. "Zur Seinsfrage". In: *Wegmarken*, Gesamtausgabe Band 9 (Frankfurt am Main: Vittorio Klostermann 1976), pp. 385–426; "On the Question of

Being", *Pathmarks*, trans. W. McNeill (Cambridge: Cambridge University Press 1998), pp. 291–322.

Heidegger, Martin. *Platon: Sophistes*, Gesamtausgabe Band 19 (Frankfurt am Main: Vittorio Klostermann 1992); *Plato's Sophist*, trans. R. Rojcewicz and A. Schuwer (Bloomington and Indianapolis: Indiana University Press 1997).

Heidegger, Martin. *Einführung in die Metaphysik*, Gesamtausgabe Band 40 (Frankfurt am Main: Vittorio Klostermann 1976, 1983); *Introduction to Metaphysics*, trans. R. Polt (New Haven & London: Yale University Press 2000).

Heidegger, Martin. "Nietzsches Wort >>Gott ist tot<<". In: *Holzwege*, Gesamtausgabe Band 5 (Frankfurt am Main: Vittorio Klostermann 1977), pp. 385–426; "Nietzsche's Word: God Is Dead", *Off the Beaten Track*, trans. J. Young and K. Haynes (Cambridge: Cambridge University Press 2002), pp. 157–199.

Heidegger, Martin. "Der Ursprung des Kunstwerkes". In: *Holzwege*, Gesamtausgabe Band 5 (Frankfurt am Main: Vittorio Klostermann 1977); "The Origin of the Work of Art", *Off the Beaten Track*, trans. Julian Young, Kenneth Hayes (Cambridge: Cambridge University Press 2002), pp. 1–56.

Heidegger, Martin. "Die Zeit des Weltbildes". In: *Holzwege*, Gesamtausgabe Band 5 (Frankfurt am Main: Vittorio Klostermann 1977), pp. 75–113; "The Age of the World Picture", *Off the Beaten Track*, trans. Julian Young, Kenneth Hayes (Cambridge: Cambridge University Press 2002), pp. 57–85.

Heidegger, Martin. *Holzwege*, Gesamtausgabe Band 5 (Frankfurt am Main: Vittorio Klostermann 1977); *Off the Beaten Track*, trans. Julian Young, Kenneth Hayes (Cambridge: Cambridge University Press 2002).

Heidegger, Martin. *Sein und Zeit*, Gesamtausgabe Band 2 (Frankfurt am Main: Vittorio Klostermann 1977); *Being and Time*, trans. J. Macquarrie and E. Robinson (New York: Harperperennial 1962).

Heidegger, Martin. *Die Grundbegriffe der Metaphysik. Welt—Endlichkeit—Einsamkeit*, Gesamtausgabe Band 29/30 (Frankfurt am Main: Vittorio Klostermann 1983); *The Fundamental Concepts of Metaphysics: World, Finitude, Solitude*, trans. W. McNeill and N. Walker (Bloomington: Indiana University Press 1995).

Heidegger, Martin. *Nietzsches metaphysische Grundstellung im abendländischen Denken*, Gesamtausgabe Band 44 (Frankfurt am Main: Vittorio Klostermann 1986); *Nietzsche, Volumes one and two*, trans. D.F. Krell (San Francisco: Harper 1991).

Heidegger, Martin. *Beiträge zur Philosophie (vom Ereignis)*, Gesamtausgabe Band 65 (Frankfurt am Main: Vittorio Klostermann 1989); *Contributions to Philosophy (from Enowning)*, trans. P. Emad, K. Maly (Bloomington & Indianapolis: Indiana University Press 1999).

Heidegger, Martin. *1. Nietzsches Metaphysik 2. Einleitung in die Philosophie. Denken und Dichten*, Gesamtausgabe Band 50 (Frankfurt am Main: Vittorio Klostermann 1990); *Introduction to Philosophy: Thinking and Poetizing*, trans. P.J. Braunstein (Bloomington: Indiana University Press 2011).

Heidegger, Martin. *Heraklit*, Gesamtausgabe Band 55 (Frankfurt am Main: Vittorio Klostermann 1979, 1994).

Heidegger, Martin. *Vorträge und Aufsätze*, Gesamtausgabe Band 7 (Frankfurt am Main: Vittorio Klostermann 2000).

Heidegger, Martin. *Besinnung*, Gesamtausgabe Band 66 (Frankfurt am Main: Vittorio Klostermann 1997); *Mindfulness*, trans. P. Emad, T. Kalary (London/New York: Continuum 2006).

Heidegger, Martin. *Die Geschichte des Seins*, Gesamtausgabe Band 69 (Frankfurt am Main: Vittorio Klostermann 1998).

Heidegger, Martin. *Logik als die Frage nach dem Wesen der Sprache*, Gesamtausgabe Band 21 (Frankfurt am Main: Vittorio Klostermann 1998); *Logic: The Question of Truth*, trans. T. Sheehan (Bloomington: Indiana University Press 2010).

Heidegger, Martin. *Metaphysik und Nihilismus*, Gesamtausgabe Band 67 (Frankfurt am Main: Vittorio Klostermann 1999).

Heidegger, Martin. *Reden und andere Zeugnisse eines Lebensweges*, Gesamtausgabe Band 16 (Frankfurt am Main: Vittorio Klostermann 2000).

Heidegger, Martin. *Grundbegriffe der aristotelische Philosophie*, Gesamtausgabe Band 18 (Frankfurt am Main: Vittorio Klostermann 2002); *Basic Concepts of Aristotelian Philosophy*, trans. R.D. Metcalf, M. Tanzer (Bloomington: Indiana University Press 2009).

Heidegger, Martin. *Zu Ernst Jünger*, Gesamtausgabe Band 90 (Frankfurt am Main: Vittorio Klosterman 2004).

Heidegger, Martin. "Das Ende der Philosophie und die Aufgabe des Denkens". In: *Zur Sache des Denkens*, Gesamtausgabe Band 14 (Frankfurt am Main: Vittorio Klostermann 2007).

Heidegger, Martin. *Der Anfang der abendländischen Philosophie. Auslegung des Anaximander und Parmenides*, Gesamtausgabe Band 35 (Frankfurt am Main: Vittorio Klostermann 2012).

Heidegger, Martin. *Überlegungen VII–XI (Schwarzen Hefte 1938–1939)*, Gesamtausgabe Band 95 (Frankfurt am Main: Vittorio Klostermann 2014).

Heidegger, Martin. *Überlegungen XII–XV*, Gesamtausgabe Band 96 (Frankfurt am Main: Vittorio Klostermann 2014).

Herrmann, Friedrich-Wilhelm von. *Wege ins Ereignis: Zu Heidegger's "Beiträge zur Philosophie"* (Frankfurt am Main: Vittorio Klostermann 1994).

Herrman, Friedrich-Wilhelm von. "Topologie und Topographie des Nihilismus aus dem Gespräch zwischen Ernst Jünger und Martin Heidegger", *Heidegger Studies* 24 (2008) 21–39.

Hesse, Hermann. *Demian* (Frankfurt am Main: Suhrkamp 1981).

Heumakers, A., Oudemans, Th.C.W. *De horizon van Buitenveldert* (Amsterdam: Boom 1997).

Ibáñez-Noé, J.A. "Heidegger, Nietzsche, Jünger, and the Interpretation of the Contemporary Age", *The Southern Journal of Philosophy* 33 (1995), pp. 57–81.

Ihde, D. *Heidegger's Technologies: Postphenomenological Perspectives* (New York: Fordham University Press 2010).

Ipema, J. "Pessimismus der Stärke. Ernst Jünger & Nietzsche". In: Ester, H., Evers, M. (eds.), *Zur Wirkung Nietzsches* (Würzburg: Königshausen & Neumann 2001), pp. 13–30.

Jünger, F. *Die Perfektion der Technik* (Frankfurt am Main. Vittorio Klostermann 1946).

Jünger, F. "Auf meinen Bruder", *Beiträge zur deutschen Literatur und Kunst der Gegenwart* 60/61 (1960).

Kiesel, H. *Ernst Jünger. Die Biographie* (München: Siedler Verlag 2007).

Koslowski, Peter. *Der Mythos der Moderne. Die dichterische Philosophie Ernst Jüngers* (München: Wilhelm Fink Verlag 1991).

Kruse, W. "Kriegsbegeisterung? Zur Massenstimmung bei Kriegsbeginn". In: Kruse, W. (ed.), *Eine Welt von Feinden. Der große Krieg 1914–1918* (Frankfurt am Main: Fischer Verlag 1997), pp. 159–166.

Lacoue-Labarthe, P. *Heidegger, Art and Politics*, trans. Chris Turner (Oxford: Blackwell 1990).

Leed, E.J. *No Man's Land: Combat and Identity in World War I* (Cambridge: Cambridge University Press 1979).

Meyer, M. *Ernst Jünger* (München/Wien: Carl Hanser Verlag 1990).

Metzger, W. "Gestalt". In: Ritters, J., K. Gründer, and G. Gabriel (eds.), *Historisches Wörterbuch der Philosophie*, Band 3 (Basel: Schwabe & Co 1974).

Müller-Lauter, W. "Heideggers Nietzsche Lekture: zum Problem des Nihilismus", *Synthesis Philosophica* 11 (1996), pp. 123–130.

Nietzsche, F. *Kritische Studienausgabe in 15 Banden* (Munchen/Berlin: DTV de Gruyter 1980).

Nietzsche, F. *Die fröhliche Wissenschaft*, Kritische Studienausgabe, Band 3 (Munchen/Berlin: DTV de Gruyter 1988).

Nietzsche, F. *Also sprach Zarathustra*, Kritische Studienausgabe, Band 3 (Munchen/Berlin: DTV de Gruyter 1993).

Nietzsche, F. *Jenseits von Gut und Böse. Vorspiel einer Philosophie der Zukunft*, Kritische Studienausgabe, Band 5 (Munchen/Berlin: DTV de Gruyter 1993).

Oudemans, Wouter. "The Man of the Crowd of: Wat Heet Informatisering?". In: Geraedts, F., de Jong, F. (eds.), *Ergo Cogito V. Pleidooi voor de filosofie* (Groningen: Historische uitgeverij 1996).

Oudemans, Wouter. *Ernüchterung des Denkens oder der Abschied der Onto-Theologie* (Berlin: Dunckler & Humblot 2008).

Peperstraten, Frans van. *Sublieme Mimesis* (Budel: Damon 2005).

Plato. *Republic*, trans. F. Cornford (Oxford: Clarendon Press 1944).

Radloff, Bernard. "Self-Overpowering Power and the Refusal of Being", *Existentia* 17 (2007), pp. 393–422.

Radloff, Bernard. *Heidegger and the Question of National Socialism* (Toronto: University of Toronto Press 2007).

Rürup, R. "Der 'Geist von 1914' in Deutschland. Kriegsbegeisterung und Ideologisierung des Krieges im Ersten Weltkrieg". In: Hüppauf, B. (ed.), *Ansichten vom Krieg. Vergleichende Studien zum Ersten Weltkrieg in Literatur und Gesellschaft* (Königstein: Verlag Anton Hain Meisenhem 1984), pp. 1–30.

Schwarz, H.-P. *Der konservative Anarchist. Politik und Zeitkritik Ernst Jüngers* (Freiburg im Breisgau: Verlag Rombach 1962).

Schwilk, H. *Ernst Jünger. Ein Jahrhundertleben* (München/Zürich: Piper 2007).

Segeberg, H. "Technikverwachsen. Zur 'organischen Konstruktion' des 'Arbeiters' bei Jünger". In: Eggert, H., Schütz, E., Sprengel, P. (eds.), *Faszination des Organischen. Konjunktionen einer Kategorie der Moderne* (München: Iudicium Verlag 1995), pp. 211–230.

Thomä, Dieter. "The Name on the Edge of Language: A Complication in Heidegger's Theory of Language and Its Consequences". In: Polt, R., Fried, G. (eds.), *A Companion to Heidegger's Introduction to Metaphysics* (New Haven: Yale University Press 2001), pp. 103–122.

Trawny, Peter. "'Was ist Deutschland'? Ernst Jüngers Bedeutung für Martin Heideggers Stellung zum Nationalsozialismus", *Heidegger Jahrbuch* 5 (2009), pp. 209–234.

Trawny, Peter. *Heidegger und der Mythos der jüdischen Weltverschwörung* (Frankfurt am Main: Vittorio Klostermann 2014).

Verhey, J. *The "Spirit" of 1914: The Myth of Enthousiasm and the Rhetoric of Unity in World War I Germany* (Berkeley: PhD thesis 1991).

Visser, G. *Nietzsche en Heidegger. Een confrontatie* (Nijmegen: SUN 1989).

Weberman, D. "Heidegger's Relationalism", *British Journal for the History of Philosophy* 1 (2001), pp. 109–122.

Wilczek, R. *Nihilistische Lektüre des Zeitalters. Ernst Jüngers Nietzsche-Rezeption* (Trier: Wissenschaftlicher Verlag Trier 1999).

Zimmermann, M. *Heidegger's Confrontation with Modernity: Technology, Politics, Art* (Bloomington, Indianapolis: Indiana University Press 1990).

Zimmermann, M. "Die Entwicklung von Heideggers Nietzsche-Interpretation", *Heidegger Jahrbuch* 2 (2005), pp. 97–116.

Index

stamps - 5 — 10
coins - 10 — 15
cards - 5 — 10
items - 10 — 30
_____   ___
        30   65

can 25 — 30
_____   ___
      55   95
USPS   10   USM - 10
_____   ___
      65   105
                  5
Furniture —   ___
                110

65190593R00095